THE
CENTRAL
LINE
OF THE
Divine Revelation

WITNESS LEE

Living Stream Ministry
Anaheim, California • www.lsm.org

First Edition, December 1995.

ISBN 0-87083-960-8

Published by

Living Stream Ministry
2431 W. La Palma Ave., Anaheim, CA 92801 U.S.A.
P. O. Box 2121, Anaheim, CA 92814 U.S.A.

Printed in the United States of America

04   05   06   07   08   09   /   11   10   9   8   7   6   5

CONTENTS

PREFACE

This book is composed of messages given by Brother Witness Lee in Anaheim, California from August to December, 1991.

The Central Line of the Divine Revelation
THE DIVINE ECONOMY
AND THE DIVINE DISPENSING

MESSAGE ONE

GOD

(1)

Scripture Reading: Gen. 1:1, 26; 2:4; Exo. 3:14-15; Gen. 15:2, 8;
Matt. 1:1, 16, 18, 20-23; Acts 2:36; 10:36; John 7:38-39; Rev.
22:17; 1:4, 8; 11:15; 20:6

I. THE ENTIRE SCRIPTURE
BEING THE REVELATION OF GOD
AS THE UNIQUE DEITY, MAINLY IN
HIS DIVINE TITLES AND DIVINE PERSON

The central line of the divine revelation begins with God.
What the Bible reveals firstly and lastly is God. Nearly every
page of the Bible reveals God. God is the main factor in the
divine revelation. The Bible shows us the titles of God and
the person of God. Then it goes on to show us His economy
and His dispensing. These four things are the alpha of the
divine revelation—God's titles, God's person, God's economy,
and the way to accomplish His economy, which is to dispense
Himself into His chosen people. Later, we will see how God
carried out His creation in the view of dispensing Himself
into His chosen people. The main things that followed God's
creation and man's fall were the age of promise and the age
of types. There were many promises and many types as pre-
figures of the things to come. In all the types we can see
God's dispensing, and in the promises it is the same.

In the New Testament, the first major item is incarnation. We want to study the incarnation this time in a very
renewed way. Then we will go on to see Christ's humanity,
including His human living, His all-inclusive death, His resurrection, and His ascension with His heavenly ministry. In

His ascension and by His resurrection, He ministers, by the divine dispensing, in the heavenlies to produce the church, to build up the church, and to consummate the church age. Then we will fellowship about His appearing. He will appear as a stone from the heavens to fall upon the human government, to smash it, and to crush it (Dan. 2:34-35, 44-45). This will bring in the manifestation of the kingdom of the heavens, the millennium, which will eventually consummate in the new heaven and new earth with the New Jerusalem. The negative things and persons in the universe are cleared up through Christ's death and His last appearing.

Still, however, the rebellious element remains within man during the millennium. Thus, at the end of the millennium, there is the last rebellion of mankind instigated by Satan (Rev. 20:7-10). This will be a final sifting of man's rebellious nature, which will be fully purged away by the Lord's final judgment on mankind. During the millennium, the heavens and the earth remain old. God uses four ages to purge the oldness out of His creation—the age before the law, the age of the law, the age of grace, and the age of the kingdom. Through these four ages, everything is brought into His divine newness. The kingdom age, the age of the millennium, will be the age of restoration, but not the age of complete newness.

Although Christ's crucifixion and His second appearing clear up the universe, the old nature of the old creation will still remain. Then there is a need of a burning through which the old heavens and old earth will become new. The new heaven and new earth are produced through a baptism, not of water but of fire (2 Pet. 3:7, 10, 12-13). The entire old heavens and old earth will be baptized into fire. The fire will renew the heavens and earth into God's divine newness, consummating in the New Jerusalem. The New Jerusalem with the new heaven and new earth will be the eternal completion, the consummation, of God's economy. This is the central line of the divine revelation.

We need to pray that we may enter into all these items of the central line of the divine revelation so that we can live Christ and be today's overcomers to change the age like

Daniel and his three companions did. For us to be over-comers we need to know the Word. In order to know the Word properly and fully, we need the help of a proper exposition. Acts 8 tells us of an Ethiopian eunuch reading Isaiah 53. The Holy Spirit told Philip to visit him because the Holy Spirit knew that the eunuch was not understanding anything. Thus, Philip asked him, "Do you really know the things that you are reading?" (v. 30). The eunuch responded, "How could I unless someone guides me?" (v. 31). This shows that we need the proper opening and expounding of the Word in order to understand it.

Zechariah 1 presents a vision of a man as the Angel of Jehovah riding on a red horse and standing among the myrtle trees (vv. 7-17). How could we understand this with-out the proper exposition? I read and studied Zechariah 1 many times without understanding this vision. This vision unveils Christ as the Angel of Jehovah in His humanity. His riding on a red horse typifies Him moving swiftly in His redemption. The myrtle trees, which are shrub-like trees growing in the valley, signify the precious yet humiliated people of Israel in their captivity. Christ as the Angel of Jehovah was remaining vigorously among the captured Israel in the lowest part of the valley in their humiliation. Without the proper expounding of Zechariah 1 in this way, this chapter is very difficult to understand. The apostle Paul was a major interpreter of the Old Testament types. His book of Hebrews is an exposition of the types in Leviticus.

After the completion of the book of Revelation and begin-ning in the second century, the fathers of the church began to study the entire Bible. They were real scholars. They saw that God is triune, and they used this term to describe God. Throughout the centuries, many scholars have studied the Bible. Today we have inherited the best interpretations of the Bible, and we are standing on the shoulders of many who have gone before us.

In this series of messages, we want to see the central line of the divine revelation. I want to help people know the Bible not merely in letter but in revelation.

II. THE DIVINE TITLES OF GOD

A. Among the Many Titles for God in the Old Testament, Only Three Being Primarily Used—*Elohim*, Jehovah, and *Adonai*

Elohim, Jehovah, and *Adonai* are the three major, divine titles used for God in the Old Testament.

1. Elohim

Elohim, a plural noun in Hebrew, implies the notions of the strong One and faithfulness, hence, the faithful, strong One. Our God is strong and faithful. He is strong in strength and faithful in word. Whatever He does, shows forth His strength. Whatever He says, He will keep. He is the strong, faithful One. *Elohim* is a uni-plural noun. The plurality of the word *Elohim* implies the Divine Trinity (Gen. 1:26a; 3:22a; 11:7a; Isa. 6:8a; John 17:11b, 22b; Matt. 28:19; 2 Cor. 13:14). This title, denoting the unique yet triune God, is used more than two thousand five hundred times in the Old Testament.

2. Jehovah

Jehovah is another divine title of God (Gen. 2:4), literally meaning "He that is who He is, therefore the eternal I AM." This title primarily denotes "the self-existent and ever-existent One" (Exo. 3:14-15; John 8:24b, 28a, 58; Rev. 1:4, 8). As Jehovah, He is the One who was in the past, who is in the present, and who is to come in the future. Revelation 1:4 speaks of "Him who is and who was and who is coming." In the past He was; in the present He is; and in the future He is to be. He is the great I AM. The Lord Jesus told the Pharisees, "Unless you believe that I am, you will die in your sins" (John 8:24b). Eventually, they asked Him, "You are not yet fifty years old, and have You seen Abraham?" Jesus responded, "Truly, truly, I say to you, Before Abraham came into being, I am" (vv. 57-58). The Lord Jesus is the great I AM in every age. He is everything. Whatever we need, He is. He is our Savior, our Redeemer, our sight, our ability, our capacity, our light, our life, our righteousness, our holiness, and our kindness. He is thousands of items to us because He is everything and He is in every time.

When Moses was called by God, Moses asked Him what His name was. Exodus 3:13 and 14 say, "And Moses said unto God, Behold, when I come unto the children of Israel, and shall say unto them, The God of your fathers hath sent me unto you; and they shall say to me, What is his name? what shall I say unto them? And God said unto Moses, I AM THAT I AM: and he said, Thus shalt thou say unto the children of Israel, I AM hath sent me unto you." As the I AM, He is the God of Abraham, the God of Isaac, and the God of Jacob—the threefold yet unique and one God (v. 15). In His person there is the Father like Abraham, the Son like Isaac, and the third One like Jacob. He is threefold, yet one unique God.

As the I AM, He is eternal. This means that He does not have a beginning or an ending. A circle is a good illustration of eternity, since in appearance it does not have a beginning or an ending. At a certain place on the circle, we may place a cross signifying the crucifixion of Christ. Where in relation to the cross on the circle would you put Old Testament saints such as Adam and Moses, and where would you put all the believers in Christ throughout the centuries? It would be difficult to say, according to such a diagram, who is before the cross and who is after. This is why it says in Revelation 13:8 that the Lamb was slain from the foundation of the world, and 1 Peter 1:20 says that Christ was foreknown before the foundation of the world. Although Christ's redemption was accomplished in time, it is an eternal redemption (Heb. 9:12). According to God's figuration, in His way of eternity, it is difficult to say what comes first and what comes last. Jehovah, the eternal One, is in every age. He was in the past, He is in the present, and He will be in the future. He existed, He exists, and He will exist. He is everything, and He is everywhere because He is eternal.

Genesis 18 records that three persons came to visit Abraham. One was Jehovah, and the others were angels. Jehovah appeared to Abraham as a real man. Abraham prepared water for Him to wash His feet, and Sarah prepared a meal for Him to eat (vv. 3-8). He was in the form of a man. Before His incarnation, He had already appeared to Abraham as a man. Surely God became a man in time at His incarnation, but with God there is no element of time. With God there is no beginning and no ending. On a certain day in time, the very God, Jehovah, entered into the womb of a human virgin and was born as a man. According to human history, this happened about two thousand years ago. But in God's sight, the incarnation is eternal.

His crucifixion is also eternal. Revelation 13:8 points out that He was slain from the foundation of the world. In God's eyes, according to His figuration, Christ was slain from the beginning of the creation. However, in time Christ was slain much later. From Adam's creation to Christ's crucifixion, there were about four thousand years. But in God's eyes, Christ was slain when creation began. With Jehovah there is no time element. He is the One who was, who is, and who is forever.

The Lord Jesus is the great I AM. When the soldiers and deputies from the chief priests and Pharisees came to arrest Jesus and told Him they were seeking Jesus the Nazarene, He said to them, "I am." "I am" is the name of Jehovah. When the soldiers heard this name, they drew back and fell to the ground (John 18:4-6). The name Jesus means Jehovah the Savior. Jesus is Jehovah. The title Jehovah, denoting the Triune God as the One who is not only eternally existing but also eternally being, is used more than seven thousand times in the Old Testament.

3. Adonai

Adonai, in Hebrew, denotes Master (Gen. 15:2, 8; Exo. 4:10; cf. Gen. 24:9, 10, 12) and Husband (cf. Gen. 18:12). In Genesis 24 Abraham's old servant called Abraham his master. A slave has a lord, and that lord is his master, his owner, his possessor. In Genesis 18:12, Sarah referred to Abraham as her lord. The husband is the lord to the wife, and the lord is the master. On the one hand, our God is our Master. On the other hand, our God is our Husband. As our Master and our Husband, He is our Lord; He is our *Adonai.*

B. The Primary Divine Titles
Used in the New Testament Being God,
Father, Lord, Jesus, Christ, and Holy Spirit

In the New Testament, the main divine titles used are God, Father, Lord, Jesus, Christ, and Holy Spirit.

1. God

God in Greek is *Theos*. God, *Theos*, equals God, *Elohim*, in the Old Testament, denoting the unique yet triune God (1 Cor. 8:4, 6; 1 Tim. 2:5a)—the Father being God (1 Pet. 1:2-3), the Son being God (Heb. 1:8), and the Holy Spirit being God (Acts 5:3-4). Theologians have accurately pointed out that the Father, Son, and Spirit are not three separate gods, but three hypostases, or supporting substances, of the one God. Later, theologians began to use the word *persons* for the three of the Godhead. *Person* comes from the Latin word *persona,* which was an actor's mask. One person can have three masks or appearances.

Since I came to the United States, I have spoken much on the Divine Trinity. Some have said wrongly that the three of the Godhead, the Father, Son, and Spirit, are separate from one another. I published something pointing out that the three of the Godhead are distinct but not separate. They are always one. When we have the Father, we have the Son and the Spirit because the three are one. When the Son is here, the Spirit and the Father are with Him. The three are not separate. They are distinct, but one.

God is three yet one. In essence God is one. In economy, in God's move, God is three. This is why the best theology refers to the essential Trinity and the economical Trinity. Essentially God is one, but economically God is three. God the Father sent the Son in His economy, in His move. The Son did things by the Spirit in His move. The Father, Son, and Spirit are three economically in Their move and administration, but not in Their essence. Essentially God is one. This is why the Bible shows that the Son is the Father (Isa. 9:6; John 14:9). Furthermore, Paul said that the last Adam, who was the Son in the flesh, after His death and resurrection became a life-giving Spirit. He said in 2 Corinthians 3:17 that the Lord, the Son, is the Spirit. In verse 18 Paul said that we are being transformed "from the Lord Spirit." The Lord Spirit is a compound title like the Father God and the Lord Christ. This means that the Spirit is the Lord and the Lord is the Spirit.

John indicates that the Son is the expression of the Father. This is why the Son said, "He who has seen Me has seen the Father" (14:9). He also said, "Believe Me that I am in the Father and the Father is in Me" (v. 11). Humanly speaking, no one can understand this. We may say that we are one with another person, but no human being can say that he is in another one and that this other one is in him. The Son is in the Father, and the Father is in the Son. This is coinherence. The three of the Godhead not only coexist but also coinhere. The Son also pointed out that He did not speak from Himself and that His speaking was the Father's speaking and working (vv. 10, 24). This is because the Son and the Father are one. Some may say that they believe that God is triune, when they actually have a tritheistic concept of three gods. The Father, Son, and Spirit are not three gods. They are one God with three aspects—the aspect as the Father, the aspect as the Son, and the aspect as the Spirit.

2. Father

Another divine title used in the New Testament is Father. Father, in Greek *Pater,* denotes that God as the Father is the origin, the source, of all the families of God's creatures (Eph. 3:15). In God's creation there are many families, such as the family of the angels, the family of mankind, and the family of the animals. The source, the Father, of these families is God.

Eventually, there is a particular family, the highest family, which is the household of the faith (Gal. 6:10). God is the Father, especially of the household of the faith, which is begotten of Him. We believers are a particular family. Actually, we are the genuine family because we were not only created by God as the Creator, the origin, the source, but also regenerated, begotten by God. God has imparted His life essence into our being.

God is the Father of the human race. Luke 3:38 says that Adam was the son of God, but that does not mean that Adam was begotten of God. Adam was only created by God. God was not his Father in life but his Father in creation as the origin. In the new creation, however, we have a Father in life who regenerated us, who imparted His very life essence into us. We are His genuine family, the family of faith, the household of faith.

The Father is also called Abba (Aramaic) Father (Greek). In the Gospels, the Lord Jesus addressed God as Abba, Father (Mark 14:36). The apostle Paul also told us we cry Abba, Father in the spirit of sonship (Rom. 8:15; Gal. 4:6). Abba, Father is an intensified expression of intimacy. When we say Father, this is sweet. When we say Abba, this is sweeter. But when we say Abba, Father, this is the sweetest.

3. Lord

Lord, in Greek *Kurios,* denotes Jesus Christ as the Lord of all, who possesses all (John 20:28; Acts 2:36; 10:36). It is often used as a substitute for the title Jehovah in the Old Testament, as in Mark 1:3. Mark 1:3 quotes the word of the Old Testament in Isaiah 40:3. In the word of the Old Testament, it was Jehovah. In the quotation in the New Testament, it becomes the Lord. This indicates that the Lord in the New Testament is a substitute for Jehovah. Another Greek word, *Despotes,* is used to denote either God or the Lord Jesus as the Master of the slaves (Luke 2:29; Acts 4:24; Rev. 6:10; Jude 4; 2 Pet. 2:1; cf. 1 Tim. 6:1-2). In the Old Testament the Master of the slaves is called *Adonai,* but in the New Testament, in the Greek, He is called *Despotes.*

4. Jesus

Jesus, meaning Jehovah the Savior or Jehovah the salvation (Matt. 1:21), denotes that Jesus is Jehovah God becoming our Savior or Jehovah God becoming our salvation. This means that Jesus is the complete God becoming a perfect man (Matt. 1:23), thus, a God-man (1 Tim. 2:5). Jesus is a God-man. He is the very God and the perfect man.

5. *Christ*

Christ, in Greek Christos (Matt. 1:16b), equals *Messiah* in Hebrew (John 1:41; Dan. 9:26). Both of these terms mean the anointed One (Psa. 2:2). Christ is God's anointed One. *Christ* is a title of commission. To be anointed means to be appointed by God to be His Christ, to be His anointed One, for the accomplishing of His eternal economy (Luke 4:18-19). The anointed One of God accomplishes God's economy in His salvation. In the New Testament the two titles, Jesus and Christ, are often used as a compound title, either Jesus Christ or Christ Jesus (Matt. 1:1b, 18a; 1 Tim. 1:15-16).

6. *Holy Spirit*

The divine title *Holy Spirit,* meaning the Spirit who is holy, refers to the Spirit of God, who is God and the Lord Himself. Acts 5:3-4 and 9 show this. In verse 3 Peter told Ananias that he lied to the Holy Spirit. In verse 4 he said that Ananias lied to God. Then in verse 9 he told Sapphira that she and Ananias tested the Spirit of the Lord. This indicates that the Holy Spirit is both God and the Lord.

I hope that this simple study of the divine titles will help us. We should do our best to remember these primary divine titles of God. The New Testament also speaks of the Spirit of God (Rom. 8:9), the Spirit of Jesus, the Spirit of Christ, and the Spirit of Jesus Christ. The Spirit of Jesus is mentioned in Acts 16:7, the Spirit of Christ is mentioned in Romans 8:9, and the Spirit of Jesus Christ is seen in Philippians 1:19. The Spirit of Jesus refers to Jesus as the One who suffered, the Spirit of Christ indicates that Jesus is the One in resurrection, and the Spirit of Jesus Christ indicates that the Lord is the One who suffered and who is now in resurrection. The divine titles in the Bible are very meaningful. In order to know our God, we need to know His divine titles. Our God is not that simple. He is *Elohim,* Jehovah, *Adonai,* God, Father, Lord, Jesus, Christ, and the Holy Spirit.

The Central Line of the Divine Revelation

THE DIVINE ECONOMY
AND THE DIVINE DISPENSING

MESSAGE TWO

GOD

(2)

Scripture Reading: Gen. 1:1, 26; 2:4; Exo. 3:14-15; Gen. 15:2, 8; Matt. 1:1, 16, 18, 20-23; Acts 2:36; 10:36; John 7:38-39; Rev. 22:17; Matt. 28:19; Rev. 1:4, 8; 11:15; 20:6

In this message, we come to the hardest point in the Bible—the person of God. In a sense, it is not very difficult to know the names of God, the titles of God. These titles are not only revealed but also printed in the Bible. But many Christians are ignorant concerning God's person. In the previous message, we pointed out that the entire Scripture is the revelation of God as the unique Deity, mainly in His divine titles and His divine person. By God's titles and His person we know that He is unique.

The first time the Bible mentions God is in Genesis 1:1, which says, "In the beginning God created...." The word for God here in Hebrew is *Elohim*. *Elohim* is a compound word, and it is a uni-plural noun. In Genesis 1:26 God speaks of Himself in the plural by saying, "Let *us* make man in *our* image." God said, "Let Us," not "Let Me." *Us* and *our* are plural. God is one and also plural.

The plurality of the word *Elohim* implies the Divine Trinity. Genesis 1:26a, 3:22a, and 11:7a all mention God, using the plural pronouns *us* and *our*. In Isaiah 6:8 God said, "Whom shall I send? Who will go for us?" *I* is singular, but *us* is plural, showing that God is uni-plural. In John 17 the Lord Jesus prayed to the Father, "That they may be one, even as

We are one" (vv. 22b, 11b). He also prayed, "That they also may be in Us" (v. 21). God the Father and God the Son are "Us"; They are plural, yet They are one.

In the past we wrote some helpful small booklets on the Divine Trinity which I would suggest for your reading. These are—*The Revelation of the Triune God according to the Pure Word of the Bible*; *What a Heresy: Two Divine Fathers, Two Life-giving Spirits, and Three Gods!*; and *The Biblical Trinity*. The truth in these booklets can be a great help to us in seeing the scriptural revelation of the Triune God. Now we want to see something concerning the person of God.

III. THE PERSON OF GOD

A. God, Denoting That God Is a Living Person Who Is Divine from Eternity to Eternity, Thus, the Eternal God

God (Gen. 1:1; 1 Tim. 2:5) is a living person who is divine from eternity to eternity (Psa. 90:2b). Thus, He is the eternal God (Rom. 16:26). God is uniquely one from eternity past to eternity future. This means God is eternal and eternally unique. He is eternally one.

B. The Divine Persons of the Divine Trinity

Now we want to see the divine persons of the Divine Trinity. Matthew 28:19 says that we need to baptize the nations into the name of the Father and of the Son and of the Holy Spirit. Here there is one name for the three of the Godhead. A person may have a first name, a middle name, and a last name, but these are all actually one name for one person. The Father, the Son, and the Spirit are not three names, but the name of the unique Triune God. Matthew speaks of a wonderful person with a compound name—Father, Son, and Spirit.

1. The Father Being the Source of the Trinity

The Father is the source of the Trinity (John 8:18; 16:27-28).

2. The Son Being the Course of the Trinity, the Embodiment of the Father for His Expression

The Son is the course of the Trinity, the embodiment of the Father for His expression (John 14:9-11; Col. 1:19; 2:9). This is particularly revealed in John 14. John 14 may be considered as the greatest chapter in the Bible. In this chapter Philip said, "Lord, show us the Father and it is sufficient for us" (v. 8). This indicates that probably before that time, the disciples spoke to one another about the Father since the Lord Jesus had often mentioned the Father. Now in John 14 Philip took the chance to ask the Lord to show them the Father. The Lord Jesus said to Philip, "Have I been so long a time with you, and you have not known Me, Philip? He who has seen Me has seen the Father; how is it that you say, Show us the Father?" (v. 9). When the Lord spoke this to Philip near the end of His earthly ministry, He had been with the disciples for a long time, close to three and a half years. The Lord went on to tell Philip that He was in the Father and the Father was in Him. He said, "The words that I say to you I do not speak from Myself, but the Father who abides in Me does His works" (v. 10). When the Lord spoke, the Father worked, because He and the Father are one.

If we had been there, we might have said, "Lord Jesus, You and the Father are one, but You *and* the Father are still two. There is a distinction." The Lord also told the disciples that He would pray to the Father. If He and the Father were one, how could He pray to Himself? He said, "I will ask the Father, and He will give you another Comforter" (v. 16). The Comforter which was given to the disciples is the Spirit of reality (v. 17). This indicates that besides the Son and the Father there would be a third One, the Spirit.

In John 14, the Lord indicated that God is three, yet one. He told us that He and the Father are one. Then He went on to say that the Spirit of reality "abides with you and shall be in you" (v. 17). Then He said, "I will not leave you as orphans; I am coming to you....In that day you will know that I am in My Father, and you in Me, and I in you" (vv. 18, 20).

Eventually, this portion of the Word shows that when the Spirit is in us, that is the Son in us. When the Son was among the disciples, that was the Father. Then when the Spirit came and entered into the disciples, that was the Son.

This does not mean that the Father existed first, then the Son followed to exist, and then the Spirit followed as the third One to exist. The heresy of modalism says that the three of the Godhead are not eternally coexistent. We need to be clear that the three of the Divine Trinity all exist together at the same time from eternity to eternity. Furthermore, the three not only coexist but also coinhere. To coinhere is to exist in one another. The Father, the Son, and the Spirit all exist in one another. They mutually indwell one another. The three of the Divine Trinity exist together, and They also coinhere with one another from eternity to eternity.

3. The Spirit Being the Flow of the Trinity

The Spirit is the flow of the Trinity, the realization of the Son for His reaching and entering into His believers (John 7:38-39; Rev. 22:1; John 14:16-20). The Father is the source, the Son is the course, and the Spirit is the flow. The source, the course, and the flow are according to the notion of our Triune God as the living water, which eventually becomes a river. At the end of the Bible, in the very last chapter, our Triune God is shown as a flowing river, the river of water of life (Rev. 22:1). Such a flowing river has a source, a course, and a flow. The source, the course, and the flow are three aspects of the one river.

In 1977 I visited Israel with a group of brothers. One day we went to the source of the Jordan River at the foot of Mount Hermon. There is a spring there with a fountain as the source. The spring has a flow, and the flow is a stream, a river. Such a river is a picture of our Triune God with the Father as the source, the Son as the course, and the Spirit as the flow. This is the biblical illustration in Revelation 22.

In Revelation 22:1 the Son is the Lamb, indicating that the Son is the Redeemer. The river of water of life proceeds out of the throne of God and of the Lamb. There is one throne for both God and the Lamb, signifying that God and the Lamb are one—the Lamb-God, the redeeming God, God the Redeemer. Revelation says that the Lamb is the lamp (21:23), and God is within Him as the light (22:5). Thus, God is in the Lamb on the throne, and out of His throne flows the river of water of life, the Spirit. When the Spirit flows it carries the Lamb. Then in the flow of the river, the Lamb becomes the tree of life (Rev. 22:2). The tree of life growing on the two sides of the river signifies that the tree of life is a vine, spreading and proceeding along the flow of the water of life for God's people to receive and enjoy. The tree of life symbolizes the Triune God to be our life supply. The Triune God is the water of life for us to drink and the tree of life for us to eat.

At this point I want us to realize that we should not study the person of God in an objective, theological way. We should not study the Divine Trinity as a mere doctrine. The Bible shows us that the Divine Trinity is for our enjoyment. Second Corinthians 13:14 says, "The grace of the Lord Jesus Christ and the love of God and the fellowship of the Holy Spirit be with you all." This verse mentions three things: grace, love, and fellowship. Actually, however, this is one thing in three aspects. The source is the divine love, the course is the divine grace, and the flow is the divine fellowship. Out of God the Father flows the grace through Christ. Then this grace flows in the fellowship of the Spirit. Second Corinthians 13:14 shows us three persons in three aspects: God the Father, Christ, and the Spirit; and love, grace, and fellowship. God the Father as love is the source, Christ as grace is the course, and the Spirit as fellowship is the flow. At the end of the Bible, we see our Triune God flowing forever. His flowing is for the purpose of supplying His redeemed with Himself as drink and food so that we may enjoy Him as the bountiful supply. In the beginning of my Christian life I did not realize this. But today I fully realize that we need to experience, enjoy, and express the Triune God—the Father, the Son, and the Spirit.

The Son is the embodiment of the Father for the Father's expression. Then the Spirit is the realization of the Son for the Son to reach us and enter into us. The Father is embodied in the Son, and the Son is realized as the Spirit. Now the Spirit reaches us and enters into us. When the Spirit enters into us, the Son is here and the Father is here. All three are here within us. The Spirit is within us as the realization of the Son, who is the embodiment of the Father.

As such a Spirit, He was not there before Christ's resurrection. In John 7:38-39 the Lord said, "He who believes into Me, as the Scripture said, out of his innermost being shall flow rivers of living water. But this He said concerning the Spirit, whom those who believed into Him were about to receive; for the Spirit was not yet, because Jesus had not yet been glorified." At that time the Spirit was not yet. The Spirit of God was there from the very beginning (Gen. 1:1-2), but the Spirit as the Spirit of Christ (Rom. 8:9), the Spirit of Jesus Christ (Phil. 1:19), was not yet at the time the Lord spoke this word, because He was not yet glorified. Jesus was glorified when He was resurrected (Luke 24:26). The Spirit of God was there in creation, but before Christ's resurrection, *the* Spirit was not there yet because Christ was not glorified in His resurrection. This indicates that after Christ's resurrection, *the* Spirit is here.

God the Spirit in eternity past was merely divine. In eternity past, He did not have humanity within Him. He was only God, but not yet man. When He created the earth and man, He was merely God. Within Him there was no humanity. At the time of the incarnation, God entered into humanity and mingled Himself with humanity. He remained in a virgin's womb for nine months and was born as Jesus, a God-man. That little infant lying in the manger (Luke 2:12) was God and man. He was not only divine but also human.

When He became thirty years old, He came out to minister. He was a wonderful person who astounded those around Him. They wondered how He could have such wisdom and perform such works of power. They asked, "Is not this the carpenter, the son of Mary, and brother of James and Joses and Judas and Simon? And are not His sisters here with us? And they were stumbled in Him" (Mark 6:3). He was wonderful in His dual life and nature. He had both the divine life and the human life. He had both the divine nature and the human nature. He was divinely human and humanly divine. He lived as a God-man. He wept, and He was hungry and thirsty. He felt what we as men feel, but He also was divine. Christ was a wonderful person on this earth, but He is not merely historical. He is living in us today as the One who is divinely human.

The biography of Christ actually starts from eternity past where He was merely divine. He, as the unique God, created billions of items with man as the center of His creation. He created man in His own image with the intention that someday He would come into this man to be man's content and man's life. But after the creation of man, He waited for about four thousand years to become a man.

About two thousand years after God's creation of man, He gave Abraham a promise, telling Abraham that his seed would be a blessing to all the earth (Gen. 12:3; 17:7-8, 19). This promise to Abraham was fulfilled in Himself, the real seed of Abraham (Gal. 3:16). He was telling Abraham that one day He would come as Abraham's seed. He would come to be born of Abraham's descendant to be a man. Thus, in incarnation He entered into man and put humanity on as a garment. From that day He has been wearing humanity and will wear humanity for eternity. Divinity wears humanity.

He lived on earth in this humanity for thirty years, and He worked and ministered for another three and a half years. Who was He? Most of the Jews never knew. The Jews always considered Him merely as a Nazarene. They did not know that He was the very God, the Creator, Jehovah, *Elohim,* whom they worshipped. But they worshipped a divine God, without humanity. Today we Christians worship God as the One who is both divine and human. Jesus is the One who is the complete God and the perfect man. Our God is different from the Jewish God. The Jewish God is just *Elohim,* not Jesus Christ. But our God is Jesus Christ, who is the very *Elohim* and the very *Jehovah,* with both divinity and humanity.

This wonderful One passed through human living and went to the cross. By His death He terminated the old creation. After three days, He walked out of death and out of Hades to enter into resurrection. By entering into resurrection, He brought the terminated humanity into divinity. His incarnation and resurrection were a two-way traffic, coming and going, He came with divinity in incarnation to bring divinity into humanity. Then He went back with humanity in resurrection to bring humanity into divinity. He blended the divine with the human and the human with the divine. This blending is also a mingling.

In eternity past God had neither entered into humanity nor experienced death. But after picking up humanity and living in humanity for thirty-three and a half years, He walked into death. We should not think that He was put to death by man's decision. If He had not been willing to go into death, no one could have put Him to death. When the soldiers from the chief priests and Pharisees came to arrest Him at Gethsemane, He said, "Do you think that I cannot beseech My Father, and He will provide Me at once with more than twelve legions of angels? How then shall the Scriptures be fulfilled which say that it must happen this way?" (Matt. 26:53-54). He walked into death and entered into death voluntarily.

After three days, He walked out of death into resurrection. By entering into resurrection, He brought humanity into divinity. The Bible tells us that resurrection was a birth to Him (Acts 13:33). In divinity He was God's only begotten Son (John 3:16), but in resurrection He brought His humanity into divinity to be born as the firstborn Son among many sons, many brothers (Rom. 8:29).

In resurrection as the last Adam, Jesus became a life-giving Spirit (1 Cor. 15:45b). As God He became a man in incarnation (John 1:14). As such a One, He also became the life-giving Spirit. This life-giving Spirit is the totality of the Triune God, the consummation of the Triune God. As the life-giving Spirit, He is the Son, and embodied in the Son is the Father. Thus, the Father and the Son are here with this life-giving Spirit, who is the consummation of the Triune God and the totality of the Triune God.

We may say that the life-giving Spirit is the consummated God, the compound Spirit. The Spirit of God was compounded with man, with Christ's death, and with Christ's resurrection. In eternity past God was merely in divinity. He had not entered into humanity, and there was no all-inclusive death or powerful resurrection in Him. But after going through incarnation, crucifixion, and resurrection, the merely divine One was compounded with humanity, with the all-inclusive death, and with the powerful resurrection. Now today our God is a God-man with the element of the all-inclusive death and with the element of the powerful resurrection. He is the life-giving Spirit. He is *the* Spirit today. This is why I call our God today the processed God, the consummated God. He is the consummated One as the life-giving Spirit to be the totality of the Triune God, the consummation of the Triune God. When I have Him, I have the Trinity—the Father, the Son, and the Spirit. When I have Him, I have everything. I not only have the divine and human Triune God but also the wonderful death of Christ and the powerful resurrection of Christ.

In Exodus 30 the compound ointment is a wonderful type of the compound Spirit. Oil is a single element, but an ointment is a compounded entity. The compound ointment has the olive oil as a base, and this olive oil is compounded with four kinds of spices: myrrh, cinnamon, calamus, and cassia. This compounding produces an ointment. The priests and the tabernacle with everything related to it were anointed with this ointment. In the New Testament, 1 John 2 speaks of the divine anointing (vv. 20, 27), and this divine anointing is the anointing Spirit, the compound Spirit.

After Christ's resurrection the Spirit of God was consummated in His process. Today the Spirit indwelling us is the processed Spirit who can give life. Without being processed, without being consummated, He could never give life. Before the resurrection of Christ, He was not called the life-giving Spirit. But now after the resurrection, He has become the life-giving Spirit, and the life-giving Spirit is a compound Spirit.

The Bible calls Him *the Spirit*. In the last chapter of the Bible, Revelation 22, verse 17 refers to the Spirit and the bride. The Spirit is the processed Triune God, and the bride is the transformed tripartite man. The processed Triune God and the transformed tripartite man are married to be one universal couple—the Spirit and the bride. Man and God, God and man, are fully blended, mingled. Through His terminating death and in His germinating resurrection, we are the new creation, which is a blending of humanity with divinity and a mingling of divinity with humanity. His death terminated the old creation and germinated, through His resurrection, the new creation. As the new creation, we have become one with the Spirit (1 Cor. 6:17).

Through the process of Christ's death and resurrection, the Holy Spirit of God has become the processed Spirit as the consummation of the Triune God (Matt. 28:19) to be the life-giving and indwelling Spirit (2 Cor. 3:6b; Rom. 8:11). We need to realize that we have the Spirit indwelling us, and the indwelling Spirit is the consummated Triune God. He is the life-giving and indwelling Spirit to seal the believers of the Son (Eph. 1:13), that is, to impart and dispense the riches of God's being as the unsearchable riches of Christ into the believers as the members of Christ for the constituting and building up of the organic Body of Christ (Eph. 3:8, 10; 4:16). The indwelling, life-giving Spirit is the sealing Spirit. The sealing ink of a seal saturates the sealed material. We are the sealed material, and we have the Spirit as the sealing ink saturating us. This saturating, this sealing, mingles us with God.

This sealing is a kind of transfusing and saturating, which is what we call the dispensing. God today, who is the life-giving Spirit indwelling us, is always sealing, saturating, transfusing, and dispensing Christ's unsearchable riches into our being to make our being blended, mingled, with the processed God. This sealing is going on to transfuse and saturate us with the processed Triune God and to impart His unsearchable riches into our being. This is the divine dispensing for the building up of the organic Body of Christ.

We are being sealed with the compound Spirit, who is God the Spirit, as the basic element, compounded with Christ's humanity, with His death and its effectiveness, and with His resurrection and its power, as typified by the compound ointment in Exodus 30:23-25. Such a Spirit is both essential in us for life and economical upon us for work (Acts 2:4; 4:31). The life-giving Spirit today is the divine essence dispensed into our being to be our very life element within us. The Spirit is also the Spirit of power upon us for us to carry out the work to accomplish God's economy.

C. The Spirit

As we have seen, the Spirit (John 7:39; Rev. 22:17) is the consummation of the Triune God for the mingling of the processed Triune God with the transformed tripartite man.

IV. THE DIVINE REVELATION
IN THE SCRIPTURES
CONCERNING THE UNIQUE AND TRIUNE GOD

The divine revelation in the Scriptures concerning the unique and triune God is progressive, beginning from God in Genesis (1:1) and culminating in the all-inclusive Christ in Revelation (1:1; 11:15; 20:6). The progressive, divine revelation begins from God and goes higher and higher to reach Christ in Revelation as the culmination, the highest point. The sixty-six books of the Bible reveal that the highest point of the divine revelation of the person of God is Christ. This Christ today is the life-giving and indwelling Spirit, and this Spirit is the consummated Triune God. When we have this Spirit, we have the three of the Triune God. We have everything related to the processed Triune God: His all-inclusive death, His powerful resurrection, and the unsearchable riches of His being. All these are here to be our portion. Day by day this life-giving, indwelling Spirit is dispensing Himself into our being to constitute us and build us up as the organic Body of Christ.

The Central Line of the Divine Revelation

THE DIVINE ECONOMY
AND THE DIVINE DISPENSING

MESSAGE THREE

THE DIVINE ECONOMY

Scripture Reading: Eph. 1:5, 9-11; 3:8-11; Acts 2:23; 1 Tim. 1:4b; Eph. 3:2; 1 Cor. 9:17

In these messages we are burdened to see the central line of the divine revelation. If we were to ask a number of students and teachers of the Bible what the central line in the Bible is, they would have different opinions. Our feeling about what the central line is depends on our understanding of the Bible, and our understanding of the Bible depends on what we are. Many Christians in the Far East prefer the book of Proverbs, while those in the West prefer the Psalms. A New Testament in Chinese will frequently have Proverbs attached to it, while a New Testament in English will frequently have the Psalms accompanying it. What one sees in the Bible can be according to his preference and based upon his culture and his natural disposition. In order to see the central line of the divine revelation, we need to empty ourselves. We need to forget the things behind, even forgetting what we heard in the past in our church life. In this series of messages, we want to present the truth concerning the central line of the divine revelation in a new way.

The first thing mentioned in the Bible is a record of God's creation. Genesis 1:1 says, "In the beginning God created the heaven and the earth." In fact, however, the first thing was not God's creation. The beginning in Genesis is the beginning of time. Time has a beginning but eternity does not. Eternity is without beginning and without ending. Only God really knows what eternity is because He is the eternal God.

The Gospel of John also uses the phrase "in the beginning." John 1:1 says, "In the beginning was the Word." In John 1:1 "in the beginning" refers to eternity past. In the beginning of time, God created, but in eternity past the Word was with God and was God.

We need to consider what God was doing in eternity past. Chapters one and three of Ephesians give us a glimpse of what He was doing before time began. I would like us to read Ephesians 1:9-11 and 3:11. Ephesians 1:9-11 says, "Making known to us the mystery of His will according to His good pleasure, which He purposed in Himself, unto the economy of the fullness of the times, to head up all things in Christ, the things in the heavens and the things on the earth, in Him; in whom also we were designated as an inheritance, having been predestinated according to the purpose of the One who works all things according to the counsel of His will." Ephesians 3:9-11 says, "And to enlighten all that they may see what the economy of the mystery is, which throughout the ages has been hidden in God, who created all things, in order that now to the rulers and the authorities in the heavenlies the multifarious wisdom of God might be made known through the church, according to the eternal purpose which He made in Christ Jesus our Lord." A number of crucial terms are used by Paul in these verses—God's will, God's purpose, God's good pleasure, God's counsel, and God's economy.

We have seen that the central line of the divine revelation starts from God. Then the divine revelation shows us the divine economy and the divine dispensing. God Himself, God's economy, and God's dispensing can be seen throughout the entire Bible. These three items are the central line of the divine revelation. The divine revelation reveals to us three main entities: God Himself, God's economy, and God's dispensing.

I. AN ISSUE OF GOD'S WILL, PURPOSE, GOOD PLEASURE, AND COUNSEL

The divine economy is an issue of God's will, purpose, good pleasure, and counsel.

A. God's Will Being God's Wish,
God's Desire

God's will is God's wish, God's desire. God's will is what
He wishes to do and wants to do. God's good pleasure is of
God's will. Ephesians 1:5 speaks of "the good pleasure of His
will." His good pleasure is embodied in His will, so His will
comes first. God's will was hidden in God as a mystery, so
Ephesians 1:9 speaks of "the mystery of His will." In eternity
God planned a will. This will was hidden in Him; hence, it
was a mystery. God's will as a mystery hidden in God issues
in God's economy, dispensation (3:9). From God's will issues
God's economy through His purpose, good pleasure, and
counsel.

B. God's Purpose Being
God's Intent Set Beforehand

God's purpose is God's intent set beforehand. God's good
pleasure was purposed in God Himself (Eph. 1:9b). This
shows that God's good pleasure is embodied not only in God's
will but also in God's purpose. We have been predestinated
according to God's purpose of the ages, which is His eternal
purpose (1:11a; 3:11). God's purpose is eternal. It is the eternal plan of God made in eternity past before the beginning of
time.

C. God's Good Pleasure Being
What God Likes, What Pleases God

God's good pleasure is what makes God happy. It is what
God likes, what pleases God. We have a hymn in our hymnal
which speaks of God's intent and pleasure (see *Hymns,*
#538). God has predestinated us unto sonship according to
the good pleasure of His will (Eph. 1:5). This means that
God likes to have sons. His predestination is unto sonship.
Unto means *for* or *in view of.* God's predestination of us is
for His sonship or in view of His sonship. God is happy and
glad about gaining sons. It is His good pleasure to have us as
His sons.

God has made known to us the mystery of His will

according to His good pleasure, which He purposed in Himself (Eph. 1:9). First, there is God's will, second God's purpose, and third God's pleasure.

D. God's Counsel Being God's Resolution Consummated in the Council by the Divine Trinity

God's counsel is God's resolution consummated in the council by the Divine Trinity. A council requires more than one person. A counsel is the decision of a council. A council is a meeting, and the counsel is the resolution made by the council, the meeting. If God is only one, how could He have a council? How could He have a meeting for discussion to make a resolution? This indicates that God is not only one but also three. He is the Divine Trinity.

Acts 2:23 says that Christ was delivered up and crucified by the determined counsel and foreknowledge of God. This indicates that in eternity past the Triune God had a meeting; there was a council among the three of the Godhead. The determined counsel was determined in a council held by the Trinity before the foundation of the world (1 Pet. 1:20; Rev. 13:8), indicating that the Lord's crucifixion was not an accident in human history but a purposeful fulfillment of the divine counsel determined by the Triune God. We should not think that Christ was crucified, killed, cut off, merely according to Pilate's judgment. His being cut off was determined in a council held by the Trinity in eternity past.

The three of the Godhead had a council among themselves, and a decision was made called a counsel. God had a will with a purpose according to His good pleasure. Then the Divine Trinity Himself had a council, a meeting, to make a decision, a resolution. This resolution is the counsel. In Genesis 1:26 God said, "Let us make man...." This shows that the creation of man was also according to the council among the three of the divine Godhead. Such a council can be compared to today's Congress in the United States government. The President cannot act without a counsel made by the Congress in a council.

E. God's Economy Being
God's Household Administration,
God's Plan and Arrangement

After God's will, purpose, good pleasure, and counsel, there is God's economy. God's economy is God's household administration, God's plan and arrangement. With an administration, there is the need of a plan, and with a plan, there is the need of an arrangement. Based upon God's will, He made a purpose. In His will and purpose, there is His good pleasure. Then the Divine Trinity had a council to make a decision, which is the divine counsel. Based upon that counsel, God made a plan with an arrangement, and this plan with this arrangement is His household administration, His economy.

God's economy (dispensation, plan) is to head up all things in Christ (Eph. 1:10). It is to bring all the items in the universe under the headship of Christ. God's economy is God's dispensation, plan, arrangement, of the mystery of His will (3:9; 1:9a). What God wanted in eternity past was a mystery. Based upon that mystery, God made an arrangement, and that arrangement is His economy.

God's economy is God's distribution of Himself in Christ in faith (1 Tim. 1:4b). At the apostle's time, there were different teachings. Thus, he asked Timothy to remain at Ephesus to charge certain ones not to teach differently but to take care of God's economy in faith (vv. 3-4). Anything other than God's economy is based upon human works, but the economy of God is based altogether upon our faith in Christ. It is based not upon our doing but upon our believing. The entire Bible reveals to us the economy of God, which is what God intends to do, what God intends to give us, and what God intends to work into us.

II. THE INTENTION OF GOD'S ECONOMY

The intention of God's economy is to dispense Himself into His chosen people, making Himself one with them. The Bible reveals that God dwells within His chosen people and that He desires to make Himself fully one with them.

God's intention in His economy is also to dispense Christ with all His riches to His believers chosen by God for the constitution of the Body of Christ, the church, to express the processed Triune God (Eph. 3:8-10). This is the central line of the divine revelation.

Finally, the intention of God's economy is to head up all things in Christ (Eph. 1:10). Today the entire universe is a mess, but when the new heaven and new earth come, everything will be headed up in Christ under His headship. In the church, Christ is heading us up so that eventually all things can be headed up in Christ in the new heaven and new earth.

III. GOD'S ECONOMY
AND THE APOSTLE'S STEWARDSHIP

In chapter three of Ephesians, Paul used the Greek word *oikonomia* with two denotations. First, this word refers to God's economy. Second, it refers to the stewardship of the apostle. Eventually, God's economy becomes the stewardship of the apostle. God's economy was made in eternity (vv. 9-11). The apostle's stewardship (Gk., economy) of God's grace was given in time to carry out God's eternal economy in grace (v. 2; 1 Cor. 9:17). The economy of God is with God Himself, but the stewardship of the apostle was not merely given to Paul as one person. The stewardship has been given to all the believers.

Paul reveals in Ephesians 3 that the economy of God was given to him as the stewardship, but as the receiver of the stewardship, he said that he was less than the least of all the saints (v. 8). If the least among the saints is qualified to receive the stewardship, all of us are qualified. Today an electrician knows more than Thomas Edison because he has inherited all the knowledge since Edison's time. Because we are later than Paul, we have inherited everything he and others have passed on to us since his time. In this sense, we are greater than Paul because he declared that he was less than the least of all the saints. In a sense, Paul was our initiation, and we are his consummation.

The economy of God has become our stewardship to dispense the grace of God. The riches of Christ are the grace. The stewardship of grace is mentioned in 3:2, and the unsearchable riches of Christ are mentioned in verse 8, so the stewardship of grace is the ministry to distribute, to dispense, the unsearchable riches of Christ to the believers as grace for their enjoyment.

We need to get into all of these items of God's doing in eternity past. In eternity past God was exercising His will for His purpose in which is His good pleasure and for which He had to make a counsel. Based upon this He made an eternal economy to dispense the riches of Christ into God's chosen people, the believers, so that He could have a church, a Body, an organism for His expression. Eventually, by this dispensing, He will head up all things in Christ. For the accomplishment of His economy, God dispenses Himself into us in a fine way. God's dispensing of Himself into us, His chosen and redeemed people, will consummate in the New Jerusalem.

The Central Line of the Divine Revelation

THE DIVINE ECONOMY
AND THE DIVINE DISPENSING

MESSAGE FOUR

THE DIVINE DISPENSING

Scripture Reading: Eph. 3:8-9; 1:4-5, 7-11, 13-14a, 19-23, 6, 12, 14b; Rev. 21:1-3, 10-11

In the previous message, we saw that the divine economy is the issue of God's will, purpose, good pleasure, and counsel; hence, God's will, purpose, good pleasure, and counsel are all for the divine dispensing. The intention of God's economy is to dispense God Himself into His chosen people, making Himself one with them. God's intention in His economy is to dispense Christ with all His riches to His believers chosen by God for the constitution of the Body of Christ, the church, to express the processed Triune God (Eph. 3:8-10). First, the divine dispensing dispenses Christ with all that the processed Triune God is, has, and has achieved. Second, this dispensing constitutes the organic Body of Christ. The church as the Body of Christ is not only built up but also constituted. Constitution takes place by the gradual dispensing of a life element.

A house is built up by adding pieces of inorganic material together, but the human body is built up by growth. A baby grows by taking in food as an organic element. Only organic things can be taken in as food to constitute our body. A typical American is the composition of all the rich foodstuffs of America. In order to be constituted with these riches, one must eat and digest them. Digestion plus assimilation issues in growth. For the constitution of the Body of Christ, we must take Christ in more and more. In this way the element of Christ, which is something altogether organic, will grow within us. The intention of God's economy is to dispense the element of Christ into us for our organic constitution and growth.

God's intention in His economy is also to head up all things in Christ. Christ is the Head not only of the church but also of all things (Eph. 1:10, 22). God gave Him as a gift to be Head over all things to the church, His Body. He is the Head of the Body. Our own body is a picture of this. Every part of our body is related in some way to the head organically through the nerves. Christ's heading up of all things takes place organically by the growth of the Body.

In the previous message, we also pointed out the relationship between God's economy and the apostle's stewardship. The stewardship of the apostle is just the carrying out of God's economy. Whatever God planned needs to be carried out. The real apostleship is to carry out God's economy.

I. THE DIVINE DISPENSING BEING THE CONSUMMATION OF THE DIVINE ECONOMY

The book of Ephesians unveils the dispensing of God as no other book in the whole Bible. In the first four chapters especially, the most crucial thing is the divine dispensing. In order to study the book of Ephesians in a thorough way, we need to study and understand the divine dispensing. In the entire book, the word *dispensing* is not used, but the fact of dispensing is there.

I use the word *dispensing* in the sense of food being eaten, digested, and assimilated into our being. Eventually, when the element of the food we have eaten is assimilated into our being, that food becomes us. Dispensing is not just to distribute. It means that the things we take in have been assimilated into us to become us.

The divine dispensing is the consummation of the divine economy. In other words, God's plan is accomplished through His dispensing. The divine dispensing consummates God's economy, God's plan. In Ephesians 3:8-9 Paul said, "To me, less than the least of all saints, was this grace given to announce to the Gentiles the unsearchable riches of Christ as the gospel and to enlighten all that they may see what the economy of the mystery is, which throughout the ages has been hidden in God, who created all things." These verses reveal God's dispensing. Paul received grace to announce the unsearchable riches of Christ as the gospel. "To announce" means to distribute. Paul's distributing of the riches of Christ to the believers was according to God's economy. This is the apostleship to carry out God's economy.

II. THE DIVINE ECONOMY BEING
THE ISSUE OF GOD'S WILL, PURPOSE,
GOOD PLEASURE, AND COUNSEL

The divine economy is the issue of God's will, purpose, good pleasure, and counsel; hence, the intention of God's will, purpose, good pleasure, and counsel is for the divine dispensing. Everything God has accomplished is for one purpose. This purpose is to dispense Himself into His chosen people.

III. THE DIVINE DISPENSING
OF THE DIVINE ECONOMY BEING CONSUMMATED
THROUGH THE DIVINE TRINITY

The divine dispensing of the divine economy is consummated through the Divine Trinity. When I first began to speak on the Divine Trinity in this country, I told people that the Trinity should not be considered as a mere theological doctrine. The Divine Trinity is not for doctrine but for our enjoyment. Second Corinthians 13:14 illustrates this: "The grace of the Lord Jesus Christ and the love of God and the fellowship of the Holy Spirit be with you all." The Trinity— God, Christ, and the Holy Spirit—is revealed here with love, grace, and fellowship. This revelation is for our experience and enjoyment of the Triune God.

The Trinity is for our experience, but if the Trinity could not be dispensed into us, how could we experience Him? Food is for our enjoyment, but if we could not eat, digest, and assimilate it into our body, how could we enjoy it? The food must be dispensed into our body so that we can enjoy it. Second Corinthians 13:14 shows us a kind of dispensing. God the Father as love is embodied in God the Son as grace. The grace is dispensed into us through the fellowship of the Spirit. The fellowship of the Holy Spirit is just the flowing and the dispensing of what the Triune God is and has into us. The Triune God is love with grace, and the grace with love becomes the flow. This flow is the fellowship, and the fellowship is the dispensing of the Triune God into our being for our experience and enjoyment.

A. The Divine Nature Being Dispensed into the Believers in Christ through God the Father's Choosing, and the Divine Life Being Dispensed through God the Father's Predestination

The divine nature is dispensed into the believers in Christ through God the Father's choosing, and the divine life is dispensed through God the Father's predestination (Eph. 1:4-5). Ephesians 1:4 says that God the Father chose us in Christ to be holy. He chose us for sanctification. To be holy is a matter of dispensing. Without the divine nature of God being dispensed into our being, we do not have the element to be sanctified. By nature we are like a muddy piece of clay. How can we become golden unless some element of gold is mingled with us? Nothing in the entire universe is holy but God Himself. When God's divine, holy element is dispensed into us persons of clay, we become holy. To be holy we need the sanctifying element to be dispensed into our being.

Ephesians 1:5 says that God predestinated us unto sonship. Predestination means to mark out beforehand. If you go to a supermarket to get some peaches, you first choose the peaches that you want and then mark them out. We were chosen by God and marked out for sonship. Sonship is a matter of dispensing. If God's life as the divine element were not dispensed into us, how could we be His sons? In order to be God's sons by birth, we must have God's divine element as life dispensed into us. Ephesians 1:4 and 5 strongly indicate that God's holy nature and life must be dispensed into our being so that we can be made holy and so that we can be His genuine sons.

B. The Divine Element, of Which the Believers in Christ Are Made God's Excellent Inheritance, Being Dispensed into the Believers through God the Son's Redemption unto God's Economy of the Fullness of the Times, to Head Up All Things in Christ

The divine element, of which the believers in Christ are made God's excellent inheritance, is dispensed into the believers through God the Son's redemption unto God's economy of the fullness of the times, to head up all things in Christ (Eph. 1:7-10). God the Son, Christ, has redeemed us. This implies that we were lost. Before we were saved, we had fallen into at least four categories of things: sin, self, Satan, and the world. Christ redeemed us through His redeeming death from these negative things into Himself. We were in sin, self, Satan, and the world, but now we are in Christ!

The phrase *in Christ* implies a sphere, a realm, and an element. We were in Adam, and Adam was our sphere. In Adam we were fallen, but now we have been redeemed into Christ. Christ has become our sphere and our realm. Christ is also our element. His element is the divine element, the divine substance. To be in Christ means that we are in the divine element. Day by day Christ Himself is being worked into us so that He can become our element. If we did not have Christ as our element, how could we be called Christians? We are Christians because we have Christ as our element. A cup is golden because it has the element of gold within it. If a cup does not have any element of gold, it cannot be called a golden cup.

Today we are in Christ, who is our element. This element has made us an excellent treasure to become God's inheritance (Eph. 1:11). In ourselves, we are pieces of clay, unworthy for God to inherit. What God desires to inherit is something excellent. Since Christ has become our element, this element makes us excellent. Thus, we are inherited by God as His inheritance. In order to be such an inheritance, the divine element, which is Christ Himself, must be dispensed into us.

When I was young, I doubted concerning my salvation because I did not have much of the divine element. One day I was reading John Bunyan's *Pilgrim's Progress*. When I got to the chapter where Christian received some kind of "certificate" which indicated that he had been saved, immediately I stopped reading and began to consider if I had this certificate. The "certificate" was faith. At that time I began to doubt my salvation, and I was very troubled. I then checked with the Scriptures in portions such as John 3:15-16 and 36, and I read them repeatedly. I doubted my salvation because I did not have very much of the element of Christ. Christ had not been that constituted into my being, so I doubted. Today, however, I have no doubts about my salvation because I have had an accumulation of Christ within me; I have a greater amount of Christ within me. Christ has been and is being dispensed into me as the element.

C. The Divine Essence, of Which the Believers in Christ Enjoy the Processed Triune God, Being Dispensed into the Believers through God the Spirit's Sealing and Pledging

First, the Father's nature has been dispensed into us. Second, the element of Christ has also been infused into us. Third, the divine essence, of which the believers in Christ enjoy the processed Triune God, is being dispensed into us through God the Spirit's sealing and pledging (Eph. 1:13-14). This sealing and pledging is very subjective.

The Spirit as the seal is the consummation of the Triune God. This seal is a wet seal, full of the divine ink. The Spirit as the seal is also the sealing ink, the divine ink, as the essence. With the seal there is the nature of the Father, the element of the Son, and the essence of the Spirit. The nature is in the element, the element is in the essence, and the essence has been sealed into us.

From the time we were first sealed with the Spirit, this wet seal has been saturating us. When a seal is stamped on a piece of paper, the ink of the seal spreads into the paper and saturates the paper. That saturation is a kind of dispensing. In the same way, we have been sealed with the Holy Spirit. We have received the dispensing of the wet seal of the Holy Spirit, which includes the Father's nature, the Son's element, and the Spirit's essence.

The essence of the element of a substance is its extract. Orange juice is the extract of an orange. When we drink the juice, we receive the essence of the orange. The Spirit as the processed Triune God is the essence. God has been processed so that we can take Him in. This is the reason that God is triune. He has to be the Father for planning His economy, He has to be the Son for the accomplishment of His economy, and He has to be the Spirit to be the extract of the Divine Trinity. As the Spirit He is available for us to enjoy and receive. When the Spirit is with us as the essence, we have the Son as the element and the Father as the nature.

IV. THE DIVINE DISPENSING
OF THE DIVINE ECONOMY CONSTITUTING
THE ORGANIC BODY OF CHRIST

The divine dispensing of the divine economy constitutes the organic Body of Christ, the church, with all that the processed Triune God is, has, and has achieved, as the issue of the processed Divine Trinity unto His glory and for His full expression, which consummates in the New Jerusalem.

Ephesians 1 is full of the truth of God's dispensing. In verses 4 through 5 God's nature is dispensed into us with His life. In verses 7 through 11 Christ's element has been dispensed into us through His redemption. In verses 13 through 14 the Spirit's essence has been sealed into our being. In verses 15 through 18 Paul prays for the church regarding revelation. Then from verse 19 to the end of the chapter, Paul speaks concerning the power which was wrought in Christ and which is now toward the believers. This power is the extract of the Triune God—God the Father in the Son as the Spirit. The Divine Trinity has become such a power. Just as electricity is the power which has been installed in our homes, the Triune God is the power which has been installed in our being.

This power raised Christ from among the dead, seated Him in the heavenlies, subjected all things under His feet, and gave Him as a gift to be Head over all things to the church (Eph. 1:20-22). All that transpired on Christ, with Christ, and in Christ is for the transmission to the church. Thus, the church is the great issue of the Divine Trinity's transfusion. The church as the Body of Christ is the result of the Triune God's transfusion. We may even say that the Body of Christ is the extract of the Divine Trinity.

The church as the Body of Christ is the fullness of the One who fills all in all (Eph. 1:23). I believe that the phrase "all in all" in Ephesians 1:23 is similar to the phrase "all and in all" in Colossians 3:11. In Colossians 3, Christ is all the members who comprise the new man and in all the members. In Ephesians 1 the church is the fullness of the One who is *in* all the believers and who *is* all the believers. The dispensing of the Divine Trinity issues in the Body of Christ as the fullness of the processed Triune God, who is all the believers and who is in all the believers.

The Central Line of the Divine Revelation

THE DIVINE ECONOMY
AND THE DIVINE DISPENSING

MESSAGE FIVE

GOD'S CREATION OF MAN IN THE VIEW
OF THE DIVINE DISPENSING
ACCORDING TO THE DIVINE ECONOMY

(1)

Scripture Reading: Gen. 1:26a; Eph. 1:11b; Matt. 28:19; 2 Cor. 4:4b; Col. 1:15a; Phil. 2:6; Heb. 1:3; 1 Thes. 5:23; Heb. 4:12b; Gen. 2:7; Zech. 12:1; Prov. 20:27; Gen. 2:8-9

Prayer: Lord, we trust in You for the study of such a deep word. Lord, open up Your secrets and show us the hidden mysteries. Lord, we like to know Your heart with Your desire. We like to open ourselves to You. Lord, do open Yourself to us that we may have a thorough fellowship with You. Lord, do cover us with Your precious blood and anoint us with the anointing ointment. We need this. Thank You, Lord. Amen.

In the foregoing messages we have covered four main things: God in His titles, God in His person, the divine economy, which is the eternal plan of God, and the divine dispensing. These four things serve as an introduction to the subject of this series of messages, which is "The Central Line of the Divine Revelation."

I have been in the Lord's ministry for over sixty-five years. Through all these years, by studying the word of God in the Bible and the writings of others, I have discovered that in the Bible there is a central line which has been missed by Christianity. In most of the Christian bookstores, it is difficult to find any publication concerning the dispensing of God or God's economy. According to my knowledge, those of the inner life spoke much about God's plan, and one of their writers, Mrs. Charles A. McDonough, published a book entitled *God's Plan of Redemption*. But the word *economy* was not used in regard to God's plan. This might be because in Ephesians 1:10, 3:9, and 1 Timothy 1:4, the main verses in which the Greek word *oikonomia* is used, some versions of the Bible rendered this word as *dispensation*. *Dispensation* is not a wrong translation, but its denotation has been spoiled. A better translation of the word *oikonomia* is *administration* or *economy*. In the denotation of the word *oikonomia,* there is the thought of a household administration. Hence, God's economy is God's household administration.

In God's economy the main item is to dispense God Himself into His chosen people. This thought is new. The word *economy* is in the Bible, but the word *dispensing* is not. Nevertheless, the fact of dispensing can be found in the Bible. The divine economy and the divine dispensing are the central line of the entire Bible.

During the past thirty years, I have nearly finished the life-study of the entire Bible. Today, I am beginning a new study of the Bible. The subject, points, and facts are the same, but the view is different. I call this study "The View of the Divine Dispensing according to the Divine Economy." The title of this message is "God's Creation of Man in the View of the Divine Dispensing according to the Divine Economy." The phrase *in the view of* in this title is used to show that God's creation of man was in the view of His dispensing. A view is different from a purpose. In doing anything, we must have a view. In setting up a school or a business, we should not do it without a view. In creating man, God had a definite view. God created man in the view of His dispensing.

I. IN ETERNITY THE TRIUNE GOD
HOLDING A COUNCIL AND MAKING A COUNSEL
CONCERNING THE CREATION OF MAN

In eternity the Triune God must have held a council and made a counsel concerning the creation of man (Gen. 1:26a; Eph. 1:11b). A council, or a conference, must have been held between the three of the Divine Trinity. A council indicates that more than one person is involved. A council or conference must be held by a group of people. In Genesis 1:26 God said, "Let us make man in our image, after our likeness." This verse indicates that before creating man, the Triune God held a council in which the three of the Divine Trinity made a counsel concerning how to make man. This counsel was God's view. God came in to create man in the view of His dispensing. Why did God create man in His own image and after His likeness? The reason is that this was God's view. Why did God create man by forming a body out of clay? And why did God form a spirit for man with the breath of life out of Him? Why did God, after His creation of man, put him in Eden in front of the two trees? Why was there a river flowing beside the tree, with three different kinds of precious materials produced in the flow of that river? The answer to all these questions is that God had a view, and this view came out of His counsel.

God's creation was mentioned in a very brief way in Genesis 1, but the details of His creation, especially concerning His creation of man, were not defined and unveiled until chapter two. Chapter one tells us only that God created man in His image and after His likeness (vv. 26-27). But chapter two tells us that God made two parts of man—his body out of clay and his spirit out of the breath of life breathed out by God (v. 7). When these two parts were combined together, the soul was produced. In other words, the combination of man's body and spirit produced a complete man.

The man created in Genesis 1 is both male and female. Man is a couple. In chapter one the male and female are mentioned (v. 27), but in chapter two the details of their creation are given. In verse 18 God said, "It is not good that the man should be alone." This indicates that it is not good for man to be a bachelor. By himself, a man is not complete. Man needs a counterpart; he needs another part to match him. A man is completed or consummated by his wife. Thus, God had to make a female to match the male. In making this counterpart, God used a small part of man, a rib, to build a woman (vv. 21-22). Hence, the woman was something that came out of man and was a part of man. All females are just parts of the males. For this reason, they cannot stand by themselves.

After the creation of the woman, God brought her to the man, and when the man saw the woman, he was very happy. Adam said, "This is now bone of my bones, and flesh of my flesh" (Gen. 2:23). The male and the female became one flesh (v. 24). Eve came out of Adam, and she went back to Adam. Adam and Eve became one couple, one corporate person. In this way God's creation of man was consummated.

God created man in a certain view, according to a certain design. This view was God's blueprint. When someone builds a house, the first thing he must have is a blueprint. Then he builds the building according to the blueprint. He builds it in the view of the design shown in the blueprint. God made a design in His divine counsel. That counsel was the view in which God created man. When God created man, He had a blueprint. That blueprint was His counsel, and that counsel was the view in which He made man.

God created man in the view of the divine dispensing, which is according to the divine economy. In eternity the Triune God had a council and made a counsel concerning the creation of man. Ephesians 1:11 says that God operates all things according to the counsel of His will. In God's creation of the heavens and the earth and in His creation of man, a counsel was made. This counsel was made in God's council. Our being chosen and predestinated to be the church as the Body of Christ was all according to the counsel that the three of the Triune God made among Themselves.

II. MAN BEING CREATED

A. By the Triune God— the Father, the Son, and the Spirit

Man was created by the Triune God—the Father, the Son, and the Spirit (Matt. 28:19). Genesis 1:26 says, "And God said, Let us make man." *Elohim,* translated *God* in this verse, is a plural noun in Hebrew, implying the Divine Trinity.

B. In Their (Inward) Image

Man was created by the Triune God in Their (inward) image. This image is Christ the Son as the expression of the invisible God in the essence of His attributes, such as love, light, holiness, and righteousness (2 Cor. 4:4b; Col. 1:15a).

The image of God refers to the inward image of the essence of God. Christ the Son is the image of the Triune God. He is the expression of the invisible God. God is invisible, yet He has an image, and this image is Christ the Son as the expression of the invisible God in the essence of His attributes. God's attributes refer to His characteristics. God is love (1 John 4:16), God is light (1:5), God is holy, and God is righteous. Eventually, God is also holiness and righteousness. God has many other attributes, including mercy and kindness, as well as power, strength, and might.

In our speaking concerning this matter, we need to be careful to distinguish between attributes and virtues. If we are not careful, we may use these terms in a wrong way. An attribute denotes the very element or essence of something that has not yet been expressed. When an attribute is expressed, it becomes a virtue. Strictly speaking, as men, we do not have the attributes of love, light, holiness, and righteousness. The true attributes of love, light, holiness, and righteousness are of God and belong to God. But when God became a man to live on this earth, the attributes of God were expressed in human virtues. The attributes are of divinity, but the expressed virtues are through humanity. Thus, the expressed attributes are virtues, and the hidden essence and element of the virtues are the attributes.

The Triune God is a constitution of all His attributes. The totality of all the divine attributes is God's inward essence. This inward essence needs an expression. The expression of the inward essence of God is His image, and this image is embodied in Christ. All the fullness of the Godhead is embodied in Christ (Col. 2:9). Christ as the image of God is the expression of the essence of God's attributes, which are His very being. According to this image and in this image, man was made in Christ by the Triune God.

All human beings bear the expression, the image, of God. God is love, and we also have a kind of love. Our love is a copy of God's love. God's love is the real love, and our love is a photograph of God's love. Human beings are pictures, figures, or photographs of God in His attributes. God is also light. We as human beings also have some amount of light. We also like light and hate to be in the dark. When we do something in darkness, we do not like to let people know. But when we do something in the light, we surely like people to see that we are bright and of the light. We also like to be holy; that is, we do not like to be common. We like to be separated from the common things. We also like to be righteous and to do things right. We do not like to cheat people, even though at times we may steal from others because of our fallen nature. Even before we were saved, we all liked to be loving, bright, holy, and righteous. In our nature we wanted to love our parents, yet very often we did not. We realized that this was not good. This proves that we have a copy of God's attributes. Hence, we bear God's image.

C. After Their (Outward) Likeness

Man was created not only in the inward image of the Triune God but also after Their (outward) likeness. This likeness is the form of God's being (Phil. 2:6), the expression of the essence and nature of God's person (Heb. 1:3). Christ existed in the form of God, that is, in the likeness of God. When He became a man, He laid aside the likeness of God and took the form of a slave (Phil. 2:7). He laid aside the form of God, but He did not lay aside the essence of God. Christ laid aside the outward likeness, the form of God's being. The form of God's being is the expression of the essence and nature of God's person. Hebrews 1:3 says, "Who [Christ], being the effulgence of His glory and the impress of His substance..." The essence of God is something within God

Himself. This essence needs an outward expression, an impress, like the impress of a seal. Christ is the impress, the outward form, of God's being.

D. As the Highest of the Created Life

Man was created as the highest of the created life. God's creation is in the way of life. According to Genesis 1, the life God created was of three categories: plant life, animal life, and human life. The first thing created on this earth by God through His Spirit was the plant life, including the grass, the trees, and the flowers. This is the life without any consciousness, the lowest form of created life. After the plant life, God created the animal life. This life is on a higher level and is stronger than the plant life. The animal life has consciousness, but the plant life does not. Even the smallest animals, such as the ants, are very conscious. Eventually, God's creation reached the highest level with the creation of human life. The human life has the highest consciousness. Although many of the animals are very clever and skillful, none of these animals can speak human language. Yet human beings have the ability to learn to speak any kind of human language. If an animal such as Balaam's donkey (Num. 22:27-30) speaks human language, that is a miracle. Yet man can speak many different languages. This is an indication that man's life is the highest among the created lives.

E. After God's Kind

Man as the highest of created life was created after God's kind (Gen. 1:26-27). Genesis 1 tells us that all the plants were created after their kind (vv. 11-12). Today, if you plant a peach tree, it will produce peaches. In the same way, if you plant an almond tree, it will produce almonds, not bananas. It is the same with the animal life (vv. 21, 24-25). Crabs in the water produce other crabs after their kind. Crabs cannot produce turtles. Crabs are in one family, and plants are in another family. Mankind, however, is after God's kind.

When two trees are grafted together, they must be very similar or they cannot grow together. For example, a branch from a peach tree cannot be grafted into an apple tree. However, a branch from a peach tree of one variety can grow together with a peach tree of a different variety. The two can grow together because they are of the same kind. In the same way, we can be grafted into God (Rom. 11:17-24) and grow together with Him (6:5) because we and God are of the same kind.

F. Man Being Tripartite

1. A Body, Formed with the Dust of the Ground, to Be Man's Outward Organ

Man was created as a tripartite being (1 Thes. 5:23; Heb. 4:12b). The first of man's three parts is his body. The body was formed with the dust of the ground to be man's outward organ, having physical consciousness to contact the physical world (Gen. 2:7a). All of our physical members, such as our legs, mouth, hands, and arms, are part of this outward organ.

2. A Spirit, Formed with the Breath of God, to Be Man's Inward Organ as God's Recipient

The second of man's three parts created in Genesis 2 is man's spirit (v. 7b). Man's spirit was formed with the breath of God to be man's inward organ as God's recipient, having spiritual consciousness to contact the spiritual world (Zech. 12:1; Prov. 20:27). Proverbs 20:27 says, "The spirit of man is the lamp of Jehovah." Jehovah enlightens us through our spirit. If we did not have a spirit, we would not have light or anything that would enlighten us inwardly. In the Old Testament the Hebrew word used most often for the spirit is *ruach*. This word in Hebrew means "spirit," "breath," or "wind." But the word for *spirit* here in Proverbs 20:27 is not the Hebrew word *ruach*, but *neshamah*—the same word used in Genesis 2:7 for breath. Hence, according to Proverbs 20:27, the breath of life in Genesis 2:7 is the very spirit of man. God formed a spirit with the breath of life. *Neshamah*, the breath of life, is the source of the spirit and the element with which the human spirit was formed. The body was formed with the element of dust, and the spirit was formed with the element of the breath of life out of God. This breath of life out of God was not God's Spirit. It was not the Spirit of God, but something very close. The source of our body is the ground, but the source of our spirit is God. Our breath is nearly identical with our very being. Without breath we would die. Yet there is still a big distinction between our breath and our self. God's breath of life was not His Spirit but the very element with which God formed man's spirit.

God created man by forming two things. First, He formed the body with the element of the dust. Second, He formed man's spirit with the element of His breath of life. Thus, our spirit is very precious because our spirit is close to God. The dust is not very close to God, but our spirit is very close to God. This is why in a quiet time even the atheists have something within them that says, "What if there is a God? What will happen to me?" Some may say that they are atheists and teach others to be such. But at night, something within them says, "If there is a God, what should I do?" This something within them is the spirit of man.

A few days ago the brothers distributed one hundred seventy thousand pieces of literature in Moscow and St. Petersburg (formerly Leningrad) in the Soviet Union, and they received twenty-four thousand names of people who wanted books and publications. The brothers reported that there was a burning thirst within the unbelieving Russians for the truth of the gospel and for God. They have been under atheism for more than seventy years, yet this teaching could not change their nature. No one can change their nature. They do have a part within them formed with the breath of God. This element remains with every human being. Thus, it is easy for an atheist to turn to God. The reason for this is that there is a recognizing organ—the spirit—within man.

3. A Soul Being Produced by the Combination of the Human Spirit and the Human Body

The soul was the third part of man's being that was produced by God's creation. In contrast to the body and the spirit, the soul was not formed with a certain element. The soul was produced by the combining of the human spirit and the human body. The soul, comprising the mind, the emotion, and a free will, is man's self and has the psychological consciousness to contact the psychological world (Gen. 2:7c). A man is a soul. When Jacob and his family went down to Egypt, the Old Testament says that seventy souls went to Egypt (Exo. 1:5). In the same way, Acts 2:41 records that three thousands souls were saved on the day of Pentecost. Man is a soul, and the soul is the totality of man's body plus his spirit. When the body and spirit are put together, the total is a soul. This soul is man himself, comprising his mind, emotion, and free will. Hence, the perfect man created by God is a soul with two organs, the body as the outward organ and the spirit as the inward organ.

III. THE CREATION OF MAN
BEING GOD'S PRELIMINARY PREPARATION
FOR THE DISPENSING OF HIMSELF
AS THE TRIUNE GOD INTO THE TRIPARTITE MAN
ACCORDING TO HIS ECONOMY

The first two chapters of the Old Testament give us a design of how God created the heavens and the earth and how He created man. The creation of man is God's preliminary preparation for the dispensing of Himself as the Triune God into the tripartite man according to His economy. This is the new way to study Genesis 1 and 2.

The Central Line of the Divine Revelation

THE DIVINE ECONOMY
AND THE DIVINE DISPENSING

MESSAGE SIX

GOD'S CREATION OF MAN IN THE VIEW
OF THE DIVINE DISPENSING
ACCORDING TO THE DIVINE ECONOMY

(2)

Scripture Reading: Gen. 2:8-24; Rev. 22:1-2a; John 7:38-39; Rom. 5:14b; 1 Cor. 15:45; Eph. 5:25-32; 1:22-23; Rev. 19:7; 21:2, 9b-10, 18-21

Prayer: Lord, how we thank You for Your mercy that You have been with us all the time over the past years. Yet, Lord, we confess to You that we are so slow in realizing what You are. We are also very slow in knowing ourselves. Today we come to You that we may learn how to be fearful and trembling before You. Lord, do teach us according to Your mind and according to Your economy. We do thank You that You have a divine economy for the entire universe. Lord, there are so many secrets, so many mysteries, hidden in Your holy Word. We need Your opening and Your unveiling. We even need You to point out these mysteries to us in a slow way. Thank You, Lord, that You did this while You were on the earth for three and a half years with the ancient disciples. Lord, we beg You to do the same thing with us today. Capture us and keep us in Your mind for this difficult study. Lord, we feel very sorry that it is difficult for us to overcome the poor background which surrounds us. We have picked up so many things from today's Christianity in America, the top Christian country with its science, culture, and religions. Be merciful to all of us, and take away all these veils and pre-occupying things. We stand with You and tell You in a strong way that we hate all these preoccupying things. Lord, be with us in a new and thorough way. We desire to be empty with nothing in our understanding. You told us that those who are poor in spirit are blessed. Lord, let us be poor in our spirit. Say something to us, teach us, and anoint us. Give us an empty heart and a humble mind. Amen.

I was saved in April 1925. From the first day I was saved, I loved to know the Bible. For the past sixty-five and a half years, I have spent nearly every day in the Bible. On some days, I might not have opened the Bible outwardly, but inwardly, from morning until evening, the Bible was in my consideration. In the first few years in my study of the Bible, I did not realize that the Bible is not easy to understand rightly. But the longer I have continued in my study of the Bible, the more I have realized that the Bible is difficult to understand. The Bible is like a deep mine; it is altogether unlimited. The more I dig into it, the more I realize that it is endless. Although I have studied the Bible for many years, I feel that this present year is my first year to study the Bible.

CHRIST BEING THE IMAGE OF THE INVISIBLE GOD IN THE ESSENCE OF HIS ATTRIBUTES

Over the past years, it has been difficult for me to under-stand what the image of God is. Colossians 1:15 says that Christ is the image of the invisible God. When I studied this verse years ago, I asked, "How could the invisible God have an image?" To me an image must be visible; but I wondered how the invisible God could have a visible image. I had no one to help me find the answer to this question. But through more than fifty years of study I have gained a better under-standing. The image of God is just the form of God's attributes. God has many attributes, and God's inward being is the totality of His attributes. An attribute is an element that belongs to God. God is love, light, holiness, righteous-ness, power, might, and strength. These and hundreds of other items are the elements that belong to God; hence, they are His attributes. When these attributes are expressed, they become virtues. First Peter 2:9 says that we are a chosen race, a royal priesthood, a holy nation, a people acquired for a possession, so that we may tell out the virtues of Him who has called us out of darkness into His marvelous light. Here Peter used the word *virtues* instead of *attributes*. Virtues are the expressed attributes, and attributes are the hidden or concealed virtues. When Christ lived on this earth, He expressed God's attributes in His virtues. He expressed the divine attributes in His humanity as virtues. All the divine attributes have an image. This image is Christ the Son as the expression of the invisible God in the essence of His attributes (2 Cor. 4:4b; Col. 1:15a).

CHRIST HAVING THE FORM OF GOD'S BEING

Man was created after the likeness of the Triune God. God's likeness is the form of God's being (Phil. 2:6), the expression of the essence and nature of God's person (Heb. 1:3). In the past I thought that the likeness referred to God's outward expression, and I told people that in the Old Testament, before He was incarnated, God had man's likeness already. But this understanding is not accurate. The likeness is the form of God's being, which is the expression of the essence and nature of God. Thus, the likeness is very close to the image.

In Philippians 2:5-8 the words *form, likeness,* and *fashion* are used. These verses say, "...Christ Jesus, who, existing in the form of God, did not consider being equal with God a treasure to be grasped, but emptied Himself, taking the form of a slave, becoming in the likeness of men; and being found in fashion as a man..." Before His incarnation, Christ existed in the form of God, but when He became incarnated, He put the divine form aside outwardly and took on the form of a slave. The form of God mentioned in these verses is the expression, not the fashion, of God's being (Heb. 1:3). It is identified with the essence and nature of God's person and, hence, expresses them. This refers to Christ's deity.

The form of God (Phil. 2:6) implies the inward reality of Christ's deity; the likeness of men (v. 7) denotes the outward appearance of His humanity. He appeared to men as a man outwardly, but as God He had the reality of deity inwardly. The word *fashion* in verse 8 refers to the outward guise, the semblance. It is a repetition in a more particular sense of the thought of *likeness* in verse 7. What Christ looked like in His humanity was found by men to be in fashion as a man.

Hebrews 1:3 says that Christ is the effulgence of God's glory and the impress of God's substance. The effulgence of God's glory is like the shining or the brightness of the light of the sun. The Son is the shining, the brightness, of the Father's glory. This refers to God's glory. The impress of God's substance is like the impress of a seal. The Son is the expression of what God the Father is. This refers to God's substance. If I have a seal containing my name and some sealing ink, when I put the seal on a piece of paper, an impress will be left on the paper. God Himself is the seal, and Christ is the impress, the expression, of the seal.

Man was made in God's image and after His likeness. God created man in such a way as a preparation for His dispensing of Himself into man for the fulfillment of His divine economy, His divine plan. Man was created in the image and likeness of God so that he can express God. Man is a photograph of God. A photograph taken of a certain person is for expression. In the same way, man was created for God's expression.

GOD'S CREATION OF MAN IN HIS IMAGE
AND ACCORDING TO HIS LIKENESS
AS A TRIPARTITE VESSEL

There are two crucial points in God's creation of man. The first crucial point is that God made man in His own image and after His likeness. Man was made according to God, just as a photograph of a person is taken according to that person. Thus, man's image and likeness are according to God.

The second crucial point in God's creation of man is that man was created with three parts (Gen. 2:7). Hence, man is tripartite. Man's body was formed of dust, and his spirit was formed of the breath of God. The breath of life out from God was not God's being, but it was close to God's being. The breath that came out of God formed man's spirit. This is proven by comparing Genesis 2:7 with Proverbs 20:27. In both verses the Hebrew word *neshamah* is used, indicating that the breath of life out from God became man's spirit.

The body is physical, but the spirit is not physical. In the study of medicine, medical doctors study mainly our physical body. But man has not only a physical part but also a metaphysical part—his spirit. The word *metaphysics,* in its popular usage, refers to the study of matters that transcend material reality. The spirit of man is above material reality, and thus it is very difficult for people to understand. The study of the spirit is more difficult than the study of medicine. If the medical doctors were to ask me about the body, I could not say very much. But if I were to ask them about the spirit, I do not think that they could answer me very well. Medical doctors know about the human body, but many of them do not know or even believe that man has a spirit.

The body is the outward organ of man, having physical consciousness to contact the physical world (Gen. 2:7a). The spirit is our inward organ not only to contact God but also to be the recipient of God (2:7b). It is like our stomach, which is a receiver of food and is also the place where our food remains until it is digested. Our spirit is for us to contact God, to receive God, and to retain God.

This morning I was very serious with myself. I considered that every minute, even every second, the Lord Jesus is in my spirit, yet my conversation was very careless. The way that I spoke made it seem as if the Lord was not in my spirit. This means that I lacked the fear of God. In Philippians 2:12-13 Paul says, "Work out your own salvation with fear and trembling; for it is God who operates in you both the willing and the working for His good pleasure." We must be full of fear and trembling because God is operating in us. If the

President of the United States were to visit us, we would immediately have a change and would adjust ourselves. We need to realize that the Lord Jesus who is with our spirit is much higher than the President. The Lord Jesus should have our highest regard. We should be full of fear whenever we assemble together with the Lord. But often we are not fearful. If we are not fearful in everything that we do, this shows that our realization that Christ is within us is not very serious. If we had a serious feeling concerning this matter, we could not exchange words with our spouse. Whenever we lose our temper, this indicates that we have forgotten that the Lord Jesus lives within us. It is a sign that we are not fearful and trembling, knowing that He is within us. Christ lives in us, and He even lives for us. He is in us not in an occasional way, but every minute and in every place. This is why we have a spirit. Our spirit as our inward organ is conscious of the spiritual things.

The body is our outward organ, and the spirit is our inward organ. Yet neither of these two organs is our person, our self. Our person, our self, is our soul. The soul was not formed of any element. The soul was brought forth by the combination of the two organs, the body and the spirit.

THE IMAGE OF GOD'S ATTRIBUTES
AND THE LIKENESS OF GOD'S BEING

We all have the image of God's attributes. That is, we have the imitation of God's attributes. God is love, and we also have love. God is light, and we also have something within us that is bright. God is holy, and we also like to be holy. We do not like to be low or common; rather, we like to be separated from being common. God is righteousness, and we also like to be right. Our love, light, holiness, and righteousness are all imitations of God's attributes. What we have is just a photograph of God's attributes. This is God's image.

Although we have the imitation of God's attributes, we may not have the likeness of these attributes in our behavior. We may lose our temper or become angry with our parents. We may also do many other improper things. This behavior is our likeness. We are not what we should be. We have the image of God, but in our behavior, we are not like God. Thus, we all have the image of God, but we may not have the likeness of God.

MAN'S SOUL COMPRISING
HIS MIND, EMOTION, AND FREE WILL

When the body and the spirit were combined together, the soul of man was produced (Gen. 2:7). The soul is our self, our very person. When we walk, we use our body. When we think, we use our mind, a part of our soul (Psa. 13:2). When we pray to God from the depths of our being, we exercise our spirit. Thus, man is a soul with two organs—the body and the spirit. Hence, he is tripartite, having a body, a soul, and a spirit. The worldly teachers, both in China and in the West, teach people that man has only the outward part, the physical body, and the inward part, the soul. The outward part, man's body, is the physical part and is visible. The inward part, man's soul, is the psychological part and is invisible. To these teachers man has only two parts. But according to the Bible, man has three parts (1 Thes. 5:23; Heb. 4:12b).

Before we were saved, our inward person was our soul with the body as its outward organ and the spirit as its inward organ. Our soul was the inward person with two organs. But when we were regenerated, Christ came into our being to be our life and our person. Thus, in regeneration our spirit was made a person, and our soul as the old man was crucified (Rom. 6:6; Gal. 2:20). Through regeneration, our spirit, which was an organ to our soul, became the person, with the soul and body as its organs. The mind, will, and emotion of the crucified soul became our inward organ, and the body remained as our outward organ. Our soul as the old man was crucified (Rom. 6:6). In other words, the life of the soul was terminated, but the faculties of the soul still remain. The three faculties of the soul—the mind, emotion, and will—should not be put aside; rather, they should be renewed. This is proven by Romans 12:2, which says, "Be transformed by the renewing of the mind." If our mind as a part of our soul should be renewed, our emotion and will should be renewed also. The three faculties of our soul should remain to be renewed, but in our living, we must learn to deny our crucified soul, which is the soulish life, the self (Matt. 16:24-26; Luke 9:25).

THE INNER MAN OF ROMANS 7
AND THE INNER MAN OF 2 CORINTHIANS 4

According to the Bible, we Christians now have two different inner men (Rom. 7:22; 2 Cor. 4:16). In Romans 7:22 Paul said, "For I delight in the law of God according to the inner man." Here Paul was describing a situation that he experienced before he was regenerated. At that time, as a Jew, he delighted in the law of God according to the inner man. This inner man is the soul. This is proven by verse 25, which says, "So then with the mind I myself serve the law of God, but with the flesh, the law of sin." The mind in verse 25 is the inner man in verse 22. Then in 2 Corinthians 4:16 Paul said, "Therefore we do not lose heart; but though our outer man is decaying, yet our inner man is being renewed day by day." The outer man is our body as its organ with our soul as its life and person. The inner man is our regenerated spirit as its life and person, with our renewed soul as its organ. Thus, in the New Testament, the inner man in Romans 7:22 is different from the inner man in 2 Corinthians 4:16.

THE CREATION OF MAN BEING GOD'S
PRELIMINARY PREPARATION FOR THE DISPENSING
OF HIMSELF ACCORDING TO HIS ECONOMY

God's creation of man as a three-part vessel was His preliminary preparation for man to receive the Triune God into his being. The Triune God's entering into our being is His dispensing of Himself into us. Before His dispensing of Himself into us, He made us with a body and a spirit to bring forth a soul. We were prepared in such a way by God. Thus, we as men are a soul with two organs: the body as the outer organ and the spirit as the inner organ. Our spirit as the inner organ is suitable to receive and contain God. This is

God's preparation for His dispensing of Himself into man according to His divine economy.

IV. AFTER BEING CREATED, MAN BEING PLACED IN THE GARDEN OF EDEN

After being created, man was placed in the garden of Eden (Gen. 2:8). A garden is a pleasant and beautiful place. In God's newly created earth, God placed man in a garden.

A. In Front of Two Trees

Man was placed in the garden of Eden in front of two trees (Gen. 2:9). One tree was the tree of life, and the other tree was the tree of the knowledge of good and evil. The tree of life symbolized God to be taken by man as his life of dependence (v. 16). The tree of the knowledge of good and evil symbolized Satan as the knowledge of independence, issuing in death (v. 17).

B. With a River, Signifying the Flow of God as Life to Bring Forth Three Precious Materials

A river flowed beside the tree of life. Eventually, this river was divided into four heads, flowing toward the four corners of the earth (Gen. 2:10-14). One of the four heads was the river Euphrates, which flows through the present country of Iraq. The river signifies the flow of God as life to bring forth three precious materials (vv. 10-14; Rev. 22:1-2a; John 7:38-39).

The first of the three precious materials was gold (Gen. 2:11b-12a), signifying God the Father's nature. The second precious material at the flow of the river was bdellium (v. 12b). It is formed from fragrant resin and signifies God the Son in His redemption. The third precious material was onyx, which signifies God the Spirit in His transformation (v. 12c). Gold, bdellium, and onyx were the three precious materials brought forth by the flowing of the river.

C. To Bring Forth a Counterpart for God

Immediately after His creation of man and after putting

man in front of the tree of life, God said, "It is not good that the man should be alone; I will make him a help meet for him" (Gen. 2:18). God then made a counterpart for Adam by putting him to sleep, opening his side, taking a rib, and from the rib building a woman (vv. 21-22). The woman became the counterpart, the second part, of man. The woman Eve was built with the rib out of Adam and returned to Adam to be one flesh with him as his counterpart.

Adam, the first Adam, typifies Christ, the last Adam, as the embodiment of God (Gen. 2:20b; Rom. 5:14b; 1 Cor. 15:45). Eve, who was built with the rib out of Adam and who returned to Adam to be one flesh with him as his counterpart, signifies the church, which came out of the side of Christ and returned to Christ to be one spirit with Him as His (the processed Triune God's) counterpart. This counterpart is the organic Body of Christ as His bride, consummating in the New Jerusalem, which is built with the processed Triune God as the gold, pearl, and precious stones (Rev. 21:18-21), which are typified by the gold, bdellium, and onyx in several portions in both the Old and New Testaments (Gen. 2:11-12, 21-24; Eph. 5:25-32; 1:22-23; Rev. 19:7; 21:2, 9b-10).

D. The Completion of God's Creation of Man in the View of His Dispensing according to His Economy Needing the Entire Bible to Fully Define

Why does the record of God's creation of the heavens, the earth, the plants, the animals, man, and billions of items occupy only two chapters in the book of Genesis? I do not believe that God wrote these two chapters merely to tell us of the creation. Actually, these two chapters do not speak mainly of the creation; rather, they unveil to us the divine dispensing according to the divine economy. Although we cannot find the expressions *the divine dispensing* and *the divine economy* in these chapters, the fact is there. The intention of Genesis 1 and 2 is to show us how God made a preparation for His upcoming dispensing according to His divine economy. Genesis 1 and 2 are a record of how God created man with the intention that He would be man's life and content.

After His creation of man, God brought man into a garden and placed him in front of two trees. One tree, the tree of life, was good for food (2:9), but the other tree, the tree of the knowledge of good and evil, issued in death (v. 17). God warned man not to eat of the tree of the knowledge of good and evil.

God Himself was embodied in the tree of life. The tree of life is mentioned again in the book of Revelation (2:7; 22:2). In Revelation 2:7 the Lord Jesus gave a promise to the overcomers, saying, "To him who overcomes, to him I will give to eat of the tree of life, which is in the Paradise of God." Then in Revelation 22:1-2 a river of water of life proceeds out of the throne of God and of the Lamb. Along the flow of the river and on the two sides of the river, a vine tree grows. The tree bears fruit every month for the supply of all the inhabitants in the New Jerusalem, and the river flows to quench their thirst. The New Jerusalem itself is constituted of the Triune God as gold, pearl, and precious stones (21:18-21). The mentioning of these precious materials, the river, and the tree of life corresponds to the record in Genesis 2. In Genesis the precious materials are there but are not built up. But at the end of the Bible, these materials have all been built into one building, the New Jerusalem. The New Jerusalem is the composition of these three materials to be the bride (19:7-8; 21:2; 22:17), the real Eve, to match the real man, the Triune God. At that time, God will have a counterpart with which to spend His eternity for His rest, joy, and satisfaction.

The entire Bible is a record of the divine dispensing of the processed Triune God into the transformed tripartite man, issuing in an entity that is not only a combination but also a blending, a mingling, of the Triune God with the tripartite man. This entity satisfies God and makes Him happy, and at the same time, it causes man to rest in God and be satisfied and happy with Him.

The Central Line of the Divine Revelation

THE DIVINE ECONOMY
AND THE DIVINE DISPENSING

MESSAGE SEVEN

GOD'S CREATION OF MAN IN THE VIEW
OF THE DIVINE DISPENSING
ACCORDING TO THE DIVINE ECONOMY

(3)

Scripture Reading: Gen. 2:8-24; Rev. 22:1-2a; John 7:38-39; Rom. 5:14b; 1 Cor. 15:45; Eph. 5:25-32; 1:22-23; Rev. 19:7; 21:2, 9b-10, 18-21

Prayer: Lord, how we thank You that we are coming to Your Word with You again. We trust in Your presence. How we thank You that on this earth there is such a book as the Bible. Now, Lord, we want to see the secrets in this Word, and through this Word we would see Your heart, Your heart's desire, Your good pleasure, even Your purpose, Your counsel, Your will. Eventually, we would come to Your economy. Lord, do show us all these secrets. We do not want to be blinded; we do not want to remain in darkness. Take away all the veils. Take away all that we already understand. O Lord Jesus, empty us. Make us poor in our spirit that we might receive something new. We do not know much; we only know a little. Lord, forgive us. Forgive us for our stubbornness. Lord, we do pray that You will give us the word. We have no trust in ourselves, in our speaking, in our ability. Lord, we need Your washing blood to cleanse us from everything that is against You. Do cover us from all the deceiving of the enemy, even from his attacks. Lord, we stand with You. So Lord, stand with us, and even be one spirit with us. Amen.

Genesis 2 gives us a particular picture of God's creation of man. God created man by forming his body of the dust of the ground and breathing into his nostrils the breath of life (v. 7). After being created, man was placed in the garden of Eden (v. 8) in front of two trees (v. 9)—the tree of life, symbolizing God to be taken by man as his life of dependence (v. 16), and the tree of the knowledge of good and evil, symbolizing Satan as the knowledge (of good and evil) of independence, issuing in death (v. 17). In the garden there was also a river that issued in four heads, signifying the flow of God as life to bring forth three precious materials (vv. 10-14; Rev. 22:1-2a; John 7:38-39)—gold, signifying God the Father's nature (Gen. 2:11b-12a), bdellium (formed from fragrant resin), signifying God the Son in His redemption (v. 12b), and onyx (a precious stone), signifying God the Spirit in His transformation (v. 12c).

After this, God caused all the living creatures that He had created to pass before Adam to see what he would call them. However, Adam could not find one that matched him (vv. 19-20). Therefore, God caused a deep sleep to fall upon Adam, took a rib from his side, and built this rib into a woman (v. 22). Then God brought this woman to the man, and Adam said, "This is now bone of my bones, and flesh of my flesh" (v. 23). The woman was a proper match for Adam, and the two of them became one flesh (v. 24). God made man in one way and the woman in another way. In making man, God formed a piece of clay to be man's body, breathed the breath of life into it, and caused it to become a living soul. In making the woman, God caused the man to sleep, and from a rib out of his side He built a woman. The man was made of two materials, clay and the breath of life out of God's mouth, but the woman was built of one material, the rib from the man's side.

At the end of the Bible a wonderful city is revealed, a city of gold with twelve pearl gates and with a foundation of precious stones. In the early days of our gospel preaching we referred to this city as a heavenly mansion and encouraged people to believe in Jesus in order to flee from the lake of fire and go to this mansion. Eventually, however, we saw that this wonderful city was not a heavenly mansion. Revelation 21:10 says that John saw the holy city "coming down out of heaven from God." In that day, if we go to heaven, we will find that the "mansion" has come down to the earth. This revelation caused us to begin to see the real significance of the New Jerusalem (see *Hymns,* #971-985). Eventually, we saw that the end of the Bible and the beginning of the Bible reflect each other. In Genesis 2 there is a garden with a tree and a flowing river, and there are the precious materials. Moreover, there is a man who marries a bride. In Revelation 21 and 22 there are the same items, but the garden has become a city. In the beginning there was a garden, not built but natural and created by God. At the end of the Bible, however, the garden is transformed into a city. In this city also there are the tree of life and the river (Rev. 22:1-2). This city is built with gold, pearl, and precious stones, which are the same as the materials in Genesis 2. Moreover, the city itself is the bride, and the Triune God in the Lamb is the Husband (Rev. 21:9-10). They are a universal couple.

Among the great writers in church history, very few have written according to this revelation. Brother Nee helped us somewhat to see this revelation. Tersteegen, a German writer of several centuries ago, indicated that the New Jerusalem is a composition of the beloved believers, and Brother T. Austin-Sparks also indicated that the New Jerusalem is not a physical city and that whatever was there in Genesis 2, including the tree of life and the river, are symbols. He said that all these items refer to the divine things. Since the divine things are spiritual and mysterious, the human mind cannot understand them. Therefore, God used symbols to symbolize, to portray, them. It is the same with the New Jerusalem. Revelation 1:1b says, "And He made it known by signs, sending it by His angel to His slave John." The Lord Jesus spoke to John with signs, not with clear words. Therefore, the book of Revelation contains many signs. The first sign is the lampstands, signifying the local churches (1:12). Another sign is the Lamb (5:6), signifying the Lord Jesus.

The city in Revelation 21 and 22 is also a symbol, a sign. Therefore, there is the need to study its significance. We have studied the New Jerusalem for more than thirty years, and bit by bit we have received a revelation. We have seen that the New Jerusalem is God's heart's desire. God desires to have such a city, and we will all be in that holy city. Actually, we have been built into the city already, because the names of the twelve apostles, who are our representatives, are written on the twelve foundations (21:14). Moreover, the names of the twelve tribes of Israel are written on the twelve gates of the city (v. 12). In our view, the building of the New Jerusalem has not yet been completed, but in God's view, the building was finished even before the creation of the world. With God, there is only eternity; there is no time. Thus, most of the verbs in the book of Revelation are in the past tense. In God's eyes, everything related to the building of the New Jerusalem has been completed already.

Genesis 2 speaks of the precious material of bdellium, while Revelation 21 mentions pearl in its place (v. 21). In Genesis 2 there was no sin, so there was no need of redemption. However, after Genesis 2, sin came in. Bdellium is a fragrant resin which comes from a tree. Pearl, on the other hand, is a substance formed from the secretion of the life juice of a wounded oyster, an animal. If we did not need redemption, we would not need the animal life and its blood. We would only need the plant life to support us. Because of sin, however, we need redemption, and redemption requires the blood of the animal life.

Revelation 21:23 says of the New Jerusalem, "And the city has no need of the sun or of the moon that they should shine in it, for the glory of God illumined it, and its lamp is the Lamb." The New Jerusalem will need no natural light because our Triune God is not only our light but also our lamp. If we have light without a lamp, the light is not properly formed. We may illustrate this by electricity. Electricity produces light, but the light is in a light bulb. Without a light bulb, the electricity by itself might harm us. Christ is the lamp, and God within Him is the light. This means that the

Triune God is our light, and He is properly formed in His embodiment, the Son. The principle is the same with the lampstand. The lampstand is the form, and within the lampstand there is the burning oil. Moreover, seven lamps are on one lampstand (Exo. 25:37; Zech. 4:2; Rev. 4:5) to express the light, and the lamps contain the light that the lampstand gives. Today our light is not only Christ but Christ as the lamp with God as the light.

Revelation 22:3 goes on to speak of "the throne of God and of the Lamb." God and the Lamb sit on one throne. They do not sit side by side. Rather, one is sitting within the other. God sits in the Lamb, and the Lamb sits in God. God and the Lamb coinhere; They are one. They are one light, and They are One sitting on one throne.

THE WAY TO RECEIVE THE DIVINE DISPENSING

In creating man, God used clay to form man's body as his outward, physical organ with the physical consciousness to contact the physical world. Then God breathed His breath of life into that body, and this breath became man's inward organ, his spirit. The combination of the body and the spirit produced man's psychological person, his soul. The spirit as man's inward, spiritual organ is higher than the body as man's physical organ, since the spirit is composed of God's breath. God's breath is not God Himself, but it is very close to God. Proverbs 20:27 says, "The spirit of man is the lamp of Jehovah, searching all the inward parts of the belly." The breath of life out of God's mouth became the spirit of man, which is the lamp of God to shine within us for God. As men, we have two organs, the physical organ and the spiritual organ, and we ourselves are living souls, living persons.

God's desire was not merely to have a man as a living soul with a body of clay and a human spirit formed of God's breath. This cannot satisfy God, because the central thought of God is that He would be one with man (*Hymns*, #972). In the garden of Eden, God was still not one with Adam. God was God and Adam was Adam. In order to carry out His desire, God put man in front of two trees, one tree, the tree of life, symbolizing God Himself, and the other tree, the tree of the knowledge of good and evil, being the embodiment of Satan. Then, God warned man to be careful about his eating. He said, "Of every tree of the garden thou mayest freely eat: but of the tree of the knowledge of good and evil, thou shalt not eat of it: for in the day that thou eatest thereof thou shalt surely die" (Gen. 2:16b-17). God's putting man in front of the two trees was a strong indication that God wanted man to take Him in by eating Him. If man would take God in, God would be life to man in his spirit. This was fulfilled in the New Testament. According to the New Testament, God came as the bread of life (John 6:35), good for us to eat. If we eat Him, we have the eternal life, the divine life, in our spirit. When we received the eternal life in our spirit, our spirit was regenerated, and we were born again. First, we were born of the flesh through our parents, but now we have been born of the Spirit in our spirit (3:6). Now we not only have God's life within us, but we are one with God. God can rejoice because He has come into man and become one with man.

To be born of God is wonderful because this birth indicates that God and we are now one. We can rejoice and shout, "Hallelujah! I am one with God and God is one with me." God can also rejoice because He has obtained His heart's desire—but not yet in full. After being regenerated, we, the God-created men, need to be transformed, renewed, and conformed to the image of God's embodiment. All that God is, is altogether embodied in the Son (Col. 2:9). Moreover, the Son became a man, and this man went through death and resurrection to become the life-giving Spirit (1 Cor. 15:45b). Today our Savior, the Son of God, Jesus Christ, is a life-giving Spirit, and He is now in our human spirit (2 Tim. 4:22). Not only so, "He who is joined to the Lord is one spirit" (1 Cor. 6:17). This is the consummation of God's being one with us. God is in us to be our life, and we are regenerated and are being transformed and conformed to His image. We were created in God's image, but that image was merely a photograph of God. Now, however, God has wrought Himself into our being to make our very being into the image of His being.

BEING BUILT UP TOGETHER TO BECOME
A COUNTERPART FOR THE PROCESSED TRIUNE GOD

God's inheritance is the New Jerusalem, and eventually, we as the precious stones will be built together to become His inheritance. On the one hand, we do not like to be built together. Instead of meeting together, we may prefer to stay at home and be by ourselves. On the other hand, however, there is something within us causing us to feel that we cannot live by ourselves. We need to come together. In the divine life there is togetherness. To come together in the divine life is to be built up. As we remain in the church in our locality, we are unconsciously being built together. God's sovereignty has put us together. Eventually, in the New Jerusalem we will recall with the brothers and sisters how God put us together in many situations. It is hard for me to go for three days without seeing a saint. I like to see the saints. Togetherness is an attribute of the divine life, and by this attribute we have the building up.

Through the building up, God will have a bride to match Him. The bride in Genesis 2 was a physical bride, but eventually, in the consummation of the building up of the New Jerusalem, the bride will be not only physical and human but also spiritual and divine. She will be a wonderful and marvelous bride. The bride will make herself ready (Rev. 19:7) in a physical, spiritual, divine, and human situation. This bride is a corporate person, yet all the components of this person are one. The Triune God, after being processed, has blended Himself with the tripartite, transformed men, causing them to all become one. This corporate person is the bride, and this bride is a mutual dwelling place of God and man. God dwells in man and man dwells in God. The New Jerusalem is the tabernacle of God (21:3), God's abode, and God and the Lamb are the temple for us to dwell and serve in (v. 22). God is our dwelling, and we are His dwelling. This is God's heart's desire and God's good pleasure. This is also God's purpose according to the counsel of His will.

God's counsel is His economy, and the economy of God is to dispense Himself into us. God's breathing His breath into man was a dispensing, and our taking in God as the tree of life is also a dispensing. In this way God has dispensed Himself into our being. The elements of His being have been dispensed into our being step by step and day by day. God's dispensing also includes transformation, conformation, and glorification. Eventually, God will be fully dispensed into us not only as our life and nature but also as our glory. Then we will all be one with Him, and He will be one with us. In this way we will become His bride as His counterpart.

What we have presented in this message concerning God's creation of man in the view of His divine dispensing according to His divine economy is what God desires. This is God's good pleasure, and this is our ministry, burden, and commission. We do not have any other burden besides this ministry of God's economy with His divine dispensing into humanity. We must learn to receive God's dispensing every day. He is dispensing Himself to us every moment and in every situation, even in the small things, for our renewal, transformation, and conformation. Eventually, we will be glorified. Then we will enjoy the consummation of His divine dispensing according to His divine economy.

The Central Line of the Divine Revelation

THE DIVINE ECONOMY AND THE DIVINE DISPENSING

MESSAGE EIGHT

IN THE PROMISES AND TYPES OF GOD'S ANTICIPATED REDEMPTION AND SALVATION

(1)

Scripture Reading: Gen. 3:15; Isa. 7:14; Matt. 1:16; Gal. 4:4; John 1:1, 14; Matt. 1:23; Heb. 2:14; Matt. 1:20-21; 1 Cor. 15:53-57; Gen. 17:8; Gal. 3:16; Matt. 1:1-2a, 6; Gen. 12:3; Gal. 3:14; John 14:17-20; 1 Cor. 15:45b; 2 Cor. 3:17-18; Rom. 8:9; Acts 26:18; Eph. 1:14a; 2 Sam. 7:12-14a; Matt. 22:42-45; Rom. 1:3; Rev. 22:16; Acts 2:30-31; Matt. 16:16-18; Acts 13:32-35; Isa. 55:3-4; 2 Tim. 2:12; Rev. 20:4, 6

THE FOUR AGES BETWEEN THE TWO ETERNITIES

The Bible covers four ages between eternity past and eternity future: the age before the law, the age of the law, the age of grace, and the age of the kingdom. The age of grace covers the entire New Testament age, from Matthew 1 through Revelation 19. The last age, the kingdom age of one thousand years, recorded in Revelation 20, will consummate in the new heaven and new earth. It will be the introduction to the new heaven and new earth mentioned in Revelation 21—22.

The Age before the Law

The period of time from the creation of Adam to Christ's first coming was about four thousand years. The first part of this period, from Genesis 1 through Exodus 19, is called the age before the law.

The Creation of Man

The first thing recorded in this period is God's creation of man (Gen. 1:26; 2:7). Although the creation of many other things is recorded in Genesis 1 and 2, the most important thing according to the life-study of the Bible is the creation of man.

Genesis 1:1 is the only verse in the first two chapters that deals directly with the creation of the heavens and the earth. Genesis 1:1-2 says, "In the beginning God created the heavens and the earth. And the earth became waste and empty; and darkness was upon the face of the deep. And the Spirit of God was brooding upon the face of the waters" (lit.). The heavens and the earth were created, and the earth became waste and empty. This became the background for the creation of life. When the earth became waste and empty, God came as the Spirit to brood over the face of the waters. This indicates the matter of life. The brooding of the Spirit in verse 2 is like the brooding of a hen over her eggs to warm them so that life can come forth.

The creation of the universe was the beginning of the creation of life. Genesis 1 is a record of the creation of life. In Genesis 1 the Spirit came in and began to do many marvelous things. First, God said, "Let there be light" (vv. 3-4). This light was not just for the creation of the earth; it was for life. Second, God divided the waters above from the waters beneath by inserting an expanse (vv. 6-8). The air, which is needed by every living thing, was in this expanse. Third, God divided the land from the water (vv. 9-10).

The most important thing on the earth is the different forms of life. I appreciate the grass, the flowers, and the trees. The plants and the trees are beautiful. Genesis 2:9 says that the trees were pleasant to the sight and good for food. Among the trees that were pleasant to the sight and good for food was the tree of life. This tree of life signifies Christ, who is both pleasant to the sight and good for food.

After the creation of the plants in Genesis 1:11-12, God said, "Let the waters bring forth abundantly the moving creature that hath life, and fowl that may fly above the earth in the open firmament of heaven" (v. 20). Next, God created the cattle, the creeping things, and the beasts of the earth, such as the dogs, cats, lions, leopards, tigers, and bears (v. 24). In New Zealand one of the most impressive things is the countless flocks of sheep. In Brazil there are many different kinds of beautiful birds. The living creatures in the air, on the land, and in the water make the earth beautiful.

After the creation of the plants and animals, God said, "Let us make man" (Gen. 1:26). Man is the highest of all the created life. Yet the highest level of life is the divine life, signified by the tree of life (2:9). The record in Genesis progresses from the plant life to the animal life to the human life to the divine life. In the creation of the plants and animals, God began from the lower forms and went to the higher forms. The record of creation in Genesis is a record of life. The entire Bible is a book of life.

Many Christians speak of God's creation of the heavens and the earth in the first two chapters of Genesis, but they neglect the matter of life. God did not tell us how He created the planets or the stars, but He spent a great deal of time in Genesis 2 to give us a detailed picture. First, this picture portrays how God made a man from the dust (v. 7), similar to the way in which a child might make a doll out of clay. He then described in detail the tree of life with the river flowing beside it (vv. 9-14). At the flow of that river, which parted into four heads, there were three precious materials: gold, bdellium, and onyx (v. 12). God used many words to describe these things, but He gave no details concerning the things that scientists study today. This is because Genesis 1 and 2 are a record of life.

The Fall of Man

The first point in the record of life in the Bible is man's creation, and the second point is man's fall (Gen. 3:1-6). When man fell, God came immediately to give man the promise of the seed of woman (v. 15). After Adam and Eve sinned, they were afraid of God (v. 10) and tried their best to cover themselves (v. 7). So God called to Adam and said, "Where are you?" (v. 9, NASB). This was the first sentence spoken by the creating God to the fallen man. Eventually, God found Adam and Eve and had a gospel visit with them. This was the first gospel visitation. According to this pattern set up by God, I would strongly encourage you to go to visit people with the gospel.

Immediately after man's fall, God came from the heavens to the earth to visit fallen man, and He began to preach the gospel to him. First, God questioned Adam concerning whether or not he had eaten of the tree of the knowledge of good and evil (v. 11). Adam answered, "The woman whom thou gavest to be with me, she gave me of the tree, and I did eat" (v. 12). Adam blamed God for giving the woman to him. God did not rebuke Adam; instead, He turned to the woman and asked her what had happened. The woman responded, "The serpent beguiled me, and I did eat" (v. 13). Then God turned to the serpent and cursed him (vv. 14-15). Within the curse on the subtle one, a promise was implied. Genesis 3:15 says, "And I will put enmity between thee and the woman, and between thy seed and her seed; it shall bruise thy head, and thou shalt bruise his heel." To bruise the head means to put to death. When He said that the seed of the woman would bruise the head of the serpent, God was saying, "Serpent, you have used the woman to spoil the man I have created. But I will use the woman to produce the seed that will bruise your head to put you to death."

God's Anticipated Redemption and Salvation

The first item in the record of the Bible is God's creation, the second item is the fall of man, and the third item is God's anticipation of His redemption and salvation for fallen man. Immediately after the fall of man, God anticipated that He would bring in His redemption and salvation for man. When God said that the seed of woman would bruise the head of the serpent, Adam and Eve were happy. Adam might have turned to Eve and said, "Eve, this is very good! You will bring forth a seed which will bruise the head of that subtle one, the serpent." God's word concerning the seed of the woman was both a promise and a prophecy. All the promises are prophecies, but not all the prophecies are promises. The best prophecies are always promises. Zechariah, a book that is full of prophecies (9:1—14:21), proves this. All the top prophecies in Zechariah are also promises. Zechariah 13:1 says, "In that day there will be an opened fountain for the house of David and for the inhabitants of Jerusalem, for sin and for impurity." This word is both a promise and a prophecy.

The anticipation of God's redemption and salvation lasted for four thousand years. The promise and prophecy concerning the seed of woman in Genesis 3:15 was given four thousand years before Christ. During those four thousand years, God did nothing to accomplish His redemption for man's salvation. Then, at the end of that period of anticipation, John the Baptist came out to announce to Israel the good news that Jehovah, the very God, was appearing to accomplish redemption for them (Isa. 40:3-5; cf. Luke 3:4-6). Eventually, that redemption would consummate in their salvation.

Adam and Eve, who had become fallen sinners, believed God's promise and prophecy that the seed of woman would come. So when Adam and Eve gave birth to their first son, Eve said, "I have gotten a man, the Lord" (Gen. 4:1, NASB margin). They named the child Cain, which means "acquired," because they thought that their first son was the fulfillment of the promise in Genesis 3:15. Cain, however, was not the seed of woman; he was the seed of the serpent. Adam and Eve were mistaken, because the seed of woman was the coming Christ.

Thirty-three hundred years from the time of Adam and Eve, the prophet Isaiah repeated the promise given to them by God. Isaiah 7:14 says, "Behold, the virgin will conceive and will bear a son, and she will call his name Immanuel." This prophecy was fully fulfilled in the first book of the New Testament, in Matthew 1:23. Jesus is the fulfillment of Immanuel, promised in Isaiah 7:14. He was a human boy, but His name was the Mighty God (Isa. 9:6). He is God with us.

The Age of the Law

The period from Adam to the present time is approximately six thousand years. This period can be divided into three sections of approximately two thousand years each: from Adam to Abraham, from Abraham to Christ, and from Christ to our present time. The law was given during the two thousand years between Abraham and Christ. The period of time from God's promise to Abraham until the decree of the law by Moses was about four hundred thirty years (Gal. 3:17). Thus, according to the entire history of the Bible, the law came very late. The law decreed by God through Moses in Exodus 20 at Mount Sinai came approximately fifteen hundred years before Christ. Then from Christ's first coming until today is a period of nearly two thousand years. From Genesis 3:15 to the time of Moses was about twenty-five hundred years. During this long period before the fulfillment of His redemption and salvation, while He was waiting and anticipating, God gave His people the law in order to test them, try them, and expose them to the uttermost.

The books of Isaiah and Jeremiah itemize all the sins of the fallen Israelites. Isaiah's list of their sins includes idolatry, the worshipping of idols and the making of idols. This indicates that they broke the first three commandments (Exo. 20:1-7). Jeremiah condemned them for their breaking of the Sabbath, which was their breaking of the fourth commandment (v. 8). According to Jeremiah, they also did not honor their parents, thus breaking the fifth commandment (v. 12). Eventually, Jeremiah shouted that there was no justice in their society. This indicates that they broke the last five commandments (vv. 13-17). Hence, they broke all the Ten Commandments to the uttermost. Eventually, the entire nation of Israel was captured, except for a small remnant. Jeremiah warned this remnant, but they would not repent. At first, they begged Jeremiah to give them the word of the Lord, but when Jeremiah received the word and gave it to them, they rejected him. Instead of receiving his word, they told him that they would go down into Egypt, and there they continued in their idolatry by worshipping the queen of heaven (the wife of Nimrod).

Eventually, God Himself came in the form of a man. When He came to the earth, Israel was full of sin. Wherever He went, the people were possessed by demons because they worshipped idols. Demon possession is an indication of idol worship. Israel's history shows that no one can keep the Ten Commandments. Thus, while God was waiting in anticipation of His coming redemption and salvation, He did only one thing: He gave people the law to test them and expose them.

CHRIST AS THE SEED OF THE WOMAN, THE SEED OF ABRAHAM, AND THE SEED OF DAVID

The promises given by God concerning Christ as our Redeemer and Savior are all regarding a seed: the seed of the woman, the seed of Abraham, and the seed of David. This is expressed in *Hymns,* #191, where the first three stanzas portray Christ as the seed of the woman, the seed of Abraham, and the seed of David. These three seeds are promised in the Old Testament; but in the New Testament, Christ as the fulfillment of these seeds has come. Matthew 1:1 says, "The book of the generation of Jesus Christ, the son of David, the son of Abraham." Both David and Abraham are mentioned at the beginning of Christ's genealogy, and Mary is mentioned at the end (v. 16). Many names are mentioned in this genealogy, but Jesus is called only the seed of the woman (Mary), the seed of David, and the seed of Abraham.

I. IN THE PROMISES

The divine economy and the divine dispensing are seen in the promises of God's anticipated redemption and salvation.

A. In the Promise of the Seed of the Woman— the Son Born of a Virgin

The first promise is the promise of the seed of the woman, who was the son born of a virgin (Gen. 3:15; Isa. 7:14). The promise of the seed of the woman was given immediately after Adam's fall. After that, God remained silent for

thirty-three hundred years. He then used Isaiah to repeat
His earlier promise given in Genesis 3:15. In Genesis God
promised that the seed of the woman would come, but in
Isaiah 7:14 He said that a virgin would conceive and bring
forth a son. This son brought forth would be the real seed
promised by God in Genesis 3:15. Between these two promises,
for thirty-three centuries man fell through four successive
steps until he had fallen to the uttermost, into idolatry, at
Babel (see *Life-study of Genesis,* Messages Eighteen through
Thirty-six).

1. Referring to the Incarnated Christ

The promise of the seed of the woman refers to the incarnated Christ (Matt. 1:16; Gal. 4:4). Mary, a female descendant
of King David, became the mother of the promised Christ
and the mother of the seed of the woman. Galatians 4:4 says
that Christ was "born of a woman."

2. Implying the Complete God Becoming
a Perfect Man through the Dispensing
of Himself into Humanity

Christ as the seed of the woman implies that the complete God became a perfect man through the dispensing
of Himself into humanity (John 1:1, 14; Matt. 1:23). God's
incarnation was a dispensing. In eternity past, God remained
in Himself. But at one point He made a counsel not to remain
in Himself any longer. He desired to bring His divinity into
humanity, and He prophesied concerning His desire in Genesis 3:15. However, this promise was not fulfilled until Mary
conceived in Matthew 1. Because He was very patient, our
God was silent for four thousand years.

At the time of the Lord's incarnation, God did not come to
visit man as He had done with Adam. This time He entered
into the womb of a virgin, remained there for nine months,
and was born of her to be a God-man. As a man, He is
Emmanuel (Matt. 1:23), God with us. Through incarnation
God dispensed Himself into humanity. From the day of His
incarnation, God no longer remained only in His divinity. He

now remains in both divinity and humanity. The incarnation of Christ was the dispensing of God Himself into humanity. Christ is a real man, a perfect man, yet within Him is also the complete God. Hence, He is the God-man.

Today in the heavens He is still a man. The subject of *Hymns,* #62 is Christ's humanity, and the fourth stanza of this hymn indicates that in the heavens Christ is still a man:

> In the time which God appointed
>   Thou wilt come, dear Lord, again,
> With the glory of the Father,
>   Still appearing as a man.
> Even on the throne of judgment
>   Son of man Thou still wilt be;
> And with this, our human nature,
>   Thou forevermore wilt be.

Stephen saw Christ as the Son of Man standing at the right hand of God after His ascension (Acts. 7:56). In His second coming, Christ will be a man (Matt. 26:64). Christ has also been appointed by God to be the Judge of the living and the dead (Acts 10:42). Because He is a man, God has given Him the authority to judge men (John 5:22, 27). According to the New Testament, God has authorized the man Jesus to judge the living at His coming, before the millennium on His throne of glory (Matt. 25:31-46), and the dead after the millennium on the great white throne (Rev. 20:11-15). In eternity He will still be a man (John 1:51).

Today on the earth the dispensing of God Himself into humanity includes not only Christ but also all of His believers. Hallelujah, Christ is the God-man, and we also are God-men. Jesus is the dispensing of God Himself into humanity, and we too are the dispensing of God Himself into humanity.

3. To Destroy Satan and to Save the Believers in Christ from Sin and Death

The purpose of the seed of the woman, the son born of a virgin, was to destroy Satan and to save the believers in

Christ from sin and death (Heb. 2:14; Matt. 1:20-21; 1 Cor. 15:53-57). To bruise the head of the serpent is to destroy the serpent (Gen. 3:15). Through His death Christ destroyed the devil (Heb. 2:14). Since Adam's fall three things have bothered mankind: Satan, sin, and death. These three things are one. Thus, in His death and resurrection Christ destroyed Satan and saved His believers from sin and death.

B. In the Promise of the Seed of Abraham

The divine economy and the divine dispensing is also shown in the promise of the seed of Abraham (Gen. 17:8; Gal. 3:16; Matt. 1:1-2a). In the beginning, God created man in His own image and after His own likeness. But man fell through four successive steps until he came to Babel, a place full of idols. Eventually, God was chased away from the earth by man's idolatry. History tells us that every brick of the tower of Babel had the name of an idol on it. Abraham was born in that land of idolatry (Josh. 24:2-3). One day while Abraham was worshipping idols, the God of glory appeared to him and called him (Acts 7:2-3). God called Abraham out of the place called Shinar, the base of Babylon, and brought him into the good land of Canaan. Once Abraham arrived in the land of Canaan, God appeared to him and made a promise to him concerning a seed (Gen. 12:7).

1. For the Blessing to All the Families of the Earth

The seed of Abraham is for the blessing to all the families of the earth (Gen. 12:3). Although He prophesied concerning the seed of the woman in Genesis 3:15, God did not do anything immediately to fulfill His promise. Instead, He allowed man to fall again and again until he reached the bottom of the fall at Babel. Then God called out one person, Abraham. In Genesis 12:2-3 His speaking to Abraham indicated only a little concerning His intention. God said that He would make Abraham great and that all the families of the earth would be blessed in him. Then in Genesis 17:7 God told Abraham that He would make a covenant with Abraham and with his *seed*. This word concerning the seed was explained clearly by

Paul in Galatians 3:16 when he said, "But to Abraham were the promises spoken and to his seed. He does not say, 'And to the seeds,' as concerning many, but as concerning one: 'And to your seed,' who is Christ."

Today we must thank the Lord that we are more clear than Abraham was concerning the promise of the seed. Abraham might have only understood that God would give him a good piece of land, a land flowing with milk and honey. It is doubtful that Abraham understood that through many centuries, through forty generations, a virgin would bring forth a boy who would be the real seed and the One through whom the earth would be blessed. Not only Abraham did not understand these things in his time; the Jews still do not understand this promise. Paul was a Jew and did not understand this matter before becoming a Christian. Eventually, after some years, Paul wrote Galatians 3, in which he said that God's promise to Abraham was His preaching of the gospel to Abraham and that the blessing of Abraham was the Spirit (vv. 8, 14). God did not promise Abraham a piece of land. The promise to Abraham was that he would receive the processed God as the all-inclusive, consummated Spirit.

2. Referring to the Promised Spirit

The blessing of Abraham refers to the promised Spirit, who is the reality of Christ (Gal. 3:14; John 14:17-20). The one seed of Abraham became the life-giving Spirit (1 Cor. 15:45b).

3. As the Consummation of the Triune God for the Dispensing of Himself into the Believers of Christ

The Spirit as the consummation of the Triune God for the dispensing of Himself into the believers of Christ is the seed of Abraham (1 Cor. 15:45b; 2 Cor. 3:17-18; Rom. 8:9). The last Adam mentioned in 1 Corinthians 15:45 is the seed of Abraham. This seed became not only our Redeemer and Savior but also the life-giving Spirit. The life-giving Spirit is a transfigured descendant of Abraham. The top blessing, the consummate blessing, to us sinners is God Himself as the life-giving Spirit. On the one hand, the life-giving Spirit is a transfigured descendant of Abraham, and on the other hand, He is the very Triune God. This life-giving Spirit is the consummated Spirit who is the consummation of the processed Triune God. This is the real blessing.

If today we had only a Redeemer who died for us on the cross and only a Savior who stretches out His hand to pull us out of the "water" of our troubles, this would not be sufficient. The Savior we need today is the One who can enter into us. We need the life-giving Spirit who dwells in our spirit and who is one spirit with us (1 Cor. 6:17). When we fall into the "water," He falls in with us. He is buoyant. If we did not have the life-giving Spirit in our spirit, we would sink in the "water" because we are not buoyant. But, praise the Lord, we do have a buoyant One within us. The third stanza of *Hymns,* #505 expresses this thought: "There's a Man in the glory / Whose Life is for me. / ...He's strong and in vigor, / How buoyant is He!" Where is Christ buoyant? He is buoyant in our spirit. He has been buoyant within me for sixty-five years. Because of this buoyant One, I can boast that I have been kept from falling. The life-giving Spirit as the seed of Abraham and as the consummation of the processed Triune God is the top blessing. As such a One, He can be in us with both His divinity and His humanity. How wonderful this is! The totality of what He is, is called *the* Spirit. The good land given to Abraham was a type of this Spirit. *The* Spirit is the blessing God promised Abraham.

4. For the Believers in Christ, Who Are Abraham's Seed, to Inherit the Consummated Spirit as Their Divine Inheritance

The seed of Abraham is for the believers in Christ, who are Abraham's seed, to inherit the consummated Spirit, the consummation of the processed Triune God, as their divine inheritance—their spiritual blessing for eternity (Acts 26:18; Eph. 1:14a; Gal. 3:14). Christ is the seed of Abraham, and all

His believers are also the seed of Abraham (v. 29). Now, as believers we are no longer merely descendants of Americans, Chinese, or Japanese. We are Abraham's seed. We are all one family, and our surname is Abraham, because Abraham is our father (Rom. 4:12).

Our spiritual blessing for eternity is to inherit the consummated Spirit, the consummation of the processed Triune God, as our inheritance. In the new heaven and new earth in the New Jerusalem, we will enjoy the processed Triune God, who is the all-inclusive, consummated, life-giving Spirit. This is our blessing. Even today, the most enjoyable thing to us is the indwelling Spirit.

C. In the Promise of the Seed of David

1. Referring to the Resurrected Christ

The divine economy and the divine dispensing are also seen in the promise of the seed of David (2 Sam. 7:12-14a; Matt. 1:1, 6; 22:42-45; Rom. 1:3; Rev. 22:16). The seed of David refers to the resurrected Christ, who carries out God's New Testament economy for the dispensing of the processed Triune God into the members of His Body (Acts 2:30-31; Matt. 16:16-18).

2. As God's Sure Mercies

The resurrected Christ is God's sure mercies, of which Christ is the center and reality, shown to David through his descendant Mary, the mother of Christ (Matt. 1:16), for the dispensing of God Himself into all the believers of Christ in His resurrection (Acts 13:32-35; Isa. 55:3-4). According to Paul's understanding in Acts 13:34 and 35 (see note 1 on verse 34), the sure mercies shown to David are Christ Himself in resurrection. In Christ as the sure mercies, God reaches us in His grace to be our enjoyment. Because our situation was miserable and could not match God's grace, Christ not only took the step of incarnation to bring God as grace to us, but He also took the further step of death and resurrection in order to become the sure mercies to us in resurrection. Through His death and resurrection, Christ, the embodiment of God's grace, became the sure mercies, and through these mercies we are now in the proper position to match God and to receive Him as grace.

3. For the Believers in Christ
to Share His Kingship

Christ as God's sure mercies shown to David is for the dispensing of God Himself into all the believers of Christ in His resurrection. This is for the believers in Christ to share His kingship in His resurrection in the eternal kingdom of God (2 Tim. 2:12; Rev. 20:4, 6).

The divine economy and the divine dispensing in the promises of the seed of the woman, the seed of Abraham, and the seed of David have a threefold purpose: first, to destroy Satan and to save us from sin and death; second, to cause us to inherit the consummated Triune God as our blessing and inheritance; and third, to cause us to share Christ's kingship. These three items cover God's full salvation in a complete way. God's full salvation is to deliver us out of the hand of Satan and out of sin and death, to bring us into the full inheritance of God Himself as our blessing, and to cause us to share the kingship with Christ as His co-kings in the kingdom age.

The seed of the woman, the seed of Abraham, and the seed of David all indicate the divine dispensing. All three of these seeds are just one seed—a human being with God dispensed into Him. Christ, the God-man, is the seed of the woman, the seed of Abraham, and the seed of David. Now, in Him, God and man, man and God, are blended and mingled together as one entity. This entity is fully signified in, with, and by the New Jerusalem. The New Jerusalem is the totality of God's dispensing of Himself into humanity.

The Central Line of the Divine Revelation

THE DIVINE ECONOMY
AND THE DIVINE DISPENSING

MESSAGE NINE

A COMPLEMENTING WORD ON CHRIST
BEING THE THREEFOLD SEED IN HUMANITY
FOR GOD'S DISPENSING OF HIMSELF
INTO THE BELIEVERS OF CHRIST

Scripture Reading: Gen. 1:26, 28b; 2:8-9, 22-24; Heb. 2:14;
John 1:29; Rom. 8:3; 2 Tim. 1:10b; 1 Pet. 1:3b; Rom 6:6a;
1 Tim. 2:14; Rom. 5:12; 1 Cor. 15:45b; Rom. 8:9b, 11; Rev.
22:17a; John 3:5-6; 2 Cor. 3:17-18; Rom. 8:29; Luke 1:31-32;
Acts 13:33-34; 5:30b-31a; 2 Tim. 2:12a; Rev. 20:4, 6; Rom.
6:3-5; Eph. 2:6; 1 Cor. 6:17; Phil. 3:10; Phil. 1:19b-21a; Acts
13:52; 4:31b; Gal. 5:16, 25; Rom. 8:4b; Rev. 2:26-27; 3:21;
1 Thes. 5:17, 19

Prayer: Lord, we look to You again for Your mercy and
blessing. Without You we are nothing and we can do nothing.
Lord, be merciful to us and speak to us. Give us grace that
we may humble ourselves as we come to You with Your Word.
We look to You that You would shine upon us and upon every
line as we read. Lord, give us light. Give us the instant utterance that we may speak what You have shown us. Amen.

Christ as the threefold seed touches the essence of the
divine revelation. The revelation of the Bible is mainly an
unveiling of Christ as the threefold seed: the seed of the
woman (Gen. 3:15; Isa. 7:14), the seed of Abraham (Gen. 17:8;
Gal. 3:16), and the seed of David (2 Sam. 7:12-14; Matt. 1:1,
6; 22:42-45; Rom. 1:3; Rev. 22:16). The promise of the seed of
the woman was given nearly six thousand years ago. The
promise concerning the seed of Abraham was given two thousand years after the first promise, and the fulfillment of that

promise came two thousand years later. The entire revelation of the Scriptures is wrapped up with the seed of the woman, the seed of Abraham, and the seed of David. This threefold seed links Christ as God to man and Christ as man to God. In other words, this seed makes Christ the mingling, the blending, of God and man.

As we pointed out in the previous message, the Bible tells us that Christ is the seed of only three persons: the woman (Mary); Abraham, the forefather of God's chosen people; and David, the one who founded the kingdom of Israel. These three are mentioned in a particular way in the genealogy of Christ in Matthew 1. In verse 1 Christ was introduced as the son of David and the son of Abraham. This indicates that Christ is the seed of David and the seed of Abraham. Then at the end of the genealogy, Matthew records that Christ was born of Mary (v. 16). Mary's husband was Joseph, but Christ was not born of Joseph; He was born of Mary. This indicates that Christ is her seed, the seed of the woman.

INCARNATION BEING THE DISPENSING OF GOD HIMSELF INTO HUMANITY

Christ's being the seed of the woman, the seed of Abraham, and the seed of David strongly implies the dispensing of God Himself into man. The seed of the woman (Gen. 3:15) refers to the incarnation of Christ. Isaiah 7:14 confirms the promise in Genesis 3:15, and the birth of Christ in Matthew 1:22-23 and 25 was the fulfillment of Isaiah 7:14. Incarnation was the dispensing of God Himself into humanity.

The incarnation was God being born into humanity. When Mary's husband Joseph purposed to put Mary away secretly, an angel of the Lord appeared to him in a dream and told him not to be afraid to take Mary as his wife, "for that which has been begotten in her is of the Holy Spirit" (Matt. 1:20). The Spirit of God, who is God reaching man, had come into Mary's womb. In the process of incarnation, God was begotten in humanity. Eventually, a child was born who was called the Mighty God (Isa. 9:6). Because He was the very God, His name was also called Emmanuel—God with us (Matt. 1:23).

Through incarnation God entered into humanity, and this entering of God into humanity was His dispensing of Himself into humanity.

The dispensing of God into man is greater than the creation of the heavens and the earth, because incarnation makes God one with man and makes man one with God. In His creation God created many things, and before His incarnation, throughout the Old Testament, He performed a number of miracles and works of power, such as the parting of the Red Sea (Exo. 14:21-22). But there is no comparison between these miracles and incarnation. Incarnation was the bringing of God into man.

Regeneration is as great an event as incarnation. With the Lord Jesus, God's entering into man was incarnation, but with us, God's entering into man is regeneration. Through regeneration we are the same as Christ; we even are little "Christs." D. L. Moody once said that regeneration is the greatest miracle. When we repented and believed, we received the Lord Jesus, and as we prayed, God entered into us. The New Testament tells us clearly that, first, God is within us (Eph. 4:6); second, Christ is within us (Rom. 8:10; 2 Cor. 13:5); and third, the Spirit is within us (Rom. 8:9). Eventually, Philippians 2:13 tells us that God is operating in us. Every day God operates in us. God's operation within us is a great matter.

CHRIST AS THE THREEFOLD DISPENSING

Christ as the seed of the woman, the seed of Abraham, and the seed of David is a threefold seed and also a threefold dispensing. God promised that the seed of the woman would bruise the head of the serpent. This is the first aspect of God's dispensing.

God's promise to Abraham that his seed would be the blessing to all the nations was the second aspect of His dispensing. This blessing to all the nations is the Spirit. The seed of Abraham is Christ as the last Adam (1 Cor. 15:45b). This last Adam, the God-man, eventually became the life-giving Spirit. A man who was the seed of Abraham became a Spirit, even a life-giving Spirit (1 Cor. 15:45b). John 1:14 reveals that the Word became flesh. Then, according to 1 Corinthians 15:45, Christ as the last Adam became a life-giving Spirit. The first time the word became is used concerning Christ is when He became a man to bring divinity into humanity. The second time is when Christ as the last Adam became a Spirit in order to give life. In order to impart God into man, the man Jesus had to die and be resurrected so that He could become a life-giving Spirit. How marvelous this is!

Christ as the seed of David was begotten through His resurrection to be the firstborn Son of God and God's sure mercies shown to David (Acts 13:33-34). This is the third aspect of His dispensing.

I. THE POSITIVE INTENTION
OF GOD'S ECONOMY

In eternity past the Triune God held a divine council. In that divine conference the Triune God made a counsel, and this counsel became His economy. The positive intention of God's economy comprises three items.

A. To Have Man
in His Image and after His Likeness
for Man to Be One with Him
That He May Express Himself in Humanity

The first item of God's positive intention in His economy is to have man in His image and after His likeness for man to be one with Him that He may express Himself in humanity (Gen. 1:26a). As a man on this earth, Jesus was made, or created, in God's image and after God's likeness. Christ was not only born but also created. When He entered into a human womb, Christ joined Himself with the created man, Adam. Hence, Christ was created in God's image and after God's likeness. As human beings, we all were begotten of our parents. But we were not only begotten; we were also created. We were created when Adam was created. Our birth merely caused us to participate in that creation. In the same way, Christ was created in God's image and after God's likeness to be one with man and one with God.

Man was made in God's image and after His likeness so that God could express Himself in humanity. God expressed Himself in the humanity of Jesus while He was on the earth for thirty-three and a half years. John 1:18 says, "No one has ever seen God; the only begotten Son, who is in the bosom of the Father, He has declared Him." When He wept, Jesus expressed God. When He was angry with the Pharisees, He expressed God. He did everything to express God in His humanity.

Although God was seen in the humanity of the one man Jesus, this was not sufficient. The man Jesus had to be duplicated, mass-produced. In Christ's incarnation, God entered into only one man, but in Christ's becoming the life-giving Spirit, God entered into millions of people. On the day of Pentecost, three thousand were produced at one time (Acts 2:41). All of these believers were made small "Christs"; that is, they were the mass production of Christ.

B. To Give Man His Dominion
over the Earth
That Man May Represent Him
in His Administration

The second item of God's positive intention in His economy was to give man His dominion over the earth and over all the creatures on the earth, in the water, and in the heavens that man may represent Him in His administration (Gen. 1:26b, 28b). Man should not only express God but also represent God in His administration. This touches the matter of God's government. The four Gospels reveal that Jesus is not only God's expression but also God's representative. The little man Jesus rebuked the wind and silenced the sea (Mark 4:39). His disciples said to one another, "Who then is this, that even the wind and the sea obey Him?" (v. 41). He was a small Nazarene, but the wind and the sea obeyed Him. This was because He had God's dominion; as a man He represented God. The Lord Jesus represented God, and we also must learn to represent God.

C. To Be Received by Man as Man's Life for Man's Inward Constitution That Man May Become the Counterpart of the Triune God

The third item of God's positive intention in His economy is to be received by man as man's life for his inward constitution that man may become the counterpart of the Triune God (Gen. 2:8-9, 22-24). Adam was created in God's image and after God's likeness. God formed man with a body of clay and with the breath of life out from God. This breath became man's spirit as a receiver and container of God. God made man in this way and put him in front of the tree of life (v. 9) because He intended to be received by man. He then told man that he could eat of all the trees in the garden, including the tree of life (v. 16). He also warned man not to eat of the tree of the knowledge of good and evil (v. 17). The tree of life signifies God as life to man. If man would have eaten of the tree of life, he would have taken God Himself into him. Without the life signified by the tree of life, man is an empty container, a vessel without any content. Today, we as God's containers have the Triune God as our life and content. Every day this life constitutes us.

Today, God is within us as our life and life supply. As our life supply, He constitutes us with Himself, making Himself our constituent. Whenever we eat food, a dispensing takes place. Once food is eaten, after about eight hours, it becomes our constitution. When the children of Israel were brought out of Egypt and journeyed in the wilderness, they had nothing to eat. They had no farms to produce their food, so every morning God dropped manna from heaven for them to eat. The children of Israel lived on manna for forty years. Wherever they went for those forty years, the manna was there. Before entering the wilderness, the children of Israel were Egyptian in their constitution because all they had eaten were the things of the Egyptian diet, including fish, cucumbers, green onions, leaks, and garlic. Such eating produced an Egyptian constitution within them. But God changed their constitution by giving them manna to eat. By eating manna for forty years, the Israelites became a constitution of manna. Their constitution was changed by their eating.

God's intention in His economy is that He would be man's life for man's inward constitution that man may become the counterpart of God. What a wonder that we can be the counterpart of God! This is fully typified as a divine revelation in Genesis 2. God created Adam (v. 7), built a wife from one of his ribs (vv. 21-22), and brought the wife back to Adam, and the two of them became one flesh (vv. 22-24). Eve became the counterpart of Adam. Today we have become the counterpart of God, a part of God that matches God. Initially, God was alone; but it was not good for Him to be alone (v. 18). God needed a counterpart. After receiving God as his life for his inward constitution, man has become the counterpart of the Triune God.

According to Ephesians 4:4-6 the Father, the Son, the Spirit, and the Body are all one. This is the oneness of the Body. It is altogether proper to say that the Father, the Son, the Spirit, and the Body are four in one. The Triune God is three, yet He now has a fourth part, a counterpart. However, only the first three are worthy of our worship. The Triune God with His counterpart are now four in one.

II. THE NEGATIVE NEED CAUSED BY MAN'S FALL THROUGH THE TEMPTATION OF GOD'S ADVERSARY SATAN

God's positive intention in His economy consists of the aforementioned three positive items. But man's fall through the temptation of God's adversary caused a negative need. This need consists of four items.

A. To Destroy Satan in Christ's Humanity through Death

The first item of the negative need caused by man's fall is

to destroy Satan, the origin of sin and the possessor of the might of death, in Christ's humanity through death (Heb. 2:14). Satan is not only God's enemy but also God's adversary. An enemy is one who is on the outside, but an adversary is one who is on the inside. God's intention is to deal with man's negative need by destroying Satan, God's enemy and God's adversary.

B. To Take Away Sin through Christ's Death in His Flesh

The second item of man's negative need is to take away sin through Christ's death in His flesh (John 1:29; Rom. 8:3). Christ as the Lamb of God took away the sin of the world.

C. To Nullify Death through Christ's Resurrection in His Humanity

The third item of man's negative need is to nullify death through Christ's resurrection in His humanity (2 Tim. 1:10b; 1 Pet. 1:3b). In His humanity, Christ nullified death through His resurrection.

D. To Terminate the Old Man Corrupted by Satan with Sin unto Death

The fourth item of the negative need caused by man's fall is to terminate the old man corrupted by Satan with sin unto death (Rom. 6:6a; 1 Tim. 2:14; Rom. 5:12). God did not create man in an old condition; He created man in a very fresh condition. Man became old when Satan came into him with sin, which is unto death. These three factors—Satan, sin, and death—entered into us to corrupt us and make us old. Being old is not a matter of age but a matter of condition. We were dirty, sinful, and destined to die because we have Satan, sin, and death within us. Our entire old being, our old man, was and still is wrapped up with these three things. However, through Christ's death on the cross in His humanity, the old man corrupted by Satan with sin unto death was terminated.

III. CHRIST AS THE SEED OF THE WOMAN
HAVING DESTROYED SATAN,
TAKEN AWAY SIN, NULLIFIED DEATH, AND
CRUCIFIED THE OLD MAN IN HIS HUMANITY

Christ as the seed of the woman has dealt with Satan, sin, death, and the old man. The first stanza and chorus of *Hymns,* #890 express the fact that Christ is the Victor over Satan, sin, and death:

> Hallelujah! Christ is Victor,
>   Tell with every breath,
> That the Savior still is conqu'ror
>   Over sin and death.

> Hallelujah! Christ is Victor,
>   Tell where'er you go,
> That the Lord is still the conqu'ror,
>   Over every foe.

Sin and death are the product of Satan. Sin came from Satan and issues in death (Rom. 5:12). However, Satan was destroyed by Christ, sin was taken away through Christ's death, and death was nullified by Christ's appearing in the flesh. Moreover, our old man, which was corrupted by Satan, sin, and death, was terminated by being crucified with Christ. All these items are included in the bruising of the serpent's head by the seed of the woman. These are the achievements of Christ as the seed of the woman.

IV. CHRIST AS THE SEED OF ABRAHAM,
THE LAST ADAM, THE GOD-MAN,
BECOMING THE LIFE-GIVING SPIRIT
TO IMPART HIMSELF AS GOD'S EMBODIMENT
AND LIFE INTO HIS BELIEVERS

Christ as the seed of Abraham, the last Adam, the God-man, has become the life-giving Spirit, the Spirit of Christ, the consummated and indwelling Spirit, the divine Spirit processed and compounded with Christ's humanity, His death and its effectiveness, and His resurrection and its power, the unique and all-inclusive Spirit, the Spirit (as the aggregate of the blessing of the full gospel of God in Christ), to impart Himself as God's embodiment and life into us that we may be regenerated and transformed and conformed to the glorious image of Christ as the firstborn Son of God (1 Cor. 15:45b; Rom. 8:9b, 11; Rev. 22:17a; John 3:5-6; 2 Cor. 3:17-18; Rom. 8:29).

The first man, Adam, was not a God-man. But the last Adam was a God-man, a man wrapped up with the element of God. As the last Adam, Christ died and resurrected, and through death and resurrection He became the life-giving Spirit (1 Cor. 15:45b). It is significant that Paul inserted the adjective *life-giving* before the word *Spirit*. We might also render the adjective *life-giving* as *life-imparting*. Christ has become the life-imparting Spirit. Since life is God Himself embodied in Christ, this life-imparting Spirit is also the God-giving, or God-imparting, Spirit, the Spirit who imparts God into us. This is implied not in the seed of the woman but in the seed of Abraham (Gal. 3:14, 16). Jesus Christ, our Redeemer and Savior, has become a Spirit who gives life, a Spirit who imparts God.

Christ as the life-giving Spirit is also the Spirit of Christ. He is not just the Spirit of God, but the Spirit of Christ. This is the consummated and indwelling Spirit. The word *consummated* implies a process. Thus, the consummated and indwelling Spirit is the Spirit who has gone through a process to become qualified and able to indwell us. The Spirit of God could not indwell us without being processed. In order to indwell us, the Spirit of God has passed through incarnation, human living, death, and resurrection as the steps of a long process. Now, because of this process, He is qualified and able to dwell within us. This indwelling is a great thing.

The steps of incarnation, human living, death, and resurrection are a real process. In the process of incarnation God Himself was confined within the womb of Mary for nine months. Then after His birth, He continued the process by passing through human living for thirty-three and a half years. Thus, human living was included in the long process of His incarnation. He then went through death and traveled through death, staying in the realm of death for three days.

Then He entered into the process of resurrection. After His glorification in resurrection (Luke 24:26), the process of the Triune God was complete, and on the day of resurrection He came back to His disciples and breathed the Spirit into them (John 20:22). Before Jesus was glorified in resurrection, the Spirit who is the Spirit of Christ and the life-giving Spirit was not yet (John 7:39). After Christ's resurrection, the Spirit, the divine Spirit, was processed and compounded with Christ's humanity, His death, the effectiveness of His death, His resurrection, and the power of His resurrection. The compound ointment in Exodus 30:23-25 is a clear type of the unique and all-inclusive Spirit, who is the Spirit. This Spirit is the aggregate of the blessing of the full gospel of God in Christ.

The eight items of blessing, including the last Adam, the God-man, the life-giving Spirit, the Spirit of Christ, the consummated and indwelling Spirit, the divine Spirit, the unique and all-inclusive Spirit, and the Spirit, are all wrapped up with Christ as the seed of Abraham. If you have Christ as the seed of Abraham, you are qualified to be blessed with these eight items. Although Confucius was a great teacher of morality, he was not qualified to receive this eightfold blessing. Only genuine, regenerated, and transformed Christians are qualified to enjoy these blessings. We are qualified with, by, in, and through the life-giving Spirit. This Spirit is the aggregate of the blessing of the full gospel of God in Christ. Christ became the life-giving Spirit so that He could impart Himself as God's embodiment and life into us that we may be regenerated, transformed, and conformed to the glorious image of Christ as the firstborn Son of God.

V. CHRIST AS THE SEED OF DAVID
BEING BEGOTTEN THROUGH HIS RESURRECTION
TO BE THE PRINCE (THE KING)
THAT WE MAY SHARE HIS KINGSHIP

Christ as the seed of David, the king anointed by God, was begotten through His resurrection to be the Prince (the King) in His humanity that we may share His kingship for

God's administration (Luke 1:31-32; Acts 13:33-34; 5:30b-31a; 2 Tim. 2:12a; Rev. 20:4, 6). If we read Acts 13:33 and receive light from the Lord, we can see clearly that resurrection was a birth to Christ. He was the unique, only begotten Son of God (John 3:16), but in resurrection He was born to be the firstborn Son of God (Rom. 8:29; Heb. 1:5-6).

When Christ as the seed of David became the firstborn Son in resurrection, He became God's sure mercies (Acts 13:33-34; see note 1 on verse 34). He also became the Prince, that is, the King, in His humanity that we may share His kingship for God's administration (Acts 5:30b-31a; see note 2 on verse 31). This is the fulfillment of the second item of the positive intention of God's economy, which is to give man God's dominion that he may represent God in His administration.

VI. OVERCOMING SATAN, SIN, AND DEATH, TERMINATING THE OLD MAN, AND PARTICIPATING IN THE ALL-EMBRACING BLESSING OF THE SPIRIT OF CHRIST AND IN THE KINGSHIP OF CHRIST

In order to overcome Satan, sin, and death, to terminate the old man, and to participate in the all-embracing blessing of the Spirit of Christ and in the kingship of Christ, we need at least six items. These items cover all the charges to the believers in the New Testament.

A. To Be Identified with the All-inclusive Christ as the Threefold Seed in His Humanity

First, we must be identified with the all-inclusive Christ, as the threefold seed in His humanity, in His death, resurrection, and ascension, so that we can be one with Him, even one spirit with Him (Rom. 6:3-5; Eph. 2:6; 1 Cor. 6:17). It is in this way that we are one with the Triune God.

B. To Live in Christ's Resurrection through His Cross

Second, we must live in Christ's resurrection through His cross (Phil. 3:10). Every day we should walk and live under the shadow of the cross. We should always remain under the cross, not doing anything in a natural way. Then we will have the experience of Christ's resurrection.

C. To Live Him as the Pneumatic Christ by the Bountiful Supply of His Spirit

Third, we must live Him as the pneumatic Christ by the bountiful supply of His Spirit (Phil. 1:19b-21a). The pneumatic Christ has a supply—the Spirit of Jesus Christ. The Spirit of Jesus Christ has the bountiful supply to support us so that we can live the pneumatic Christ, who is not in the flesh but in the spirit, in the *pneuma*.

D. To Be Filled with the Spirit Within and Without and to Walk according to the Spirit in Our Spirit

Fourth, we must be filled with the Spirit within and without, and we must live and walk according to the Spirit in our spirit (Acts 13:52; 4:31b; Gal. 5:16, 25; Rom. 8:4b). To be filled with the Spirit within and without is to be filled inwardly and outwardly. To be filled inwardly is to have the infilling of the Spirit, and to be filled outwardly is to experience the outpouring of the Spirit.

E. To Overcome Individualism, Sectarianism, and Christianity, and to Live the Life of the Body of Christ

Fifth, we must overcome individualism, sectarianism, and Christianity, and we must live the life of the Body of Christ (Rev. 2:26-27; 3:21). We must overcome every kind of "anity" and "ism," including Christianity and "church-anity." We must also learn to live the life of the Body of Christ.

F. To Receive God's Constant and Instant Dispensing Continuously through Unceasing Prayer, Not Quenching the Spirit

Sixth, we must receive God's constant and instant dispensing continuously through unceasing prayer, not quenching the Spirit (1 Thes. 5:17, 19). When we become such persons, we will overcome Satan, sin, and death, we will experience the termination of the old man, and we will participate in the all-embracing blessing of the Spirit of Christ and in the kingship of Christ. This is our experience through the daily, moment by moment, dispensing of the Triune God.

The Central Line of the Divine Revelation

THE DIVINE ECONOMY
AND THE DIVINE DISPENSING

MESSAGE TEN

THE AGGREGATE OF THE ALL-EMBRACING BLESSING
OF THE FULL GOSPEL OF GOD IN CHRIST
FOR THE DIVINE DISPENSING
ACCORDING TO THE DIVINE ECONOMY

(1)

Scripture Reading: 1 Cor. 15:45b; Gal. 3:14; John 20:22; 14:9-11, 16-20; 16:13-15; 1 Cor. 2:7-12; 2 Cor. 13:14; Rom. 8:2, 6, 9-11; John 16:7b-11; 3:5-6; 1:12-13; Gal, 4:6; Rom. 8:15; 2 Cor. 3:3b; Eph. 1:11a, 13; 4:30b; 2 Cor. 1:22a; Eph. 1:14; 2 Cor. 1:22b

Christ is the center and totality of the entire Bible, especially the New Testament. As portrayed in the four Gospels, Christ is God, a man, a King, and a Slave. However, this is not a full and proper definition of who and what Christ is. The Bible is a record of Christ as a threefold seed in humanity who became a life-giving Spirit, as the consummation of the processed and consummated Triune God, for our portion. The very Triune God became a man as the human seed of three persons—the woman (Mary), Abraham, and David. At the beginning of the Old Testament, Genesis 3:15 says, "And I will put enmity between thee and the woman, and between thy seed and her seed; it shall bruise thy head, and thou shalt bruise his heel." The seed of the woman accomplished many things on the negative side. He destroyed Satan (Heb. 2:14), took away sin (John 1:29), nullified death (2 Tim. 1:10), and terminated our old man (Rom. 6:6). Then, in the middle years of the Old Testament history, God promised Abraham a

seed who would become the blessing to the entire world
(Gen. 12:2-3; Gal. 3:16). The seed of Abraham as the
God-man, the very Triune God in a man, is the very God
given to and enjoyed and experienced by man as the blessing.
In the whole universe only God Himself is a blessing; all
else is vanity of vanities. If we have God, we have the blessing. However, the way for God to be our blessing involved a
process. For food to become our blessing, it must be cooked.
In the same way, God had to be "cooked" in order to be our
blessing. Before passing through a process, God was a "raw"
God. By passing through a process, God became the "cooked"
God and was "put on the table" as our food supply. This God
in His totality is the processed, consummated, all-inclusive,
life-giving, indwelling, compound Spirit. He as the wonderful
Spirit is the blessing from God to us.

As the seed of David the king, Christ is the successor to
David's throne. According to Isaiah 55:3 and Acts 13:34, this
seed of the king is the sure mercies of David. The resurrected
seed of David is the sure mercies that God covenanted to
David. Mercies are the initiation of God's blessing. God gives
Himself to us as a blessing through many kinds of mercies as
the initiation.

At the end of the Bible, Revelation 22:17 says, "The Spirit
and the bride say, Come." This verse indicates that the
Spirit and the bride are a couple. The term *the Spirit* indicates the process of the Triune God. The processed Triune
God will marry the redeemed and glorified tripartite man,
and together they will become a universal couple. Revelation 21 and 22 show us that the New Jerusalem is a
compound, a mingling, a blending, of this processed Triune
God with the chosen and glorified tripartite saints. This is
the blessing given to us based on God's sure mercies.

After Christ as the human seed lived and consummated
His ministry on earth, He became a life-giving Spirit (1 Cor.
15:45b). From that point onward, whatever has taken place
related to Christ has been something of this Spirit. Today the
very God whom we have received and are worshipping and
serving is the consummated Triune God, the reality of whom

is the life-giving Spirit, who is the realization of the man Jesus, the threefold seed. This is the central line, the contents, the substance, and the essence of the entire Bible.

I. THE ALL-INCLUSIVE SPIRIT BEING THE AGGREGATE OF THE ALL-EMBRACING BLESSING OF THE FULL GOSPEL OF GOD IN CHRIST FOR THE DIVINE DISPENSING ACCORDING TO THE DIVINE ECONOMY

The all-inclusive Spirit, whom the all-inclusive Christ (as the threefold seed in humanity) has become, is the aggregate of the all-embracing blessing of the full gospel of God in Christ (Gal. 3:14) for the divine dispensing according to the divine economy. This all-embracing blessing comprises many items. To know these items is to have a "master key" to open every book of the Bible.

A. The Processed and Resurrected Christ Coming Back to His Disciples and Breathing Himself as Such a Life-giving Spirit into His Disciples

On the day of His resurrection, the processed and resurrected Christ, who has become the life-giving Spirit as the consummation of the processed Triune God, came back to His disciples and breathed Himself as such a life-giving Spirit into His disciples for them to receive as the Holy Spirit to be their life, their person, and their everything (John 20:22). Some who hold a tritheistic concept of the Trinity have opposed us for saying that Christ is the Spirit. However, there is a clear word in the Bible that says that the very Christ who is our Redeemer and Savior is now the Spirit. First Corinthians 15:45b says, "The last Adam became a life-giving Spirit," and 2 Corinthians 3:17a says, "And the Lord is the Spirit," which Spirit is "the Lord Spirit" who transforms us (v. 18). Brother Nee received this light concerning the Spirit almost fifty years ago, and the light we have received in recent years is even stronger and more profound. Today we have the boldness to say that the life-giving Spirit is the consummation of the Triune God.

To repeat, on the day of His resurrection, the processed and resurrected Christ, who has become the life-giving Spirit as the consummation of the processed Triune God, came back to His disciples and breathed Himself as such a life-giving Spirit into them. John 20:22 says, "And when He had said this, He breathed into them and said to them, Receive the Holy Spirit." In the Old Testament the title *the Holy Spirit* was not used; this title was not used until the beginning of the New Testament, when God was incarnated (Matt. 1:18, 20; Luke 1:35). The title *the Holy Spirit* definitely denotes a person. The use of this title in John 20:22 makes the breathing in that verse different from the breathing in Genesis 2:7. The breathing in Genesis 2:7 was the breathing of a breath, not of a person. But the breathing in John 20:22 is called the Holy Spirit. Surely this denotes not merely a breath but a person, the breather Himself. The Holy Spirit whom we are to receive is the Triune God reaching us. The Father is the source, the Son is the course, and the Spirit is the flow and also the reaching of the Triune God. The Spirit is the ultimate expression of the Triune God; thus, when we receive the Holy Spirit, we receive the totality of the Triune God.

The old creation of man came out of the breathing in Genesis 2:7. The new creation also came out of a breathing. In Genesis we can see only the breathing of a breath, not of the person of the Divine Trinity, for the creation of man as a part of the old creation. The breathing in John 20:22 took place after Christ had passed through the processes of incarnation, human living for thirty-three and a half years, crucifixion, and resurrection. Before His ascension, on the day of His resurrection, Christ came back to His disciples. He did not teach them, but He breathed something into them. What He breathed into them was the Holy Spirit, who is the life-giving Spirit whom Christ became. This Spirit who was breathed out by Christ was the ultimate consummation of the Triune God. When God breathed His breath into Adam to animate the man of clay with a human spirit, He consummated the old creation. But the breathing in John 20:22 was after Christ had accomplished His New Testament work.

The Old Testament work of God's old creation was to create the physical things. But the New Testament work of Christ was not like that. Christ's New Testament work was of four steps. First, He became a man in incarnation. Before His incarnation He was the only begotten Son of God (John 1:18) with divinity only; but through incarnation He put on blood and flesh (Heb. 2:14a) as His humanity. Then He lived with the disciples for three and a half years. This living was His working. After this, He entered into an all-inclusive death, and then He entered into resurrection. His incarnation was to bring God into humanity; His crucifixion was to terminate that humanity; and His resurrection was to bring the crucified humanity into divinity, that is, to bring man into God. In His resurrection Christ's humanity was "sonized," and in His "sonized" humanity He was born to be the first-born Son of God (Acts 13:33). Christ's coming from God to become a man to bring God into humanity and His going through death and entering into resurrection to bring humanity into divinity was a blending, a mingling, a compounding of God with man and man with God. It was in such a condition that Christ came to the disciples and breathed Himself into them, to compound, mingle, and blend Himself with them.

When Peter, John, James, and the other disciples were meeting in that small room, they represented the entire Body of Christ. When the Head breathed into the Body and told the Body to receive the Holy Spirit, we were there also. After this breathing and receiving took place, the compounding, blending, and mingling of God with man was consummated. At the time of the incarnation there was only one God-man. After John 20:22, however, there were at least one hundred twenty God-men. Today this God-man has replenished the whole earth. Everywhere we can see God-men, who are the blending, the mingling, the compounding of God with man. The realization that we are the blending of God with man should uplift our estimation of our worth. We are the blending, the compounding, of God with man. No words can tell how great a blessing this is.

B. As the Realization of God the Son, Who Is the Embodiment of God the Father, Coming to Be the Reality of the Triune God Not Only with God the Son's Believers but Also in Them

The all-inclusive Spirit, as the realization of God the Son, who is the embodiment of God the Father, came to be the reality of the Triune God, not only with God the Son's believers but also in them, for the dispensing of the Triune God into them (John 14:9-11, 16-20). First Christ, who became the life-giving Spirit as the transfiguration, the realization of the threefold human seed, breathed Himself into the disciples, and the disciples received Him. Then, based on this breathing, the Spirit whom He became came to be the realization of Him as the embodiment of the Father within the believers. In this way the Triune God entered into us to be one with us.

Before Christ's resurrection the Triune God was not able to enter into man. After He went through incarnation, human living, death, and resurrection, He was qualified to breathe Himself into His disciples as the Holy Spirit, the consummation of the Triune God, for them to receive. This life-giving Spirit is the realization of the Son, who is the embodiment of the Father. As such a One, He comes into His disciples to be in their intrinsic being. What a blessing this is!

C. As the Spirit of Reality Declaring, Transmitting, the Triune God into the Son's Believers for the Glorification of God the Son

As the Spirit of reality, the Spirit declares, transmits, to the believers what He receives of God the Son, to whom all that God the Father has is given, transmitted, for the dispensing of the Triune God into the Son's believers, making them one with the Triune God, for the glorification of God

the Son (John 16:13-15). John 16:13-15 says, "But when He,
the Spirit of reality, comes, He will guide you into all the
reality; for He will not speak from Himself, but what He
hears He will speak; and He will declare to you the things
that are coming. He will glorify Me, for He will receive of
Mine and will declare it to you. All that the Father has
is Mine; for this reason I have said that He receives of
Mine and will declare it to you." First, what the Father has is
given, or transmitted, to the Son. This is the first step of the
transmission. Then, what the Son has is received by the
Spirit. This is the second step of the transmission. Finally,
what the Spirit has received is declared, or transmitted, to
the disciples. This is the third step of the transmission. This
transmission involves four parties—the Father, the Son, the
Spirit, and us, the believers. What the Father has is given,
transmitted, to the Son; what the Son has is received by the
Spirit; and what the Spirit receives is declared, transmitted,
to us. This is the transmission of the Triune God into the
Son's believers.

The Spirit's declaring is His transmission. What the
Spirit declares is not doctrines but spiritual realities. In the
universe there is the reality that whatever God the Father
has is given to the Son; whatever the Son has is received by
the Spirit; and all the things of the Father and the Son are
declared by the Spirit to us, the disciples. Thus, there is a
wonderful transmission in the universe—the transmission of
the Triune God into our being.

The transmission of the Triune God into the Son's believers makes them one with the Triune God for the glorification
of God the Son. Our being made one with the Triune God is
to glorify the Son, that is, to express the Son as glory. If we
live a life in the transmission of the Triune God, we will be a
glorious expression of Christ.

D. As the Revealing Spirit,
Showing Us the Deep Things of God concerning
Christ as Our Portion for Our Enjoyment

As the revealing Spirit, the Spirit shows us the deep

things of God concerning Christ as our portion for our enjoyment, foreordained, prepared, and given to us by God but having never been seen or heard by man and having never come up in man's heart, for the dispensing of all the mysterious riches of Christ into our spiritual being for our glory (1 Cor. 2:7-12). Christ is rich in many items. According to 1 Corinthians, Christ is rich first in His being the power of God and the wisdom of God (1:24), and then in His being righteousness, sanctification (holiness), and redemption to us (v. 30). He is rich in at least twenty items in the book of 1 Corinthians. The final and consummate item of Christ's riches in that book is that He is the life-giving Spirit. If Christ were not the life-giving Spirit, we could not receive Him as wisdom and power and as our righteousness, sanctification, and redemption. For us to receive Him, He must be the life-giving Spirit.

The dispensing of all the mysterious riches of Christ into our spiritual being is for our glory. We are whatever we live. If we live such a rich Christ, how glorious we will be! The way to live such a Christ is by the bountiful supply of the Spirit of Jesus Christ (Phil. 1:19). By the Spirit of Jesus Christ, we can participate in His bountiful supply in order to magnify Christ by living Him. What a glory this is!

E. As the Spirit
of the Divine Fellowship,
the Divine Flow, Imparting, Dispensing,
the Love of God in the Transfusion
of the Grace of Christ for Our Enjoyment

As the Spirit of the divine fellowship, the divine flow, the Spirit also imparts, dispenses, the love of God in the transfusion of the grace of Christ for our enjoyment (2 Cor. 13:14). Second Corinthians 13:14 says, "The grace of the Lord Jesus Christ and the love of God and the fellowship of the Holy Spirit be with you all." This is the blessing in the transfusion of the Triune God in three aspects—love, grace, and fellowship—into us for our enjoyment. We enjoy the Triune God—the Father as love, the Son as grace, and the Spirit as the fellowship, the flow. These riches are a great blessing to us.

F. As the Spirit of God, the Spirit of Christ, and the Spirit of Life, Indwelling Us to Dispense the Divine Life into Our Spirit, Soul, and Body

As the Spirit of God, the Spirit of Christ, and the Spirit of life, the Spirit indwells us to dispense the divine life into our spirit, soul (signified by the mind), and body (Rom. 8:2, 6, 9-11). The same wonderful Spirit is the Spirit of God, the Spirit of Christ, and the Spirit of life. Such a Spirit indwells us; He is the indwelling Spirit. By the Spirit's indwelling, the divine life is dispensed into our three parts: first, it is dispensed into our spirit; then, it spreads into our soul; and finally, it reaches our body. The Spirit's indwelling is not passive; rather, it is very active, but still it is quite slow and very loving. Every day we must realize that we have an Indweller within us. He is not like a roommate, dwelling with us outwardly. Whatever we do, He indwells us. Even during our sleep, He indwells us quietly, slowly, and lovingly.

G. As the Comforter, Convicting the Sinners and Regenerating Them That They May Become the Children of God

As the Comforter, the Spirit convicts us, the sinners, concerning sin, righteousness, and judgment, that we may repent and believe in the Son, and He regenerates us by imparting Christ as the divine life into our being that we may become the children of God (John 16:7b-11; 3:5-6; 1:12-13). The Comforter's convicting leads us to repent and believe. Then through repenting and believing we are regenerated. Conviction leads to regeneration. Regeneration cannot take place without conviction. Thus, in our preaching of the gospel, we must help people to have this conviction.

John 16:8 says, "And when He comes, He will convict the world concerning sin and concerning righteousness and concerning judgment." This verse implies three persons who are involved with us. Sin refers to Adam, righteousness refers to Christ, and judgment refers to the devil, Satan. We were born in Adam; hence, we are sinful. However, there is a way for us to get out of that position. By believing into Christ, we have Christ as our righteousness; sin is gone and righteousness is here. If we do not believe, however, we will participate in the punishment, the judgment, that is assigned to Satan. A sinner should be convicted in this way. Then he will repent and believe, and the Spirit will immediately come to regenerate him.

The Spirit regenerates us by imparting Christ as the divine life into our being that we may become the children of God. The Triune God not only comes into us to bring Himself to us but also to regenerate us that we may be born of God to be His children. Not only is the Triune God within us as the blessing, but we are now the children of such a One. This is a further blessing to us.

H. Becoming the Spirit of Sonship for Us to Call God "Abba, Father"

After our regeneration, the regenerating Spirit becomes the Spirit of sonship for us to call God "Abba, Father" (Gal. 4:6; Rom. 8:15). *Abba* is an Aramaic word, and *Father* is from the Greek word *Pater*. In Mark 14:36 the Lord Jesus called the Father "Abba, Father." We also should call God the Father "Abba, Father." This calling is sweet because to have such a Father is a great blessing to us. A mother can love us and sympathize with us, but a father is a blessing to us because a father can do many things for us. If we have a good, strong, capable, and rich father, we are very blessed. God is our begetting Father; we have been begotten of Him. This is a blessing to us.

I. As the Writing Ink, Sealing and Saturating Us

As the writing ink, the all-inclusive Spirit seals us as a mark of God's inheritance by saturating us to dispense the substance of God into us to form the image of God (2 Cor.

3:3b; Eph. 1:11a, 13; 4:30b; 2 Cor. 1:22a). A seal on something forms the image of the seal on that thing. The Spirit is the writing ink, the sealing substance. The more He seals, the greater is His mark upon us and the greater is His image within us. We bear the image of the sealing God. This is a deeper blessing.

J. Being the Pledge of God as Our Inheritance

As the pledge of God, the Spirit is our inheritance that we may enjoy God today as a foretaste unto the glorification (the redemption) of our body, to guarantee that God will be our full taste in the ages to come (Eph. 1:14; 2 Cor. 1:22b). The pledge is a guarantee that our God is our inheritance. As God's inheritance, we need the sealing, but for God to be our inheritance, we need the guarantee, the pledge. Today we have the Spirit as a foretaste of God, and this foretaste is a guarantee of the coming full taste. Both the foretaste and the full taste are God Himself for us to enjoy.

The preceding points are some of the items of the aggregate of the all-embracing blessing of the full gospel of God in Christ. This all-embracing blessing is Christ, the threefold seed in humanity, becoming the Spirit. The entire Bible is a book that is concerned with the Spirit. Thus, the more we touch the Spirit, the better. To touch the Spirit requires that we contact Him in prayer and in fellowship with Him.

The Central Line of the Divine Revelation

THE DIVINE ECONOMY
AND THE DIVINE DISPENSING

MESSAGE ELEVEN

THE AGGREGATE OF THE ALL-EMBRACING BLESSING
OF THE FULL GOSPEL OF GOD IN CHRIST
FOR THE DIVINE DISPENSING
ACCORDING TO THE DIVINE ECONOMY

(2)

Scripture Reading: Rom. 8:23, 14-15; 2 Cor. 1:21; 1 John 1:20-27; 5:6; John 14:16-20; Phil. 1:19b-21a; Rom. 6:5; Col. 2:12; Eph. 3:16-19; 4:3-6; Rom. 6:19b, 22b; 15:16b; 1 Thes. 5:23; 2 Pet. 1:4b; Titus 3:5; Eph. 4:23; Rom. 12:2a; 6:4; Hosea 14:8

In the previous message we saw that the threefold seed issues in the Spirit. This Spirit is the life-giving Spirit. The life-giving Spirit is the compound Spirit, and the compound Spirit is the all-inclusive Spirit, because He has been compounded with the elements of divinity, humanity, Christ's death with its effectiveness, and Christ's resurrection with its effectiveness. The Bible tells us that, after passing through incarnation, human living, death, and resurrection, Christ became a life-giving Spirit. His becoming a life-giving Spirit is the consummation of all the processes He has passed through.

At least four thousand years after He created man, the complete God entered into a "tunnel," a process. This "tunnel," this process, was quite long and had at least four sections. The first section of the "tunnel" was incarnation. Incarnation, as Isaiah shows us in chapter fifty-three, included His human living and lasted thirty-three and a half years in addition to the nine months He was in the womb. The second section was His all-inclusive death, which, strictly speaking, lasted only six hours, from nine o'clock in the morning until three o'clock in the afternoon. However, the preparation for His death lasted at least one week. Before His crucifixion, He went to Jerusalem voluntarily. According to the types and prophecies in the Old Testament, He had to be cut off on the day of the Passover (Exo. 12:3-6) and in that particular year (Dan. 9:25-26). Otherwise, the type concerning the Passover and Daniel's prophecy concerning the seventy weeks (vv. 24-27) could not have been properly fulfilled. He knew the year, He knew the month, and He knew the day. Thus, He went to Jerusalem according to the foreordained date. He entered into Jerusalem and stayed there for one week, including the day of His death (John 12:1; see note 1 in Mark 12:37). Therefore, it took Him at least one week to pass through His death. In those six days prior to His death, He was dying there; He was being slaughtered. To kill Him was not a simple matter. Before being arrested, He was tested by several groups of people, including the chief priests, the Sadducees, the Pharisees, the Herodians, the scribes, and the elders.

The third section of the "tunnel," or process, was His resurrection. In His resurrection He entered into another realm—the divine, spiritual, and heavenly realm. Before His resurrection He was in our realm, and before His incarnation He was in the eternal realm with the Father. Now He is in the fourth section—ascension.

In the first section of His process He was the complete God becoming a perfect man in humanity with blood and flesh. Then, after thirty-three and a half years He became a life-giving Spirit. This brought Him into another realm. His incarnation brought Him out of the heavenly, eternal realm into the world in which we are. He stayed here for thirty-three and a half years. Then, through the processes of death and resurrection, He was brought into another realm. Now, in this other realm He is in resurrection and in ascension. His resurrection always goes along with His ascension. Today He is there in ascension busily doing many things.

He has become the life-giving Spirit, and this Spirit has been compounded with divinity, humanity, His all-inclusive death with its effectiveness, and His powerful resurrection with its effectiveness. These are the elements with which the life-giving Spirit has been compounded. Now He has become a compound Spirit. This compound Spirit is the all-inclusive Spirit. If we want God, we must come to Him. Outside of Him there is no God. If we want to see a genuine, true, real, and perfect man, we must come to Him. Jesus is this man, and today Jesus is in the Spirit. If we want to enjoy, experience, and partake of His death with its effectiveness, we must come to this Spirit. The element of His death is in the Spirit. If we want to experience His resurrection with its power, we also must come to this Spirit. Today this Spirit is the reality of the divine person, the Triune God. This Spirit is also the reality of the unique and perfect man. In this Spirit we also have the reality of the death of Christ and the reality of the resurrection of Christ.

I feel very sorry that many dear ones who have been in the Lord's recovery for years have never delved into these deeper truths. This is why their Christian life is unstable, weak, and fluctuating. I am thankful to the Lord that He has kept me for more than sixty-six years through these deeper truths. Every step of our human education, from kindergarten through the four years of college, causes us to undergo certain changes in our behavior, our speaking, and our attitude. In order to serve the Lord properly, we need a certain amount of human education, and we also need to be filled, saturated, and infused with the adequate spiritual education that will cause us to know the Bible not in the black and white letters but in its spiritual, heavenly, and divine significances. We all need to spend some time to obtain the heavenly, divine, and spiritual education. I particularly encourage you young ones to study these truths; this will help you to grow. When I was young and I obtained a weighty spiritual book, I did not let the sun go down before I endeavored to study that book, even to some extent not caring for my eating or sleeping. The reason that I have lived such a long and healthy life is my studying of the truths of the Bible. Studying has been my "hobby." Regardless of how many things came to offend me, I found that the best way to put the offending things aside is to study the divine truths in the holy Word.

I. THE ALL-INCLUSIVE SPIRIT BEING
THE AGGREGATE OF THE ALL-EMBRACING BLESSING
OF THE FULL GOSPEL OF GOD IN CHRIST,
FOR THE DIVINE DISPENSING
ACCORDING TO THE DIVINE ECONOMY

In this message we shall consider another ten items of the all-inclusive Spirit as the aggregate of the all-embracing blessing of the full gospel of God in Christ, for the divine dispensing according to the divine economy.

K. Being the Firstfruits of Our Enjoyment
of God as Our Inheritance

The all-inclusive Spirit is the firstfruits of our enjoyment of God as our inheritance, dispensing His riches into us until the redemption (the glorification) of our body, that is, our divine sonship of glory. Romans 8:23 tells us that the Spirit today is the firstfruits. The firstfruits of the Spirit are simply the Spirit Himself as the firstfruits of the coming harvest of what God is to us. The Spirit, the compound Spirit who is the consummation of the Triune God, has been given to us as the firstfruits. These firstfruits are the firstfruits of God as our inheritance. God has given Himself to us as our inheritance. Acts 26:18 says strongly that we, the saved ones, are being sanctified unto an inheritance (see note 6 there), and that inheritance is God Himself (Rom. 8:23; Eph. 1:14). On this earth we might have an inheritance of houses, stocks, and shares in large corporations. But we need to realize that whatever we have will eventually become nothing, for when death comes, everything will be taken from us. Therefore, this kind of earthly inheritance is vanity of vanities (Eccl. 12:8). However, Christ as the threefold seed in humanity issues in the Spirit, and this Spirit is the firstfruits of the divine inheritance. In other words, the Spirit as the firstfruits is the first item of God as our inheritance. This Spirit as the firstfruits is no doubt for our enjoyment. Thus, He is the firstfruits of our enjoyment of God as our inheritance. As such, He dispenses the riches of God, who is our inheritance, into us for the redemption of our body. The redemption of our body in the future will be an issue of this dispensing.

Today we are enjoying the dispensing of the riches of the divine inheritance, which is God Himself, and this dispensing issues in the glorification of our body. That glorification will not be merely a sudden thing that will take place when the Lord Jesus comes again; it will be the issue of our enjoyment today. Our enjoyment is unto, for, and in view of that glorification. Verses such as Ephesians 1:13-14 and Ephesians 4:30 say that the Spirit seals us unto the redemption of our body. Therefore, the future redemption of our body will be an issue of our enjoyment of God, which is always accompanied by His dispensing His element into our being. This changes us and transforms us in view of the upcoming redemption and glorification of our body.

L. As the Spirit of Our Sonship, Leading Us, the Sons of God, by the Father's Life and Nature

The all-inclusive Spirit, as the Spirit of our sonship, leads us, the sons of God, by the Father's life and nature dispensed into our being in our daily life, that we may be the sons of God in practicality (Rom. 8:14-15). Romans 8:14 says, "For as many as are led by the Spirit of God, these are sons of God." As sons of God, we should live, walk, and have our being according to the leading of the Spirit. However, if we were to go to a movie, we might not have the confidence that we were practicing the practical sonship. I was deeply impressed when I read the story of a prominent American preacher. He moved into a new house and invited his father to see the house and all its furnishings. His father looked at the rooms and the furnishings and said, "Son, everything is very nice, but there is a big lack: there is no sign or indication that you are a son of God." Matters such as the way we comb our hair, the way we dress, and the way we decorate our homes are signs indicating whether or not we are practical sons of God. We are not speaking of sonship in doctrine but of sonship in practicality. The reality of our sonship in practicality is manifested in our living—in the way we conduct ourselves, in the way that we dress, in the places that we go. All these are signs of the practicality of our sonship.

M. As the Compound Spirit, Compounded with the Divine Nature and the Human Nature of Christ, and with Christ's Death and Resurrection, to Be the Anointing Ointment

The all-inclusive Spirit is the compound Spirit, compounded with both the divine nature and the human nature of Christ, and with both Christ's death and resurrection, to be the anointing ointment, anointing us with all His compounding elements, that we may abide in the Lord to receive His dispensing for our knowledge of the truth of the Divine Trinity in God's economy (2 Cor. 1:21; 1 John 2:20-27). An ointment is different from oil. Pure oil is of one element, but ointment, like paint, consists not of one element but of a base plus a few additional elements. These elements are compounded together to become an ointment as a kind of paint. The all-inclusive Spirit is the compound Spirit as an anointing ointment, anointing us with all His compounded elements.

The Spirit's anointing us with all His compounded elements is typified in the Old Testament. Exodus 30 tells us that after Moses made the compound ointment (vv. 23-25), God told him to anoint the tabernacle, all its utensils, the altar, and the priests (vv. 26-30). Everything that was related to God's service and worship had to be anointed by this ointment. This indicates that everything concerning us that is related to God's worship and service needs to be anointed by the compound Spirit.

First John 2 is a chapter on the anointing Spirit (vv. 20-27). The compound Spirit anoints us with all His compounded elements that we may abide in the Lord (v. 27). The Bible tells us to abide in the Lord (John 15:4), but many Christians do not seek to know the way to do so. Nearly fifty years ago I desired to know how to abide in Christ. One day I found the book *Abide in Christ,* by Andrew Murray. In this book Murray said that to abide in Christ we need to consecrate ourselves to the Lord. However, my experience was that I had consecrated myself to the Lord many times, but I still did not know how to abide. Surely that was not the way. After many years of reading 1 John 2, I found out that the way to abide in the Lord is to be anointed. The anointing is the way. As long as you are anointed with this anointing compound ointment, you are abiding in the Lord. First John 2 tells us to abide in the Lord according to the anointing (v. 27). The anointing is actually the Lord Himself moving. He anoints us that we may abide in Him to receive His dispensing for our knowledge of the truth of the Divine Trinity in God's economy. First John 2 teaches us the truth of the Divine Trinity in God's economy. Eventually, that truth is the teaching of the anointing. When we have the anointing of the compound Spirit, we have the Son, and when we have the Son, we have the Father. Thus, in the anointing we have all three—the Father, the Son, and the Spirit. This is the Divine Trinity in God's economy.

N. As the Reality of God, of Christ, and of the Divine Life

The Spirit is the reality of God, of Christ, and of the divine life, imparting the element of God, Christ, and the divine life into us as the life supply for our divine and spiritual support (1 John 5:6; John 14:16-20; Phil. 1:19b). According to 1 John 5:6 the Spirit is the truth, the reality. The reality mentioned in this verse must be the reality of the Triune God, Christ, and the divine life. This reality supplies us divinely and spiritually, causing us to have the divine and spiritual support. As mentioned in Philippians 1:19, this supply and support eventually become the bountiful supply of the Spirit of Jesus Christ. John 14:16-20 speaks of the Triune God—the Father, the Son, and the Spirit—telling us that the Father is embodied in the Son and the Son is realized as the Spirit. Thus, the Spirit is the realization of the Son, and the Son is the embodiment of the Father. When we have the realization, we have the embodiment, and we also have the Triune God. This becomes the bountiful supply that supports us in our spiritual life.

O. As the Reality
of Christ's Resurrection with His Death

The all-inclusive Spirit is also the reality of Christ's resurrection with His death, dispensing Christ's death with its effectiveness and Christ's resurrection with its power into our being that we may be identified with Christ and experience His death and resurrection (Rom. 6:5; Col. 2:12). Just as we cannot separate Christ's ascension from His resurrection, we cannot separate Christ's resurrection from His death. If we have Christ's resurrection, we will surely enjoy His death. However, we do not experience Christ's resurrection first; rather, we experience His death first.

In the same year that I was saved, I began to read books by Brother Watchman Nee. In those books he taught mainly that we need to realize and reckon that our old man has been crucified with Christ (Rom. 6:6). I began to consider how I could be crucified with Christ. Christ was crucified two thousand years earlier on Mount Calvary outside Jerusalem. With respect to time, He was crucified two thousand years earlier, and with regard to space, He was quite far from where I lived. He was He and I was I. How could I have been crucified with Him?

A. B. Simpson, the founder of the Christian and Missionary Alliance, published a number of books and wrote quite a few excellent hymns on the experience of Christ's death and resurrection (see *Hymns,* #481, 482, 484, and 692). One of his hymns (#692) says, "There's a little word that the Lord has giv'n / For our help in the hour of need: / Let us reckon ourselves to be dead to sin, / To be dead and dead indeed." The chorus goes on to say, "Let us reckon, reckon, reckon, / Let us reckon, rather than feel; / Let us be true to the reck'ning, / And He will make it real." I tried to "reckon, reckon, reckon" and found out that this surely does not work. When I reckoned myself dead, I became more living. Brother Nee spoke of reckoning in his earlier ministry. For example, the messages given by Brother Nee that were published as *The Normal Christian Life* were given before 1938. Later, he began to see the Body of Christ, and his ministry became more mature. He then said that the real experience of Christ's death is in the Spirit, as covered in Romans 8. He said that Romans 6 could be experienced only in Romans 8. Romans 6 contains the doctrine, the fact, of our identification with Christ in His death and resurrection, but the experience of this fact is in Romans 8 by the Spirit. If we live, walk, and do everything according to the Spirit, we will have the experience of Christ's death and of His resurrection. It is in this way that we are identified with Christ and experience His death and resurrection.

P. As the Spirit of Jesus Christ, Supplying Us with His Bountiful Supply

The all-inclusive Spirit is the Spirit of Jesus Christ, supplying us with His bountiful supply that we may magnify Christ by living Him (Phil. 1:19b-21a). Quite early in my Christian life I was told that I should live out Christ and magnify Christ. However, I did not have the way to do this. Philippians 1:20 speaks of magnifying Christ, and verse 21 mentions the matter of living Christ, but I did not see that the way to live and magnify Christ is found in verse 19. This verse speaks of the bountiful supply of the Spirit of Jesus Christ. It does not mention the Spirit of God or the Spirit of Jehovah, but the Spirit of Jesus Christ. Surely this is the processed Spirit, the compounded and consummated Spirit. The Spirit of God has become the Spirit of Jesus Christ because God the Spirit has been processed and has been consummated. With this Spirit there is a bountiful supply, and the bountiful supply of this Spirit is the way for us to magnify Christ by living Him. The Spirit's supplying is undoubtedly a dispensing. The bountiful supply is dispensed into our Christian life, and then we magnify Christ by living Him.

Q. As the Indwelling Spirit, Strengthening Us (through the Divine Dispensing) into the Inner Man

The life-giving Spirit, the compound Spirit, the all-inclusive Spirit, is the indwelling Spirit, strengthening us (through the divine dispensing) into our inner man that Christ may make His home in our hearts, that we may be full of strength to apprehend with all the saints the breadth, length, height, and depth, that we may be filled unto all the fullness of God, which is the church (Eph. 3:16-19). In Ephesians 3:16 Paul prayed that God would strengthen us through His Spirit into our inner man. To live in the outer man does not require us to do anything. Every morning when we rise up we are in the outer man. If we are not watchful, we will be in the outer man the whole day. We talk in the outer man, we laugh in the outer man, we express our attitude in the outer man—we do everything in the outer man. We are just an outer man. But we should live in the inner man. However, this can take place only by our entering into our inner man. According to Ephesians 3:16, the way to enter into the inner man is by the strengthening of the Spirit. The Spirit strengthens us into the inner man.

When we have morning watch and experience a morning revival, we are in the inner man. Before that time we might have wanted to argue with someone in the outer man; but after ten minutes we were in the inner man by being strengthened through the Spirit. However, ten minutes later we might be back in the outer man. At that point we need to pray. This is why the Bible tells us to pray unceasingly (1 Thes. 5:17). Only prayer and calling on the name of the

Lord can strengthen us into the inner man and keep us in the inner man. This kind of strengthening is also a dispensing. It dispenses the divine element into our being and strengthens us into the inner man that Christ may make His home in our hearts. Christ is in our spirit, but He needs to spread from our spirit into our hearts to make His home there that we may be full of strength to apprehend with all the saints the breadth and length and height and depth, that is, the dimensions of Christ. We need to know this unlimited Christ that we may be filled unto all the fullness of God. The fullness here simply means the manifestation, the expression, of God, which is the church. The church is the expression of God. When Christ makes His home in our hearts, we will be able to know His dimensions. Then we will be filled unto all the fullness of God. This is altogether by the inner dispensing of the Spirit. First the Spirit strengthens us into the inner man; then the Spirit strengthens us so that Christ may make His home in our being, making us the expression of God, that God may be fully expressed.

R. As the Spirit of the Oneness
of the Body of Christ,
Being the Essence of the Body

The Spirit is the oneness of the Body of Christ, being the essence of the Body, which is constituted with Christ as the element, out from the origin of God the Father, to consummate the mingling of the Triune God with the Body of Christ through the divine dispensing (Eph. 4:3-6). Christ is the element of the Body, and the Spirit is the essence. This element is out from the origin of God the Father. Thus, with the Body of Christ, the Father is the origin, the Son is the element, and the Spirit is the essence. This is the Triune God—the origin, the element, and the essence. These three are blended and mingled with the Body of Christ.

The Body of Christ, the church, is four in one: the Father, the Son, the Spirit, and the Body. Ephesians 4:4-6 speaks of one Body, one Spirit, one Lord, and one God the Father. In the Body the Spirit is the essence. The essence needs the element, which is the Lord Christ. The element must have an origin, a source, which is the Father. The Father is the source, the origin. Out of the Father there is the element, and within the element there is the essence. God is the origin, the Son is the element, the Spirit is the essence, and the Body is the very constitution. These are four-in-one. However, only the first three are worthy of our worship; the fourth, the Body, should not be deified as an object of worship.

The Spirit as the oneness of the Body of Christ is the essence of the Body to consummate the mingling of the Triune God with the Body of Christ through the divine dispensing. Today something is going on to mingle the Father as the origin, the Son as the element, and the Spirit as the essence with the Body. This mingling is continuing today and will be consummated. The Spirit is the essence of the Body to consummate this mingling.

S. As the Consummation of the Processed God, Sanctifying Us with the Divine and Holy Nature of God

The Spirit is the consummation of the processed God, sanctifying us with the divine and holy nature of God that we may be separated and made holy unto God (Rom. 6:19b, 22b; 15:16b; 1 Thes. 5:23; 2 Pet. 1:4b). The Spirit today is a consummated Spirit as the consummation of the processed Triune God. This Spirit is sanctifying us with the divine and holy nature of God. This sanctifying is surely a dispensing of the divine and holy nature of God into our being that we may be separated and made holy unto God. The nature of God is the very element with the essence of God's holiness. With this essence we can be and will be sanctified unto God.

T. As the Regenerating Spirit, Renewing Us with the Newness of Christ's Resurrection Life and with the Freshness of the Ever-existing God

The all-inclusive Spirit is the regenerating Spirit,

renewing us with the newness of Christ's resurrection life and with the freshness of the ever-existing God as the green fir tree (Titus 3:5; Eph. 4:23; Rom. 12:2a; 6:4; Hosea 14:8). Regeneration is a renewing. The regenerating Spirit renews us with the newness of Christ's resurrection life and with the freshness of the ever-existing God as the green fir tree. Hosea 14:8 tells us that God is like a fir tree, which is green the year round. This greenness is a kind of freshness. We need the newness of Christ's resurrection life, and we need the freshness of what God is. The regenerating Spirit renews us with these two things. This renewing is also a dispensing. Without the dispensing of the newness of Christ and of the freshness of God, we could never be renewed. To be renewed, we need some element, and that element is the newness of Christ and the freshness of God.

By all the foregoing items we can see that whatever this life-giving, compounded, all-inclusive Spirit does is a dispensing. Primarily, He dispenses Christ as God's embodiment with all His experiences of incarnation, crucifixion, resurrection, and ascension. The Spirit dispenses this triune processed God into our being that He may be everything to us. This is the aggregate of the all-embracing blessing of the full gospel of God.

The Central Line of the Divine Revelation

THE DIVINE ECONOMY
AND THE DIVINE DISPENSING

MESSAGE TWELVE

THE AGGREGATE OF THE ALL-EMBRACING BLESSING
OF THE FULL GOSPEL OF GOD IN CHRIST
FOR THE DIVINE DISPENSING
ACCORDING TO THE DIVINE ECONOMY

(3)

Scripture Reading: Rom. 8:2; Acts 13:52; Eph. 3:8; 1:23; Acts 1:8a; 2:4a, 17, 33; 4:4, 8, 30; Luke 24:49; Acts 16:6-10; 2 Cor. 3:17-18; Rom. 12:2a; 8:29; 1 John 3:2; Rom. 8:30b; Heb. 2:10a; 1 Pet. 5:10a; Col. 1:27; Rev. 1:4; 4:5; 5:6; 2:7, 11, 17, 26-29; 3:5-6, 12-13, 21-22; 22:17a; 21:1-3, 9-23; 22:1-2, 14

This message is a continuation of the foregoing messages concerning the thirty-one items of what the all-inclusive Spirit is as the aggregate of the all-embracing blessing of the full gospel of God in Christ for the divine dispensing according to the divine economy.

UNDERSTANDING THE DIVINE TRUTH

I have discovered that without the proper help, it is very difficult to understand the Bible. The secret to understanding the Word is like a master key that opens the door of a large house. If you have the key, you can use the key to open every door in the house. I did not get such a key until I began to have direct personal contact with Brother Watchman Nee.

I began to correspond with Brother Nee in 1925, the first year of my salvation. Then in 1932 the Lord brought the two of us together. After I had begun to serve the Lord full time, I went to see Brother Nee, and he asked me to remain there with him. During that time with him I received the key to understanding the Bible. The more I stayed with Brother Nee, the more of the secret to understanding the Word I received. Before being with Brother Nee, I did not know the crucial things of the church, the Spirit, life, and identification with Christ in His death, resurrection, and ascension. But from 1933 I began to know these crucial things, and my entire being began to be occupied with them. I found out that the church, the Spirit, life, and identification with Christ are bottomless mines. The more I have dug into these things, the deeper they have become. I have discovered that the spiritual, heavenly, and divine significances of these things in the Bible can never be exhausted.

Progressing in Understanding the Bible

Brother Nee was saved at the age of seventeen, and he began to minister in 1922 at the age of twenty. In that year the first local church in mainland China was raised up through his ministry. Brother Nee's ministry spanned three decades, from 1922 to 1952. In 1952 he was put into prison, where he stayed until his death in 1972. In his early ministry, from 1922 to 1932, his knowledge on certain matters was not yet full or complete. Then from 1932 to 1942, his understanding improved. But from 1942 to 1952, he reached the stage of maturity in his ministry. Whatever he spoke or published from 1940 until the end of his ministry was very accurate. Brother Nee continually progressed in his understanding of the depths of the Bible. We need to keep this in mind as we read Brother Nee's writings through the three decades of his ministry.

For example, the book *The Normal Christian Life* consists of messages given by Brother Nee in northern Europe and in China before 1938. In that book Brother Nee stressed the matter of reckoning ourselves to be dead to sin and alive to God, according to Romans 6:11. But eventually many discovered that reckoning did not work in their experience.

The book of Romans does not end at chapter six. Romans has sixteen chapters, which can be divided into four sections.

These four sections and their main subjects are: chapters one
through four, on justification; chapters five through eight,
on sanctification; chapters nine through eleven, on God's
selection; and chapters twelve through sixteen, on the Body
life, which consummates in the local churches. To say that
chapters five through eight deal with sanctification is a
superficial understanding of that section. Actually, the
subject of these chapters is the pneumatic Christ, that is,
Christ as the Spirit. In chapter eight, Christ is in us (v. 10),
and the Spirit of Christ also is in us (v. 9). Christ is the
Spirit of Christ, and the Spirit of Christ is one with Christ. It
is in the pneumatic Christ that we experience Christ's
death and resurrection. It is not by reckoning but by identification with Christ. This Christ with whom we are identified
is not merely the incarnated or crucified Christ, but the
Christ who became pneumatic in His resurrection. Unless
we see this, we can never experience what is revealed in
Romans 5—8.

The fourth section of Romans begins with the Body life in
chapter twelve and consummates with the local churches
in chapter sixteen. Ultimately, the entire book of Romans is
a book on the gospel of God (1:1; 16:25). Hence, the local
churches are a part of the gospel of God. Without the local
churches as part of the gospel of God, the gospel of God
would not be complete. Romans begins with sinners in chapter one and ends with local churches in chapter sixteen.
Thus, Romans reveals that God in His sovereign economy is
able to cause sinners to become the local churches.

Apprehending the Spiritual Significance
in Studying the Bible

We need to enter into the Word of God, not in the natural
way of merely studying the geography, the history, and the
Hebrew and Greek words in the Bible, but in the way of
apprehending the spiritual significance of what is revealed
in the Bible. We need to enter into the Lord's way of interpreting the Bible. In Matthew 22:23-33 the Sadducees came
to the Lord with a question concerning resurrection. They

did not believe in resurrection (Acts 23:8), and they wanted to argue with the Lord Jesus concerning this matter. The Lord answered them by interpreting Exodus 3:6. According to the Lord's interpretation, the clause "I am the God of thy father, the God of Abraham, the God of Isaac, and the God of Jacob" implies resurrection. The Lord said that God is "not the God of the dead, but of the living" (Matt. 22:32). God could never be the God of dead persons; He is the God of living persons. As God is the God of the living and is called "the God of Abraham, the God of Isaac, and the God of Jacob," so the dead Abraham, Isaac, and Jacob will be resurrected. Such a title of God implies resurrection. Simply to remember the title itself is easy and is of little value; but the implication of this title is of great significance. This is the way to interpret the Bible, and this is the way that we must learn to study the Bible. Paul also quoted and interpreted many portions from the Old Testament in this way, such as in the book of Hebrews, which is an interpretation of the book of Leviticus. We should not only read the Word according to the black and white letters. Rather, we must read, study, and pray, asking the Lord to show us the real significance of the words that are printed in black and white.

BUILDING THE CHURCH WITH LIFE,
THE SPIRIT, AND THE TRUTH

Today there is a great debate concerning the way to build up the church. Those in the Pentecostal movement say that the way to build the church is by the Spirit. But this is a shallow understanding of the way to build up the church. The Pentecostal movement in the United States began at the turn of the twentieth century. In 1906 it spread to Azusa Street in Los Angeles. In this movement there was an outpouring and a burning from the Holy Spirit among the believers for a time. But later they found out that they could not build the church just with the Spirit. The Assemblies of God, one of the groups within the Pentecostal movement, made this discovery, set up a printing press, and began to educate their people. They told their people that they could not go out to build up the church by the Spirit alone; they had to build by the proper teaching of the Bible. Within the fifty years after the founding of the Assemblies of God in 1914, that denomination had the highest rate of increase among all the major Christian denominations. They increased because they exercised themselves in the matter of teaching. This is proof that in order to build up the church, there is the need of proper teaching.

The Southern Baptists also have stressed the matter of teaching. They have stressed the Word of God and have discouraged their preachers from speaking about the Spirit. To them the Word is solid, but the Spirit is too abstract and mysterious. They have also depended upon the teaching of the Bible in their Sunday school classes. They use so-called laymen to teach the Sunday school classes, and they have built up their churches by the teaching of the Bible.

Others have said that to build up the Body of Christ, only life is needed. Brother T. Austin-Sparks was a typical example of those with this view. I knew him very well, and I went to stay with him for about five weeks. He was very strong not to use any teaching or doctrine, but to stress only life, especially the resurrection life. In the 1920s Brother Nee and I both appreciated his books. In those years Brother Nee translated a number of his books into Chinese. Brother Sparks was very much for the resurrection life, but he missed the importance of the teaching of the Bible. The effectiveness of his ministry in building up the church was diminished because of this.

Because we have learned the lessons of church history, we stress life, the Spirit, and the truth continually. The truth is a kind of doctrine or teaching, but not all doctrine or teaching is truth. We need to realize that these three things—life, the Spirit, and the truth—are of one essence. John 6:63 says, "The words which I have spoken to you are spirit and are life." In this verse the word, life, and the Spirit are combined together. Then John 17:17 says, "Sanctify them in the truth; Your word is truth." According to this verse, God's word, which may be considered as doctrine or teaching, is the truth. Thus, the word, the Spirit, life, and the truth are all one. To receive "truth" from the word and yet not touch the Spirit is emptiness. Whenever we touch the truth, we should touch the Spirit. The Spirit always goes along with the truth. Actually, the word and the Spirit are one. The word is the truth, and the truth is the Spirit (1 John 5:6b). Furthermore, the Spirit is called "the Spirit of life" (Rom. 8:2). Thus, the word is the Spirit and the life. When we touch the word as truth, we surely need to touch the Spirit, and this Spirit is life. Actually, there is no difference between the Spirit and life. It is by these things—life, the Spirit, and the truth—that the church is built up.

The word, the Spirit, and life are all wrapped up with our spirit. Thus, we must learn to study the Word by exercising our spirit, and we must also learn to study with prayer. Whatever we study, we must turn into prayer, and then we must turn our prayer into our experience. When the word in the Spirit becomes our experience, the issue is life. The issue of the word and the Spirit is the experience of life. The only way for us to grow is by touching the word with prayer and turning the word with prayer into the Spirit, which issues in the experience of life. With the life of the Spirit from the word, we can build up the church.

The word is the base for the building up of the church. Because they realize their shortage of the word, some of the elders invite speakers to come to their locality. But this is the practice of the old way. The new way is to replace the speakers by equipping all the saints to prophesy. By the practice of prophesying, the need for the word on the Lord's Day morning is met. Otherwise, the burden of giving a message each Lord's Day would become a killing burden to the elders. Even when there are good speakers in a locality, after two years they will be exhausted, and the listeners will lose their taste for their speaking. The God-ordained way is to replace the speaking of one or two speakers with the prophesying by all the saints.

To prophesy is not merely to speak. To speak may be to talk loosely, but to prophesy is to speak something from the

Word with definite points. The sisters as well as the brothers must prophesy. The New Testament shows us clearly that the sisters can prophesy (1 Cor. 11:5; 14:31). But the sisters should not teach with authority in the way of defining doctrine (1 Tim. 2:12). To do so is to overstep their limit. The sisters should prophesy to minister Christ, to minister life, to others. This is for the building up of the church.

I. THE ALL-INCLUSIVE SPIRIT BEING THE AGGREGATE OF THE ALL-EMBRACING BLESSING OF THE FULL GOSPEL OF GOD IN CHRIST, FOR THE DIVINE DISPENSING ACCORDING TO THE DIVINE ECONOMY

The all-inclusive Spirit, whom the all-inclusive Christ (as the threefold seed in humanity) has become, is the aggregate of the all-embracing blessing of the full gospel of God in Christ (Gal. 3:14), for the divine dispensing according to the divine economy. This all-inclusive Spirit comprises many items.

U. As the Spirit of Life, Filling Us Inwardly with Himself as the Life-giving Spirit

As the Spirit of life, this Spirit fills us inwardly with Himself as the life-giving Spirit that we may be saturated and permeated with the unsearchable riches of Christ to be the fullness of Christ for His expression (Rom. 8:2; Acts 13:52; Eph. 3:8; 1:23). The words *saturate* and *permeate* are similar in meaning, but each bears a special denotation. To saturate means to fill to capacity, to soak thoroughly, and carries the thought of "in depth." To permeate means to spread or flow throughout, to pervade completely, and carries the thought of "in breadth." It would be more meaningful to say that a room is permeated, rather than saturated, with the smell of perfume. The Spirit of life fills us inwardly that we may be both saturated and permeated with the unsearchable riches of Christ. The unsearchable riches of Christ are always with the life-giving Spirit. Christ as the threefold seed in humanity is now the life-giving Spirit. The life-giving Spirit is the essential Spirit, who is the spiritual, divine, and heavenly essence of all the riches of Christ. When these riches fill us, we are saturated with Christ, and when He fills us further, we are permeated with Christ. Eventually, we are full of Christ both vertically and horizontally. Vertically, we are saturated with Christ, and horizontally we are permeated with Christ. This is the infilling of the Spirit of life (Acts 13:52).

V. As the Spirit of Power
Filling Us Outwardly with Himself
as the Outpoured Spirit

The all-inclusive Spirit as the Spirit of power fills us outwardly with Himself as the outpoured Spirit that we may be clothed with the power from on high as our authority for us to be engaged in the Lord's work according to God's economy (Acts 1:8a; 2:4a, 17, 33; 4:4, 8, 30; Luke 24:49). The Greek word used in reference to the inward filling is *pleroo,* and the corresponding word used in reference to the outward filling is *pletho.* According to their usage in Acts, *pleroo* denotes the filling of a vessel within, as the wind filled the house inwardly in Acts 2:2, and *pletho* denotes the filling of persons outwardly, as the Spirit filled the disciples outwardly in Acts 2:4.

The Spirit of power is the economical Spirit for the carrying out of God's economy. This aspect of the Spirit is different from the aspect of the Spirit as the Spirit of life, or the essential Spirit. On the day of Pentecost, what was poured out on the disciples was not the essential Spirit but the economical Spirit, not the Spirit of life but the Spirit of power (Acts 2:4), because on the day of Pentecost what was needed was not primarily life but power (1:8). The power that was poured out from on high was the economical Spirit to clothe the disciples as their authority. Today, when driving on the street, you may be fearful if you see a policeman in uniform. This is because his uniform is his authority. A large truck may be full of strength and power, but when the policeman in uniform signals for the driver in the truck to stop, the truck must stop. To drive a truck is a matter of power, but to stop the truck at the wave of a hand is a matter of authority. The power from on high is our authority. Everyone who truly speaks for the Lord has this authority. His speaking is the authority. The power from on high becomes the authority for us to be engaged in the Lord's dispensing according to His economy.

W. As the Holy Spirit and the Spirit of Jesus, Directing the Move of the Ministers of Christ through the Inward Guidance by the Divine Dispensing

The all-inclusive Spirit as the Holy Spirit and the Spirit of Jesus directs the move of the ministers of Christ through the inward guidance by the divine dispensing (Acts 16:6-10). In Acts 16 Paul and his co-workers were traveling in Asia Minor. They wanted to turn toward Asia, but they were forbidden by the Holy Spirit (v. 6); then they attempted to go to Bithynia, but they were prohibited by the Spirit of Jesus (v. 7). Eventually, they stopped, and in the night Paul had a vision concerning a Macedonian man who entreated the brothers to come over to help them. Paul and his co-workers concluded that God had called them to bring the good news into Macedonia (vv. 9-10). They crossed the Aegean Sea and entered into eastern Europe and into the major city of that region, Philippi (vv. 11-12).

Paul and his co-workers had both the outward guidance and the inward guidance. The dream in which the Macedonian man said, "Come over into Macedonia and help us" was the outward guidance. The inward guidance came as they considered the dream and concluded that God had called them to announce the good news to the Macedonians. This inward guidance was through the Spirit by the divine dispensing. Through the leading of the Spirit, Paul and his co-workers received some amount of dispensing. This was their inward guidance.

Today we must take this as our pattern. Often the co-workers come to me and say, "Brother Lee, I have received an invitation to go to a certain place. Should I go or not?" Usually, I do not say whether or not they should go. I simply tell them to pray. When I say this, my consideration is that they should receive a "Macedonian call." Once they receive the call, following Paul's pattern, they need to consider. This consideration is inward in the human spirit with the divine Spirit.

X. As the Renewing Spirit, Transforming Us with All the Attributes of Christ into the Glorious Image of the Resurrected and Glorified Christ

As the renewing Spirit, the all-inclusive Spirit transforms us with the attributes of Christ into the glorious image of the resurrected and glorified Christ that we may bear His image for His glory (2 Cor. 3:17-18; Rom. 12:2a). The attributes of Christ include many items, such as His humility, His patience, and His kindness. When they are expressed outwardly, these items are Christ's virtues, but within Christ, they are His attributes.

Y. As the Transforming Spirit, Conforming Us, His Many Transformed Brothers, to His Image

As the transforming Spirit, the all-inclusive Spirit conforms us, His many transformed brothers, to His image, the image of the firstborn Son of God, that we may fully be what He is (Rom. 8:29; 1 John 3:2). The Spirit's transformation has a goal, and that is to conform us to the image of the firstborn Son of God. Christ as the firstborn Son of God is the model, the mold, to which we all must be conformed. In baking bread, there is the need of a mold. Once we have the mold, the dough can be placed into the mold so that it will have the same image as the mold. Christ is the mold, and we are the dough. Before being placed in the mold, we are without a proper image. But once we are put into the mold, we have the proper image. All the saints bear the same image because they have all been placed into the same mold.

Colossians 1:15 tells us that Christ "is the image of the invisible God, the Firstborn of all creation." Verse 16 then says that all things were created in Christ. Christ is the mold. Before God created anything, He first created Christ as the mold, the model. In this model all the other creatures were created. How could Christ be created first? He was created by putting on human nature. By putting on human nature, Christ became a creature. But how could His putting on human nature, which took place after Adam was created, cause Him to be the Firstborn, the first creature? The answer is that there is no element of time with God. With Him there is only the fact. In the universe there is the fact that Christ was created first among all the creatures. Then, this Firstborn of creation became a mold, or a model, for a mass production.

Was Christ crucified before Adam or after Adam? According to Revelation 13:8 Christ was slain from the foundation of the world. This indicates that He was crucified before Adam was created. After drawing a circle, we will not be able to locate the starting point or the ending point. If we put a dot on some point on the circle, it would be difficult to say what is before that point and what is after it. Adam was before Christ, and he was also after Christ. Christ is actually the first because He is the center and centrality of God's move (Col. 2:16-17). It is difficult to say whether we are before or after Him. According to human history, Abraham was before Christ. But in John 8:58, Jesus said, "Before Abraham came into being, I am." The proper grammar for the phrase "I am" should be "I was." Because Abraham was in the past, the Lord Jesus was grammatically wrong. But according to actual fact, He was right because He is eternal. As the great I Am, He is the eternal, ever-existing God. Hence, He was before Abraham and is greater than Abraham. With Him there is no element of time.

The transforming Spirit will conform us to the image of the firstborn Son of God that we may fully be what He is. First John 3:2 says, "Beloved, now we are children of God, and it has not yet been manifested what we will be. We know that if He is manifested, we will be like Him because we will see Him even as He is." The real meaning of this verse is that the glorified Christ in our spirit will both saturate us vertically and permeate us horizontally, filling us that we may express Him. Eventually, we will be conformed to His glorified image and be exactly as He is.

Z. As the Conforming Spirit, Glorifying Us with the Divine Glory of God and of Christ

As the renewing Spirit, He transforms us, and as the transforming Spirit, He conforms us. Then as the conforming Spirit, He glorifies us with the divine glory of God and of Christ that the divine glory within us today may be expressed outwardly, in which we will be the same as Christ is in the glory of God (Rom. 8:30b; Heb. 2:10a; 1 Pet. 5:10a; Col. 1:27). To be glorified in the divine glory is not merely objective. In my early Christian life I was taught that although we are very mean and low pieces of clay, one day, when the Lord Jesus comes, we will be brought into the glory of God. At that time I did not understand the matter of glorification, so I accepted this teaching. Later, I realized that this kind of teaching is too objective. If we as pieces of clay are put into glory, we will remain pieces of clay. The only difference will be that today we are clothed with clay, but in that day we will be pieces of clay clothed with glory.

The way that we are glorified is not objective but very subjective. Christ as the glory today is already within us as the hope of glory (Col. 1:27). He is not in us in a dormant way, but He is saturating and permeating us to bring us through the process of conformation. His conforming us is also His glorifying us. When this glorifying reaches its climax, our body will be redeemed (Phil. 3:21; Rom. 8:23). At that time, we will no longer be clay. Rather, our clay will be transformed and conformed to the expression of Christ in glory.

AA. As the Seven Spirits of God, as the Seven Lamps of Fire, and as the Seven Eyes of the Lamb

As the seven Spirits of God, as the seven lamps of fire, and as the seven eyes of the Lamb, the all-inclusive Spirit searches through enlightening and infuses through

observing the churches with all the saints by the divine dispensing (Rev. 1:4; 4:5; 5:6). The seven Spirits are the Spirit of
God intensified sevenfold. The seven Spirits as the Spirit of
God are the seven eyes of the Lamb, Christ (5:6). This
strongly contradicts traditional theology which says that the
three of the Divine Trinity are separate persons. In Revelation 5:6 the third of the Divine Trinity, who is the Spirit, is
the eyes of the second, who is the Lamb, Christ the Son of
God. Are these two separate persons or are they one person?
The eyes of a person cannot be separated from that person to
become another person. The third of the Divine Trinity is one
with the second of the Divine Trinity. How wonderful this is!

The seven Spirits of God as the eyes of the Lamb are also
seven lamps of fire (Rev. 4:5). Whenever we close our eyes, we
find that we are in darkness; we have no "lamps" by which
we can see. Thus, our two eyes are two lamps. If we were
blind, we would have no light, because we would have no
lamps. To have light, we need a lamp. Without our eyes, we
would have no light, no lamp, to enlighten us. This illustrates
how the eyes are the lamps. Because our eyes are our lamps,
we must pray so that the Lord will open our eyes that we
may have light (Acts 26:18; Eph. 1:18). Proverbs 20:27 says,
"The spirit of man is the lamp of the Lord" (lit.). Our spirit is
the lamp to bring in the Lord as the light. Our spirit is not
the light; it is the lamp to receive the light. But without the
lamp, we cannot receive the light. Hence, we must exercise
our spirit, which is the lamp, to have a clear conscience so
that the light can shine within us.

The seven lamps of fire are for searching through enlightening. If we are going to search a dark room, light is needed.
The seven eyes of the Lamb are for infusing through observing. When I observe you, my eyes dispense something into
you. If I am angry with you, my eyes dispense anger into you
and cause you to be angry; but when I am joyful, my eyes dispense joy into you, causing you to become joyful. This means
that either my joy or my anger is dispensed into you. Thus,
before we look at others, we must be full of the Spirit. Then

our looking at others will dispense the Spirit into them, just as the Lord does when He looks at us.

BB. As the Seven Spirits,
the Sevenfold Intensified Spirit,
Speaking to the Churches as Christ Himself

As the seven Spirits, the sevenfold intensified Spirit, the all-inclusive Spirit speaks to the churches as Christ Himself to transfuse and infuse all that Christ is, as Christ declared at the beginning of each of the seven epistles, to the saints who are seeking to be overcomers (Rev. 2:7, 11, 17, 26-29; 3:5-6, 12-13, 21-22). In each of the seven epistles in Revelation 2 and 3, Christ Himself as the speaker declared who or what He is. Then, at the end of each epistle, we are told that the Spirit speaks to the churches. This indicates that the Spirit and Christ are one. This also indicates that the speaking Spirit dispenses the very Christ into the churches with all the saints. He transfuses and infuses all that Christ is into the saints who are seeking to be overcomers. Because we are seeking to be overcomers, every morning we must listen to the speaking of the Spirit. As we listen, something of Christ is transfused and infused into our being. This is His dispensing.

CC. As the Consummation
of the Processed Triune God, Marrying
the Transformed, Tripartite, Redeemed Saints,
That He and We May Be a Universal Couple

The life-giving Spirit, who today is sevenfold, is the consummation of the processed Triune God. This consummated Triune God marries the transformed, tripartite, redeemed saints, that He and we, we and He, may be a universal couple for His redeemed ones to enjoy the riches and fullness of the processed Triune God as the all-inclusive blessing of the New Jerusalem through His dispensing according to His economy for eternity (Rev. 22:17a). The entire Bible of sixty-six books ends with the New Jerusalem, the embodiment of the blessing of the gospel of God. Galatians 3:14 reveals that the

Spirit is the blessing of the gospel. The New Jerusalem is the aggregate of the Spirit, who is the blessing allotted to us in the gospel of God for our eternal enjoyment.

DD. As the All-Embracing Blessing of the Full Gospel of God in Christ, Consummating in the New Jerusalem in the New Heaven and New Earth

The life-giving Spirit, as the all-embracing blessing of the full gospel of God in Christ, consummates in the New Jerusalem in the new heaven and new earth as the aggregate, the totality, of Christ's being the threefold seed in humanity (Rev. 21:1-3, 9-23; 22:1-2, 14). The Spirit is the consummation of Christ as the threefold seed of Mary, Abraham, and David.

EE. This Total Blessing Being the Mingling, the Blending, of the Processed and Consummated Triune God with His Chosen and Glorified Tripartite Saints as the Conclusion of the Divine Revelation for Eternity

This total blessing is the mingling, the blending, of the processed and consummated Triune God with His chosen and glorified tripartite saints as the conclusion of the divine revelation for eternity. This is the end of the Bible, and this is the central line of the divine revelation.

The Central Line of the Divine Revelation

THE DIVINE ECONOMY
AND THE DIVINE DISPENSING

MESSAGE THIRTEEN

THE AGGREGATE OF THE ALL-EMBRACING BLESSING
OF THE FULL GOSPEL OF GOD IN CHRIST
FOR THE DIVINE DISPENSING
ACCORDING TO THE DIVINE ECONOMY

(4)

Scripture Reading: Gal. 1:16a; 3:2; 4:29b, 6; 3:27; 2:20

Prayer: Lord, we look to You for Your teaching, Your instruction, Your guidance, even Your interpretation of Your Word. We need You to teach us, to guide us into Your light. Lord, do cleanse us and anoint us and render us much help that we may know You through Your Word. Amen.

This message concerns the way to receive, experience, and enjoy the all-inclusive Christ as the all-inclusive life-giving Spirit—the aggregate of the all-embracing blessing of the full gospel of God—in the book of Galatians. It is Galatians that tells us that the blessing of the full gospel of God is the promised Spirit (3:14). This promised Spirit, when He comes to us in His consummation, is the life-giving Spirit. According to Paul's interpretation, the promise God gave to Abraham was the blessing of this life-giving Spirit. We need to spend some time to see the logic by which Paul said this. Paul was very logical doctrinally, spiritually, and economically according to God's plan.

The book of Galatians presents to us the very Christ who is the threefold seed in humanity. He was the complete God in eternity. Then He came in to promise something to the fallen race, beginning with the first couple, Adam and Eve (Gen. 3:15). I believe that He directed this promise particularly to the wife, Eve, because Eve very much regretted what she had done. She was the one who spoke to the serpent, and as a result the serpent damaged her and also her husband through her. Therefore, she was fully responsible for that mistake, which led to man's fall (2 Cor. 11:3; 1 Tim. 2:14). After the fall, the complete God as Jehovah came from heaven down to the earth to the garden of Eden, seeking the fallen sinner: "And the Lord God called unto Adam, and said unto him, Where art thou?" (Gen. 3:9). That was the first visit for the purpose of preaching the gospel. Then God gave them the promise. That promise was the first preaching of the gospel. In that promise, in that first preaching of the gospel, the complete God made a promise to the couple, especially to Eve, by cursing the serpent (v. 14). The first preaching of the gospel was the pronouncing of a curse. When God was cursing the damaging serpent, He promised the damaged persons that the seed of the woman would bruise the serpent's head (v. 15). In the entire Bible of sixty-six books there is such a reality as the seed of the woman. This is not a small thing. In Galatians 4:4 Paul purposely said that the Coming One, Christ, was born of a woman. This indicates that Paul knew what God had promised in Genesis 3:15. Paul knew the Bible, the Old Testament; therefore he said, "God sent forth His Son, born of a woman."

After the first promise in Genesis 3:15, twenty-seven centuries passed until the time of Isaiah, who repeated God's promise: "Behold, the virgin will conceive and will bear a son, and she will call his name Immanuel" (Isa. 7:14). This son borne by the virgin is the seed of the woman. For two thousand years after the first promise was given, nothing took place to fulfill that promise. Man continued to fall step by step, all the way to the bottom, to Babel (Gen. 11:1-9). However, God called Abraham out of the fallen race and promised him that he would be a blessing to all the nations on the earth (12:1-3). Eventually, God gave more details, saying that not through Abraham directly but through his seed all the nations of the earth would be blessed (22:18). This became the promise to Abraham concerning the seed of Abraham. Then, approximately one thousand years later God promised David that He would establish the throne of his seed forever (2 Sam. 7:12-13). This was the promise to David concerning the seed of David.

These three promises, concerning the seed of the woman, the seed of Abraham, and the seed of David, were fulfilled four thousand years after man was created (Matt. 1:1, 18-23). The Lord was very patient. First He promised; then four thousand years later He fulfilled the promise. In the middle of the four thousand years He repeated the promise to Abraham, and after another thousand years He repeated the promise to David. One thousand years after that, Jesus came to fulfill the three promises.

Christ as the threefold seed in humanity is a great subject in the entire Bible. The Triune God, the complete God, created man and then purposed to be born of fallen man to become a threefold seed. The first aspect of this seed was to destroy Satan to deliver fallen man out of sin, death, and self. The second aspect was to be a blessing to the fallen race. He Himself would be the blessing in His Trinity. By this we can see that the Trinity is not a doctrinal matter but a matter of dispensing and enjoyment to the fallen race. The seed of Abraham is the consummated God. This is the truth the Lord has shown us in His recovery. Before the incarnation, God was complete, yet He was not consummated. Eventually, His intention was to become a God-man. We need to realize that today our God is absolutely different from the God of the Jews and from the God of the Moslems. The God of both the Jews and the Moslems is only a divine person, not a God-man. But our God today is God plus man, the God-man. Our God is a God who is one with man to the extent that He became a man, a God-man. Now, in His constitution He has both divinity and humanity as His elements.

Nearly every page of the sixty-six books of the Bible is occupied with the threefold seed in humanity. This threefold seed in humanity is God who became a man. First, He became the seed of the woman to overcome all the enemies— Satan, sin, death, and man's self. Second, He became the seed of Abraham to be the consummated Triune God. This consummation began with incarnation and ended in resurrection. In resurrection this incarnated One became the life-giving Spirit (1 Cor. 15:45b). This is a great truth in the Bible. The Nicene Creed does not mention this, nor does it mention the sevenfold Spirit in Revelation 1:4, 4:5, and 5:6. The Triune God has not only been consummated as the life-giving Spirit; He has been intensified sevenfold. This is the clear revelation of the Bible. Paul, in 1 Corinthians 15:45, saw only the life-giving Spirit, but John saw not only the consummated Triune God but also the consummated Triune God intensified sevenfold.

The conclusion of my study of the Bible is that the Triune God, the complete, eternal God, one day became a threefold seed in humanity, first, to destroy God's enemies, second, to cause Himself to be consummated for the blessing of His chosen people, and third, to be the seed of David to bring in the kingdom. He came not just to be a blessing to His chosen people but to set His chosen people up as a kingdom. This kingdom is the great mountain in Daniel 2:34-35 that will fill the whole earth. The great mountain is the corporate threefold seed in humanity, which includes all the believers in Christ. We are all incorporated in that great mountain.

The threefold seed in humanity first dealt with all the enemies; second, He became the consummated Triune God as our full blessing, intensified sevenfold; and third, He made His chosen people His kingdom that fills not only the earth but also the heavens, causing the whole universe to become His great kingdom. The enemies are gone, the blessing is here, and we are in the kingdom. This is the revelation of the entire Bible. How wonderful this is!

II. THE WAY TO RECEIVE, EXPERIENCE, AND ENJOY
THE ALL-INCLUSIVE CHRIST
AS THE ALL-INCLUSIVE LIFE-GIVING SPIRIT—
THE AGGREGATE OF THE ALL-EMBRACING BLESSING
OF THE FULL GOSPEL OF GOD

A. The Way in the Book of Galatians

The way to share in, partake of, and participate in the threefold seed can be seen in the book of Galatians. In the short book of Galatians Paul presents the fact that the very Christ whom he ministered to people is the consummated God as the Spirit to be our blessing (3:14). I studied Martin Luther's exposition on Galatians, and I appreciate his interpretation of chapter three. However, he did not see that the blessing of God's gospel is the consummated Triune God as the consummated Spirit. Nevertheless, Paul presented this to us, and we thank the Lord that He has opened our eyes to see this.

1. By God's Revealing of Christ in Us

The way to receive, experience, and enjoy the all-inclusive Christ as the all-inclusive life-giving Spirit, the aggregate of the all-embracing blessing of the full gospel of God, is first by God's revealing of Christ in us (Gal. 1:16a). Apart from God's revelation, none of us, not even Paul, has a way. Paul said that he formerly was zealous for his fathers' religion (v. 14) and that he had advanced in that religion beyond many of his contemporaries. Paul was fighting absolutely for his fathers' religion against Jesus Christ. On a certain day he was traveling from Jerusalem to Damascus to bind the followers of Jesus and bring them to the high priest for sentencing. As he went, he drew near to Damascus; suddenly a light from heaven shone around him, and he fell on the ground and heard a voice saying to him, "Saul, Saul, why are you persecuting Me?" (Acts 9:3-4). That shocked him. He thought that he was persecuting the followers of Jesus on the earth. How then did a voice come from heaven? Paul responded, and spontaneously he called this One "Lord." He said, "Who are You, Lord?" (v. 5). He did not know who this

One was, yet he called Him "Lord." By this he was saved, for "whoever calls upon the name of the Lord shall be saved" (Rom. 10:13). The Lord answered Paul, "I am Jesus." From that time the revelation began to shine within Paul. He received a revelation of Christ, and he also received a burden to preach, to minister, and to present this One to others.

The New Testament tells us that Paul was a pattern to all the believers (1 Tim. 1:15-16). Therefore, since God revealed Christ into Paul, it should be the same with us. God must reveal Christ into each of us. Those who have been genuinely regenerated and saved can testify that since the time they heard the gospel, within them there has been an unveiling. After they heard the gospel, the scenery of a person, Jesus, began to shine within them. From that time onward, nearly every day something more concerning this One is unveiled to them. We have not just heard something; we have seen something within. We could not have been saved unless we had had such an unveiling of Christ within us.

The Christ whom we have seen is a profound Christ, One whose size is the dimensions of the entire universe. The dimensions of the universe are unlimited. No one can tell the length, the breadth, the height, and the depth of the universe. However, Paul said that if we allow Christ to make His home in our hearts, we will have the ability to know with all the saints the breadth, the length, the height, and the depth of this universe, that is, the dimensions of Christ (Eph. 3:17-18). From 1960, when I was in Taiwan, I began to count how many items of Christ are revealed in the Bible. They are endless. It was from that year that I began to preach the unsearchable riches of Christ (v. 8). Oh, the riches of Christ are unsearchable!

Today Christ is still shining in me, and I am continually seeing more of Him. We all need such an unveiling. This is God's doing. Every aspect of the Christian life comes out of this unveiling. We live the Christian life according to the Christ whom we have seen. My Christian life is not according to the teachings I picked up from reading the Bible or from listening to messages. My Christian life comes out of the Christ whom I have seen day after day. Christ must be revealed not only into us but in us. This means that something is going on within us. Since the day we believed in the Lord Jesus, God's unveiling of Christ has been going on in us. This unveiling never ceases.

2. By Our Receiving of Christ as the Spirit out of the Hearing of Faith

Day after day we see more of the Lord Jesus. As God, on His side, is revealing, we, on our side, are receiving. In our receiving, we receive Christ as the Spirit out of the hearing of faith (Gal. 3:2). The Spirit whom we receive is the indwelling, life-giving, compound, sevenfold intensified Spirit. We need to receive Christ as such a Spirit.

When we were saved, we received the Spirit out of the hearing of faith. Here *faith* does not refer to the action of believing but to the things we believe in. The word *faith* denotes first the things we believe in; then, based on what we believe in, we have the action of believing. In Galatians 3:2 the word *faith* means belief, referring to what we believe in. We have received Christ out of our hearing of the belief. The Christian belief is Christ Himself in His person and His redemptive work. Christ's person and Christ's work together constitute our belief.

When we preach the gospel, we preach this belief, that is, the person of Christ and the redemptive work of Christ. When the audience hears our preaching, they hear the faith; that is, they hear the belief. They hear about Christ's person, and they hear about Christ's redemptive work. As they are hearing of the person and work of Christ, something rises up within them, that is, a believing. By hearing, we believe.

Romans 10 says that faith comes out of hearing, and hearing comes out of preaching (vv. 14, 17), and preaching comes out of being sent (v. 15). Recently I received a letter from a dear brother who had just returned from a trip to eastern Europe to visit Czechoslovakia, Poland, and Hungary. The impression I received from this report is that there is the need for the preaching of what we believe. Those countries need our young people to go there to teach the people our belief, our faith. I do believe the Lord will afford us the way to go. We need to send a good number of young people to these countries. But where are the people who will go? The Lord said to Isaiah, "Whom shall I send? Who will go for us?" (Isa. 6:8). Would you answer, "Lord, I am here. I will go"? You do not need to care for your living. Jesus will feed you. Some of you can go to those countries to teach English. As you teach English to the people, you can teach them the truth, the faith, the belief, and the holy word that you have heard. If you would go there and take care of just ten people, I believe that in half a year you would bring all these ten to the Lord and into the truth.

3. By Being Born according to the Spirit and Being Given the Spirit of God's Son into Our Hearts

The third way in the book of Galatians to receive, experience, and enjoy the all-inclusive Christ as the all-inclusive life-giving Spirit is by being born according to the Spirit and by being given the Spirit of God's Son into our hearts (Gal. 4:29b, 6). Galatians 4:29 refers to being born according to the Spirit. This being born surely refers to our regeneration. Our regeneration was according to the Spirit; that is, it was accomplished according to the Spirit within us.

At one time you had never believed in the Lord Jesus because you had never heard about Him. However, one day you did hear. While the preacher was speaking, something was going on within you. The Spirit within you either showed you the preciousness of the Lord Jesus or convicted you of your sins or showed you how pitiful you were in your human life. As a result, you regretted and repented. Even before anyone asked you to do anything, something within you spontaneously brought you to pray and to say, "O Lord, I want to believe; I want to take You. You are too good." You might also have said, "Lord, I am an evil person." This was your repentance. Your repenting just this much was sufficient for you to be saved. Or you might have said, "Lord

Jesus, You know my situation. Look at my situation. How pitiful I am!" Just by saying this much, you were saved.

This is to be regenerated according to the Spirit. We were not regenerated merely *by* the Spirit; we were regenerated *according to* the Spirit. After the gospel meeting you might have gone back home, and your inward feeling continued. Actually, that was not your feeling; that was the moving of the Spirit. This might have continued for a week. According to the recollection of my experience, this moving of the Spirit within me lasted quite a long time. As a result, I began to lose my taste for all the worldly things. I began to think about my attitude toward my mother. That was not just my thinking or my feeling by myself; that was the moving of the Spirit. Perhaps after one week or after ten days, you thoroughly realized your regeneration.

It is right to say that regeneration is instantaneous. However, regeneration is also a process. This process is the moving of the Spirit within us to regenerate us. Therefore, we were regenerated according to the Spirit. To be regenerated by the Spirit is instantaneous, but to be regenerated according to the Spirit implies a process. I do know of some who were regenerated not just in one week but in six months. The Spirit began to move in them a little, but they did not pay much attention to that. However, the Spirit continued to move within them. This process lasted for quite a time, until they fully realized that they were regenerated.

Doctrinally speaking, regeneration is immediate and instantaneous. However, although regeneration is instantaneous, with some persons the process is not quick but, rather, very slow.

It was according to the process of the Spirit's moving within us that we were regenerated. Therefore, our regenerated being is absolutely spiritual. Immediately after this regenerating birth, God sent the Spirit of His Son into our hearts (Gal. 4:6). We were born according to the life-giving Spirit, and immediately after our birth, God gave us the life-giving Spirit. This is a double portion. We were born according to the life-giving Spirit, and God gave us a gift—the Spirit of sonship. This gift is also the life-giving Spirit, and this life-giving Spirit is the consummated Triune God. Therefore, we were born according to the consummated Triune God, and after our birth we received the gift of the consummated Triune God. This One is the threefold seed in humanity. Every aspect of our spiritual experience is nothing less than the processed and consummated Triune God.

4. By Putting on Christ through the Baptism That Puts Us into Christ

We receive, experience, and enjoy the all-inclusive Christ as the all-inclusive Spirit also by putting on Christ through the baptism that puts us into Christ (Gal. 3:27). To put on Christ is to be clothed with Christ. We were once naked, without any covering. To be naked is a shame. However, at the time we believed and were baptized, something was put on us to clothe us. We were clothed with Christ through baptism. Matthew 28:19 says, "Go therefore and disciple all the nations, baptizing them into the name of the Father and of the Son and of the Holy Spirit." We baptize people not only into water but also into the Triune God. In so doing, we put Christ upon them; we clothe them with Christ through baptism.

Baptism puts us into Christ. When we go to preach the gospel, we need to have the full realization that when we baptize people, we are putting them not only into water but also into the consummated, processed Triune God. We should tell them, "From today onward you are no longer naked; you are clothed and covered with the processed, consummated Triune God." This is the way to receive, experience, and enjoy the all-inclusive Christ as the all-inclusive life-giving Spirit, who is the aggregate of the all-embracing blessing of the full gospel of God.

5. By Being Identified with Him in His Death So That It May Be No Longer We Who Live but He Who Lives in Us

The fifth way in Galatians to experience the all-inclusive

Christ as the life-giving Spirit is by being identified with Him so that it may be no longer we who live but He who lives in us; and the life which we now live in the flesh we live in the faith of Christ (Gal. 2:20). To be identified with Christ is to be made one with Christ. Baptism identifies us with Christ by making us one entity with Christ. We are identified with Christ especially in His death. Romans 6:3 says, "Or are you ignorant that all of us who have been baptized into Christ Jesus have been baptized into His death?" We have been baptized into two things—into Christ and into His death. Therefore, we are now one entity with Christ in His death. This means that He died, and we died also. His death is our death. With Him, His death is history, but with us, it is a present, living, vivid experience. When we are baptized, we are put into Christ's death, making Christ's death ours. Since we are dead and buried, how could we live any longer? We have been identified with Christ in His death that it may be no longer we who live but He who lives in us; and the life which we now live in the flesh we live in the faith of Christ.

To live in the faith of Christ means that the very Christ who lives in us becomes our faith. Galatians 2:20 says that it is no longer we who live, but it is Christ who lives in us. It then goes on to say that the life that we now live, we still live in the flesh, yet we live this life by Christ as our faith. Christ is living within us, and this living Christ within us eventually becomes our faith. It is by this faith, which is the very realization of Christ, that we still live in the flesh. This kind of living is actually not we who live but Christ who lives in us. Christ's living in us means that we still live in the flesh by Christ as our faith. Thus, the life spoken of in Galatians 2:20 is a life that is absolutely Christ. People may say, "Since you are still eating, sleeping, studying, working, and doing things, you are still living." To this we may reply, "Yes, I am still living, but I do not live by anything of myself; I live by Christ as my faith. And this Christ is the One who lives in me. So actually this is not my living. This is Christ's living, because I live no longer, but Christ lives in me. I still have a kind of living, but this living is not by me but by Christ as my faith. The more He lives in me, the more I realize His preciousness. The more I appreciate His preciousness, the more faith is within me. This, therefore, is altogether not a life by myself but a life by Christ. As for me, I am terminated; I am finished; I have been crucified and even buried. It is no longer I who live but Christ who lives in me. I am still living, yet I am living not by something of myself but by Christ Himself as my faith."

It is in this way that we enjoy, experience, and receive this wonderful Christ. Paul's presentation concerning the way is not simple. It is very deep and very logical. This is the Christian life. I do not believe that such a truth is being adequately taught among Christians today. We thank Him that He has opened both His Word and our eyes so that today we can see something. I hope that you all will learn such things. Then you will spontaneously have more experience of Him, and you will have something as a testimony or a teaching of the truth to render to others. Today the whole world is in need. The entire earth is in a famine like that at the time of Joseph (Gen. 41:30-31). Therefore, we need to be raised up in His stewardship to dispense all the riches of our Father's great household. I hope that many of you will be stirred up to sacrifice all the things that are considered by people as blessings so that you may gain the real blessing. The whole world is starving, waiting for help from the proper sources. We all need to realize the Lord's sovereignty in raising up the present world situation. We also need to realize that God's ordained way is not to use a big speaker but to raise up all His chosen people to prophesy for Him. We all have accumulated quite much of the Lord's riches in His Word; therefore, now the time is ripe for all of us to go and minister to the hungry ones what we have received.

The Central Line of the Divine Revelation

THE DIVINE ECONOMY
AND THE DIVINE DISPENSING

MESSAGE FOURTEEN

THE AGGREGATE OF THE ALL-EMBRACING BLESSING
OF THE FULL GOSPEL OF GOD IN CHRIST
FOR THE DIVINE DISPENSING
ACCORDING TO THE DIVINE ECONOMY

(5)

Scripture Reading: Gal. 2:20; 5:16, 25; 4:19; 6:7, 8b, 14-15, 18

In this message we will continue to fellowship concerning the way to receive, experience, and enjoy the all-inclusive Christ as the all-inclusive life-giving Spirit—the aggregate of the all-embracing blessing of the full gospel of God.

First, I would like to present something further regarding the matter, mentioned in the previous message, of our being identified with Christ in His death that it may be no longer we who live but Christ who lives in us (Gal. 2:20). To be identified with someone, we must first have a union with him. We cannot have communion, that is, fellowship, without first having union. In the Old Testament, the priests laid their hands on the sacrifices that they offered. This signified their union with the offerings. Actually, however, the priests were still the priests, and the offerings were the offerings. Union is not by a physical means; union must be by the Spirit. If the Lord were not a Spirit or if we did not have a human spirit, it would be impossible for the Lord and us to have a union. First Corinthians 15:45b says, "The last Adam became a life-giving Spirit," and 1 Corinthians 6:17 says, "But he who is joined to the Lord is one spirit." To be identified with the Lord means to be one spirit with Him and even to be one entity with Him. To be one entity with the Lord means that we become Him and He becomes us, that is, that He and we become one. This is a deeper union than that of a husband and wife. A couple's union is not absolute; they can still be divorced. However, just as our body cannot divorce our head, it is impossible for us to "divorce" the Lord. We are one entity with Him.

We become one with the Lord by believing into Him. Certain verses in the New Testament, such as John 3:16, speak of our believing not merely *in* Christ but *into* Christ. Our believing into the Lord is a fact, not merely a saying. Galatians 3:27 says, "For as many as were baptized into Christ have put on Christ." To realize that we have been baptized into Christ and have put on Christ requires the exercise of our believing ability. Many times when we preach the gospel to sinners we do not speak concerning deep spiritual matters because we believe that they will not be able to understand them. This is wrong. We should tell people, "Dear friends, today you can be in Christ, and Christ is waiting to enter into you. Let me tell you how this can be. God is a Spirit, and one day two thousand years ago this God became a man by the name of Jesus. This man lived on the earth for thirty-three and a half years. Then He went to the cross to die for you and for your sins. He was buried and was resurrected on the third day. Now I will tell you a wonder: on the third day this Jesus in His resurrection became a life-giving Spirit. In brief, Jesus became a Spirit. You might have heard the name of Jesus, but you probably do not know who and what Jesus is. Jesus is God the Spirit. He is in me, and I am bringing Jesus as the Spirit to you. While I am speaking to you, He is speaking. If you believe in Him and call on Him, you will get into Him and He will get into you."

To be identified with the Lord is to be one Spirit with Him. It is a fact that Jesus today is the Spirit waiting to enter into anyone who believes in Him. If a person exercises his inner being to call on Jesus, regardless of his race, color, or culture, Jesus comes as the Spirit and enters into him. Following this, the person must be baptized. To be baptized is to be put into Christ, signifying what we have received through our believing. To be baptized is also to put Christ upon us. In baptism there is a two-way traffic. We enter into Jesus, and we put Jesus upon us. This is not a form or ritual; it is a fact. When we baptize people, we should tell them that we are not putting them only into the water; we are putting them into Jesus Christ as the Spirit. From the time that he is baptized, the baptized person is in Christ, and Christ is upon him like a garment. This is a fact in which we must believe, and we must have the assurance and boldness to tell this to people.

Matthew 28:19 says, "Go therefore and disciple all the nations, baptizing them into the name of the Father and of the Son and of the Holy Spirit." It is easy for us to believe that we are baptizing people into water, because water is visible; but because of our lack of realization, we may not have the boldness and assurance to tell people that we are baptizing them into the Triune God. Because of our weakness, the Lord did not say here that we should baptize people into the Triune God directly, but that we should do this indirectly by baptizing people into the name of the Father and of the Son and of the Holy Spirit. In reality, however, the name is the sum total of the Divine Being, equivalent to His person. To baptize someone into the name of the Triune God is to immerse him into all that the Triune God is. If we go out to contact others without this assurance and boldness, we will have no power. We ourselves must have the experience that we are really in Jesus and that Jesus is really in us. Then we can go out to preach what we have experienced with boldness and full assurance.

We must believe what we preach, and we must believe that when we baptize people, we put them into the Triune God. The baptized one is in the Triune God; he is in Jesus and Jesus is in him. Now he and Jesus, Jesus and he, are one. They are two persons united together to be one person. Therefore, the baptized one is identified with Christ. If we are those who have this assurance, we will not preach the gospel in a poor and weak way to others. Before we go out to preach to others, we must first pray ourselves into the Spirit and into the Word of God. We should pray for at least twenty minutes, not mainly for sinners to be saved but for ourselves. We may pray, "Lord, be merciful to empower us. Put us into Yourself. When we go out, go in us and cause us to go in You. We do not want to go out without being in You." After twenty minutes, we will have the assurance that He is in us and that we are in Him. Then we will have the genuine boldness and power. This assurance, boldness, and power added together, equals the Spirit.

After a person has been baptized, we should go back to him to tell him that he is one with Jesus. Jesus died on the cross, and since we are one with Him, we died there also (2 Cor. 5:14). We are identified with Him in His death in order that it may be no longer we who live. This was the reason that we died with Him. We needed to be terminated, and now we have been germinated. Now Christ lives in us. This is the higher gospel that we need to preach to the newly baptized ones. We must believe that people are able to understand such a gospel.

Christ's living in us must be a fact, not merely a doctrine or a declaration. When we awake in the morning, we should call on the Lord a number of times before we do anything else. If we will do this, by the time we have made our beds, we will be different persons. Calling on the Lord in this way will help us to experience Christ living in us. Copying two verses from the Bible after our morning revival and taking them in a little at a time throughout the day will also help us to experience Christ living in us. We should not care merely for the doctrine of Christ living in us. We should care for the fact.

According to Galatians 2:20, the life which we now live in the flesh we live in the faith of Christ. We live a life in the flesh, but we live this life in the faith of Christ. We do not live such a life in our faith but in Christ's faith, even in Christ as our faith. When we live in this way, we enjoy Christ and appreciate Christ, and Christ within us becomes our present faith. This means that we put ourselves absolutely aside. Nothing is left within us but Christ. Christ is everything to us to such an extent that He even becomes our faith. This is a great matter.

We all need to see that our believing in Jesus and our being baptized into Him means that He comes into us and we are put into Him so that He and we become one. He is in us, and we are in Him. This is possible only because of the two spirits. He is the divine Spirit, and we have a human spirit. The divine Spirit is in our human spirit. Therefore, in our spirit we are one spirit with Him. He died, and we died in Him. We live, but He lives in us. We are still living, yet we live this life not by anything of ourselves but by Him as everything, even as our faith. We all need to see this. This is not merely a doctrine; it must be our experience.

6. By Living and Walking by the Spirit

The sixth way to receive, experience, and enjoy the all-inclusive Christ as the all-inclusive life-giving Spirit is by living and walking by the Spirit (Gal. 5:16, 25). Living and walking by the Spirit is equivalent to having our being by the Spirit. The Spirit is in our human spirit (Rom. 8:16). It is often difficult in Paul's writings for translators to determine whether *spirit* should be capitalized or not. The spirit in Paul's writings is the mingled spirit, the Spirit who is in our spirit.

After rising up in the morning, we should do everything by our spirit. We must begin our day by living and walking in our spirit. If we rise up in a loose way, we will spoil the whole day. The best thing to do after rising up is to call on the name of the Lord. When we call "O Lord Jesus," we are in the spirit (1 Cor. 12:3). Calling in this way brings us back from everything to our spirit. Then we will have a good beginning of the day, and we will be able to face any situation. We will be able to encounter every circumstance by our spirit. This is to live and to walk by the Spirit. This experience follows the experience of being identified with Christ in His death in order that He may live in us. Without experiencing the identification with Christ, we cannot live and walk by the Spirit.

7. By Having Christ Formed in Us through Travail

The way to receive, experience, and enjoy Christ as the Spirit is also by having Christ formed in us through travail. Galatians 4:19 says, "My children, with whom I travail again in birth until Christ is formed in you." In Galatians 1:16 Christ is revealed in us; in 2:20 Christ lives in us; and in 3:27 Christ is upon us, clothing us like a garment. Now, in 4:19 Christ is formed in us.

The second stanza of *Hymns,* #499 says,

> Oh, what a joy! Oh, what a rest!
> Christ now is being formed in me.
> His very nature and life divine
> In my whole being inwrought shall be.
> All that I am came to an end,
> And all of Christ is all to me.

The last two lines in the Chinese say that all that we are has been terminated, and Christ's all in all has become our element. Now His element is everything to us. This is the meaning of Christ's being formed in us. In his writings Paul also used the words *transformed* (2 Cor. 3:18) and *conformed* (Rom. 8:29). If we are not transformed, Christ has not been formed in us. Christ's being formed in us depends on our being transformed. We are transformed to His image, and He is formed in us. Our being transformed and His being formed cause us to be conformed to His image. Our being conformed to His image is His being formed in us further.

Romans 12:2a says, "And do not be fashioned according to this age, but be transformed by the renewing of the mind." Here the term *renewing* is used with *transformed.* This indicates that to have Christ formed in us is to have the three parts of our soul—our mind, emotion, and will—renewed. Our mind is the leading part of our soul. To have our mind renewed is to have Christ "invade" our mind. Our mind, emotion, and will are filled with our self and the world. To be renewed in our mind is to remove our self and the world from our mind, emotion, and will and replace them with Christ. If we are renewed in this way, Christ will be formed in us, and our mind, emotion, and will will be like Him. Every part of our inner being will bear the image of Christ. This is to have Christ formed in us. When we think, we will be like Christ. When we love or hate, like or dislike, we will be like Christ. When we choose or reject, we will be like Christ.

However, most of us are not like this yet. At times we may think noble thoughts, but in our practical life our mind is not like Christ. Our mind simply expresses our self with the world. It is the same with our emotion. We may love, laugh, and weep by the self and the world, not by Christ. This indicates that Christ has not been formed in us. Christ has not invaded our mind, emotion, and will to replace the self and the world with Himself. Many times when people talk, their talk is full of the self and the element of the world. The mind, emotion, and will of such persons are filled with the self and the element of the world. What is formed in them is the self with the world, and they are the expression of the self and the world. We can never be an expression of Christ until Christ has invaded our entire inner being to chase the self and the world out of our mind, emotion, and will and replace them with Himself. Then our inner being will bear the form, the image, of Christ.

According to Paul's usage in the New Testament, the form is the outward expression of the inner being (see Phil. 2:6 and note 2 there). If we are full of the self and love the world in our inner being, our outward form will simply be the self and the world. In selecting a pair of shoes, a necktie, or a car, our choice will express the world and indicate that our emotions, our likes and dislikes, are full of the self and the world. But if Christ has invaded, conquered, and subdued us and has chased the self and the world out of our inner being and replaced the self and the world with Himself, we will express Him. What we are is expressed in our outward form. If Christ replaces the self and the world in our mind, emotion, and will, we will have the form of Christ. The Galatians were occupied by Judaism; thus, in their outward form they expressed Judaism. Therefore, Paul said, "My children, with whom I travail again in birth until Christ is formed in you."

Paul had to suffer like a mother, travailing for the Galatians until Christ replaced the self and the world in them with Himself.

8. By Sowing unto the Spirit
with the Desire and Aim of the Spirit in View,
to Accomplish What the Spirit Desires

Another way to receive, experience, and enjoy the all-inclusive Christ as the all-inclusive life-giving Spirit is by sowing unto the Spirit with the desire and aim of the Spirit in view, to accomplish what the Spirit desires (Gal. 6:7, 8b). Our human living is a sowing. Whatever we do, we are sowing seeds, and whatever we sow, we will reap. If we sow something high and good, we will reap the same, and if we sow something mean and low, we can expect to reap the same thing. Everything that we do in our daily life is a sowing. We should not think that the way we comb our hair is a small matter. Even this is a sowing. After a certain period of time, we will reap what we have sown. Galatians 6:8 says, "For he who sows unto his own flesh will reap corruption of the flesh, but he who sows unto the Spirit will of the Spirit reap eternal life." We must endeavor to sow properly. If we sow according to the Spirit, we will reap according to the Spirit.

Our sowing unto the Spirit is with the desire and aim of the Spirit in view. Our desire and aim are not ours but the Spirit's. Christ lives in us, but our sowing may be according to our own desire. We may comb our hair in a certain way because of our own desire. However, when we comb our hair, we must have the desire and aim of the Spirit in view. Our desire and aim should be that the style of our hair would express the Lord whom we love, who is the Spirit within us, that people could even see Christ in our hair style. In our sowing we must have the desire and aim of the Spirit in view, to accomplish the aim of the Spirit. Whatever we have, wear, or do should correspond with the Spirit's purpose, desire, and intention. What we will reap depends on what we sow.

To sow to the Spirit in this way is to receive, experience, and enjoy the Spirit as the all-embracing blessing of the gospel. If we live a life without the Spirit and sow according to the flesh, we cannot expect to enjoy Christ as the all-embracing blessing. Several years ago the major denominations in America came together to consider a joint work to evangelize the world. Their conclusion was that they could not do this because of the shortage of persons. There are many millions of Christians in America today, but how many of them are living Christ? How many are living Christ in the way that they comb their hair or purchase shoes? This is not a small matter. Our purchasing of a necktie is a sowing. The reaping will come when we stand before people with our tie to preach the gospel. If the tie is too worldly, our preaching will be empty. If we are not dressed according to the Spirit, people will not have the heart to listen to our message. To sow to the Spirit is to live Christ, and this is to receive, experience, and enjoy Christ.

9. By Boasting in the Cross of Christ and Living a New Creation

The way to receive, experience, and enjoy Christ as the Spirit is also by boasting in the cross of Christ and living a new creation, which is neither religion nor nonreligion (Gal. 6:14-15). The cross of Christ is our boast. We boast in the fact that everything has been terminated on the cross. The love of cars, the love of a big house, and the love of stylish fashions have all been terminated. Everything has been "crossed out." This is our boast. Now we are living a new creation. Since we boast in the cross, we cannot live in the old creation; we must live in the new creation. Everything must be new because we are a new creation in Christ. This is the way to enjoy Christ.

10. By the Grace of Our Lord Jesus Christ with Our Spirit

The consummate way to receive, experience, and enjoy Christ as the Spirit is by the grace of the Lord Jesus Christ with our spirit. The book of Galatians concludes with 6:18: "The grace of our Lord Jesus Christ be with your spirit, brothers. Amen." The grace of the Lord Jesus Christ being with our Spirit is the way to receive, experience, and enjoy Christ.

The Central Line of the Divine Revelation

THE DIVINE ECONOMY
AND THE DIVINE DISPENSING

MESSAGE FIFTEEN

THE AGGREGATE OF THE ALL-EMBRACING BLESSING
OF THE FULL GOSPEL OF GOD IN CHRIST
FOR THE DIVINE DISPENSING
ACCORDING TO THE DIVINE ECONOMY

(6)

Scripture Reading: John 1:1, 14, 16

II. THE WAY TO RECEIVE, EXPERIENCE, AND ENJOY
THE ALL-INCLUSIVE CHRIST
AS THE ALL-INCLUSIVE LIFE-GIVING SPIRIT—
THE AGGREGATE OF THE ALL-EMBRACING BLESSING
OF THE FULL GOSPEL OF GOD

B. The Way in the Gospel of John

The way to receive, experience, and enjoy the all-inclusive
Christ as the all-inclusive life-giving Spirit—the aggregate
of the all-embracing blessing of the full gospel of God—comprises at least twenty-five items in the Gospel of John. In
this message we will cover the first thirteen items.

Most Christians are very familiar with the Gospel of
John. After I was saved, I spent time in the Gospel of John
and discovered that there were many things in it that were
difficult to understand. I had many questions which could
not be answered even by the Christian workers, such as,
What is the Word (1:1)? What is regeneration (3:6)? and
What is eternal life (3:16)? The Gospel of John may be very
familiar to us, but we should not consider that it is a shallow
or superficial book. It is a book that is full of depth.

Therefore, we need to "dive" into these depths and "mine" the treasures in the depths of this book.

The apostle John used very simple words and language in his Gospel. This is a strong characteristic of his writings. The language he used is simple, but the matters conveyed by his words are very profound. Because many things in the Gospel of John are quite deep, few have spent the time to dig out the things in this Gospel. Thank the Lord that through the years, by reading their books, we have received help from others. The Bible has been read again and again throughout the past twenty centuries by millions of Christians. We are standing on the shoulders of all the foregoing saints. I am grateful to the Lord that the top understanding of those in the past was preserved in their books. Today, because of their writings we are able to know what the brothers in earlier years understood.

1. By Receiving Christ as the Son of God through Believing into Him, to Be Born of God

The first way to receive, experience, and enjoy the all-inclusive Christ as the all-inclusive life-giving Spirit in the Gospel of John is by receiving Christ as the Son of God through believing into Him, to be born of God (1:12-13).

In 1964 I was invited to speak to an independent Bible church in the city of Las Vegas. While I was there, I spoke on man's heart and spirit. I said that God created man with a heart to love Him and a spirit to receive Him. I said that man can receive God by means of his spirit and that he can love God with his heart. During my visit, I stayed in the home of one of the leaders of the congregation. I found out that the wife of that brother was very bothered about my speaking concerning the difference between the heart and the spirit. To her realization the two were the same. She felt that I had gone too far in differentiating between the heart and the spirit. The next morning she served us breakfast. As she was coming with the eggs, I said, "Sister, give me an egg." As she gave me an egg, I said again, "Sister, give me an egg." At this, she said, "Brother Lee, here it is." I said, "I surely would love to have an egg." As I said this, I kept my hands off the egg. At first, she did not understand what I was demonstrating. Then I said, "Sister, I would like to show you the difference between receiving and loving. You cannot receive the egg with your heart, and you cannot love the egg with your hands. To love the egg, you must use your heart, but to receive the egg, you must use your hands. God created us with a heart so that we can love Him. But just as I cannot receive the egg without hands, I cannot receive God without a receiving organ. This is why God created a spirit within man as well as a heart." After this brief explanation, the sister received a complete understanding and was very happy.

The word *receive* is used in a strong way in the Gospel of John. John 1:14 and 16 say, "And the Word became flesh... full of grace and reality....For of His fullness we have all received, and grace upon grace." Many Christians know that the word *believe* is used many times in the Gospel of John, but few know that the word *receive* is also used very strongly in this Gospel. John 1:12-13 says, "But as many as received Him, to them He gave the authority to become children of God, to those who believe into His name, who were begotten not of blood, nor of the will of the flesh, nor of the will of man, but of God." Verse 12 speaks first of receiving the Son of God; then it speaks of believing into the Son of God. Thus, to receive Christ is to believe into Christ. When we believe into Christ, we receive Christ and thus gain Him.

The purpose of believing into Christ is to be born of God. Before regeneration we were created by God but were not born of Him. We were His creatures, but we were not His children. John 1:12-13 says that those who receive the Son of God through their believing into Him are born of God to be children of God. How wonderful that we fallen, sinful human beings can be born of God to be His children! When the Lord Jesus spoke to Nicodemus about his need to be born anew (John 3:3), Nicodemus misunderstood the Lord's word to mean that he needed to go back to his mother's womb and be born again physically. However, his need was to receive

Christ as the Son of God through believing into Him so that he could be born of God to be a child of God.

2. By Taking Christ as the Lamb of God Who Takes Away the Sin of the World

To receive, experience, and enjoy the all-inclusive Christ, we must take Him as the Lamb of God who takes away the sin of the world (1:29, 36). Christ's being the Lamb of God is one of the deep items in the Gospel of John. The Lamb of God, no doubt, is Jesus, yet He is certainly not a lamb with four legs and a tail. Jesus was called the Lamb of God because in the eyes of God He was the sacrifice, the offering, for the sin of the world. The world here is a composition of the people of the world. The people who constitute the world are sinful, and the world as the composition of these people also is sinful. According to Isaiah 53:7, Christ was led like a lamb to the slaughter. All the people who dealt with Him at the time of His crucifixion led Him like a lamb to the cross, the place of slaughter. On the cross God collected all our sins and put the totality of sin upon Him. Thus, in the eyes of God, He became the Lamb of God. Through His death He took away the sin of the world. When we believe into Christ as the Lamb of God, we gain Christ. This is the basic way to take Christ and to enjoy Him.

3. By Following Christ as Messiah (God's Anointed One)

To receive, experience, and enjoy Christ as the all-inclusive Spirit, we must follow Christ as Messiah (John 1:37, 40-41, 43-45). The word *Messiah* in Hebrew is the equivalent of the word *Christ* in Greek. *Christ* means "the anointed One," and the anointed One is also the appointed One. We must follow the One who has been appointed and anointed by God to be the Executor of God's economy. We need to realize that the very Jesus whom we are following is the Messiah, God's elected One, His chosen One, the One anointed and appointed by God.

4. By Being Born Anew of the Spirit

To receive, experience, and enjoy the all-inclusive Christ, we need to be born anew of the Spirit (John 3:3, 5-6). John 3:6 says, "That which is born of the flesh is flesh, and that which is born of the Spirit is spirit." This verse indicates that to be born again is altogether a matter of the two spirits, God the Spirit and our spirit. We were born again not in our physical body but in our spirit, not of blood or flesh but of the Spirit of God. Our human spirit was born of God's Spirit. To be born again is a very subjective way for us to gain Christ for our enjoyment.

The entire Gospel of John is on the enjoyment of Christ by the Spirit. Without the Spirit we do not have the way to enjoy Christ. Receiving, experiencing, and enjoying Christ are absolutely related to our spirit and the Spirit of God. Before being born again, the Spirit and our spirit were separated and far apart. But through regeneration, the two spirits have been brought together as one spirit (1 Cor. 6:17). Through this one spirit we have the way to receive, enjoy, and experience Christ.

5. By Receiving the Spirit from Christ Not by Measure

We also receive, experience, and enjoy the all-inclusive Christ by receiving the Spirit from Him not by measure (John 3:34b). If the Spirit whom we receive from Christ were measurable or limited, He would not be adequate for us to enjoy. The Spirit whom we receive of Christ is without measure and is unlimited. Not only the Spirit is without measure, but the receiving of this Spirit also is without measure. Hence, the enjoyment of Christ is unlimited.

6. By Drinking the Living Water Which Christ Gives and Which Becomes in Us a Spring of Water Gushing Up into Eternal Life, through Worshipping God as the Spirit in Our Spirit

The way to receive, experience, and enjoy the all-inclusive Christ is by drinking the living water which He gives and which becomes in us a spring of water gushing up into eternal life, through worshipping God as the Spirit in our spirit (John 4:10, 14, 24). As we drink the living water, it becomes a spring of water within us, gushing up into eternal life. To drink the living water is to drink eternal life. According to the clear revelation of the New Testament, eternal life is God embodied in Christ and dispensed into us by the Spirit (11:25; 14:6; 16:13-15). Thus, eternal life is the Triune God Himself. We are drinking the Triune God, and our drinking is counted by God as our worship of Him.

According to John 4, to drink Christ as the living water is the genuine worship to God (vv. 10, 14, 24). The real worship of God is not to give something to Him or to kneel down before Him; the real worship of God is our enjoyment of Him by drinking Him. The more we enjoy Him, the more we worship Him. The angels may sing to God, but they do not have the capacity to receive Him. God's real desire is to have some who will drink Him. Man was made with a capacity to receive God and to drink Him as the living water. This is the real worship of God.

In the night in which He was betrayed, the Lord Jesus took bread, and having given thanks, He broke it and said, "This is My body, which is given for you; this do unto the remembrance of Me." Similarly, He took the cup also and said, "This cup is the new covenant established in My blood; this do, as often as you drink it, unto the remembrance of Me" (1 Cor. 11:23-25). Our eating and drinking of Christ are our remembrance of Him, and our remembrance of the Lord is our worship to Him as the processed Triune God. Eating and drinking Christ is the way to worship Him, and it is also the way to receive, experience, and enjoy Him.

7. By Hearing Christ's Word and Believing the Father Who Sent Him, That We May Live in Our Spirit and Have Eternal Life

We receive, experience, and enjoy Christ also by hearing Christ's word and believing the Father who sent Him, that we may live in our spirit and have eternal life (John 5:24a, 25). We were saved first by hearing the word of Christ concerning the Father, and then by believing in the Father, who sent Christ. The Father sent Christ so that we could live in our spirit and have eternal life.

Eternal life is difficult to explain, but according to our experience we can testify that from the day we believed into the Lord Jesus, the Triune God—the Father, the Lord Jesus Christ, and the life-giving Spirit—entered into us. This Triune God is eternal life (John 14:6; 1 John 5:12; Rom. 8:2). Because the Triune God is within us, we can live in our spirit. The worldly people do not have the capacity to live in their spirit, because they do not have eternal life in their spirit. After we believed into Christ, the Triune God entered into us as the eternal life, giving us the capacity to live in our spirit. This capacity is the Triune God Himself. As we live in our spirit, we live the Triune God.

8. By Eating Christ
(Taking Him as Food into Our Spirit)
and Living because of Him

We receive, experience, and enjoy Christ also by eating Christ (taking Him as food into our spirit) and living because of Him (John 6:57). We eat Christ by taking Him as food into our spirit. To eat physical food, we must take it into our stomach. Similarly, the Triune God embodied in Christ and realized as the Spirit to be our spiritual food and life supply must be taken into our spirit. In this way we live because of Him.

Before I speak in the meetings, I often feel empty within. So I must have some time with the Lord by myself to look to Him, to pray to Him, and to talk to Him. Sometimes, after only five minutes I am filled. At the beginning I feel like a "flat tire," but after a few minutes my "flat tire" is filled with "air." At that time I have the assurance, the boldness, and the power to speak. This power is just the Spirit. We need to come to this Jesus, to this Spirit, to take Him as our spiritual food and life supply.

9. By Eating the Word
Spoken by Christ as Spirit
and as Life

Another way to receive, experience, and enjoy Christ is to eat the word spoken by Christ as spirit and as life. John 6:63 says, "The words which I have spoken to you are spirit and are life." Christ speaks the word, the word is the Spirit, and the Spirit is life. Thus, the word, the Spirit, and life are three-in-one. The Speaker of the word is the processed Triune God, and His speaking transmits the processed Triune God into us in the form of the word. After entering into us, this word becomes the Spirit, and the Spirit is life. Then, when we utter this Spirit out to others, the Spirit becomes the word to them. When others receive the word into them, it becomes the Spirit again. Then, when they speak the Spirit out to others, He again becomes the word. Hence, when we receive the word into us, the word becomes the Spirit, and the Spirit becomes our very life. This is the transmission of the Triune God into us as our life supply, first in the form of the word, then in the form of the Spirit, and ultimately in the form of life. In this way the Triune God becomes our enjoyment.

10. By Drinking the Spirit
through Believing into Christ
to Flow Rivers of Living Water
out of Our Innermost Being

The way to receive, experience, and enjoy Christ is also by drinking the Spirit through believing into Christ to flow rivers of living water out of our innermost being (John 7:37-39). The rivers of living water are the many flows of the different aspects of life (cf. Rom. 15:30; 1 Thes. 1:6; 2 Thes. 2:13; Gal. 5:22-23), originating from the one unique river of water of life (Rev. 22:1), which is God's Spirit of life (Rom. 8:2). The one river in Genesis 2:10-14 became four heads. In the same way, not just one river but many rivers flow out of our innermost being.

11. By Following Christ to Have the Light of Life and by No Means Walk in Darkness

Another way to receive, experience, and enjoy Christ in the Gospel of John is by following Him to have the light of life and by no means walk in darkness (8:12). By following Christ, we shall by no means walk in darkness. I am grateful to the Lord that I have the feeling that I am walking in the light and that I am not in darkness. A living person has light, but a dead person is altogether in darkness. An electric light may shine intensely, but a dead person will receive no light because he has no life. He will remain in darkness. However, a living person under the same light will immediately receive light because he has life.

12. By Leaving the Sheepfold of Religion and Following Christ according to His Voice to Enjoy the Freedom of His Salvation and Partake of the Riches of His Feeding Pasture

Another way to receive, experience, and enjoy the all-inclusive Christ in the Gospel of John is by leaving the sheepfold of religion and following Christ according to His voice to enjoy the freedom of His salvation and partake of the riches of His feeding pasture (10:1-4, 9). Nearly every person on this earth has a religion. If he does not have another person's religion, he has his own religion. A person may say that he does not have a religion and that he does not believe in God. However, such a person is his own god and is his own religion.

Every religion is a sheepfold. Buddhism, Islam, and Judaism are all sheepfolds. Judaism was the sheepfold mentioned by the Lord Jesus in John 10. In a positive sense, a sheepfold keeps and protects people, but in a negative sense, it imprisons people. For years we were imprisoned within many different sheepfolds. Even we ourselves were a prison to ourselves. Then one day we believed into the Lord Jesus and were released from our prison.

If we would receive, experience, and enjoy Christ, we must leave all the religious sheepfolds and follow Him according to His voice. In John 10:27 the Lord Jesus said, "My sheep hear My voice, and I know them, and they follow Me." Today, we must not follow Christ according to any kind of religion, nor should we follow Him according to our own thought, which in reality is our own self-made religion. We must follow Him according to His voice. This is why we must pray to Him and listen to both His living speaking within us and the holy Bible outside of us. We need the holy Bible outside of us because our listening to His voice within may be inaccurate. The holy Word is our safeguard. Therefore, we must know the Bible. Today the Lord Jesus always speaks to us as the Spirit according to the Bible and through the Bible.

By leaving the sheepfold and following Christ according to His voice, we enjoy the freedom of His salvation and partake of the riches of His feeding pasture. The Lord Jesus said that we would go in and go out to find pasture (v. 9). This is freedom. Christ Himself is the rich pasture upon which we feed all the time. By feeding upon Him as the rich pasture, we enjoy Him.

13. By Taking Christ as the Resurrection and the Life through Believing into Him to Live the Eternal Life

In the Gospel of John we receive, experience, and enjoy the all-inclusive Christ by taking Him as the resurrection and the life through believing into Him to live the eternal life. In John 11:25 the Lord Jesus told Martha, "I am the resurrection and the life; he who believes into Me, even if he should die, shall live." It is difficult to understand such a verse, but it is very easy to experience Christ according to this verse. If you tell the Lord, "I believe that You are the resurrection and the life," immediately you will live the eternal life in all kinds of situations. If you repeat this prayer before having any dealings with your wife, you will live the eternal life. But if you do not pray such a prayer, you may lose your temper and be altogether in the flesh. Praying such a prayer will save you out of your flesh and transfer you into another realm, the realm of eternal life. This is not superstition or psychology. Many students of Confucius love his teachings very much, but they also mistreat their wives. But I have never seen one person who could say, "Lord Jesus, You are the resurrection; You are the life," and then turn around and mistreat his wife. The reason for this is that Christ is the unique One who is living and real.

Christ is the resurrection and the life. He is not only life but also the life that overcomes death. He is the resurrection. He is living and powerful. If you mention His name, immediately He will "electrify" you, and you will become a different person. By calling on Him, speaking to Him, and praying to Him, you will experience and enjoy Him. Many experienced brothers and sisters have written hymns concerning their enjoyment of calling on the name of the Lord Jesus many times a day (see *Hymns,* #208 and #73). To call on the Lord a thousand times a day, or even every minute, is not too much. By calling on Him we enjoy Him.

The thirteen items mentioned in this message are the subjective ways to receive, experience, and enjoy the all-inclusive Christ. Eating, drinking, and calling on the name of the Lord are all subjective. When we exercise our spirit to contact Him as the life-giving Spirit, He becomes our experience and enjoyment.

The Central Line of the Divine Revelation

THE DIVINE ECONOMY
AND THE DIVINE DISPENSING

MESSAGE SIXTEEN

THE AGGREGATE OF THE ALL-EMBRACING BLESSING
OF THE FULL GOSPEL OF GOD IN CHRIST
FOR THE DIVINE DISPENSING
ACCORDING TO THE DIVINE ECONOMY

(7)

Scripture Reading: John 1:1, 14, 16

II. THE WAY TO RECEIVE, EXPERIENCE,
AND ENJOY THE ALL-INCLUSIVE CHRIST
AS THE ALL-INCLUSIVE LIFE-GIVING SPIRIT—
THE AGGREGATE OF THE ALL-EMBRACING BLESSING
OF THE FULL GOSPEL OF GOD

B. The Way in the Gospel of John

The beginning of the Gospel of John says, "In the beginning was the Word, and the Word was with God, and the Word was God" (1:1). Verse 14 goes on to say, "And the Word became flesh and tabernacled among us (and we beheld His glory, glory as of the only Begotten from the Father), full of grace and reality." Verse 16 says, "For of His fullness we have all received, and grace upon grace." The fullness of God is the expression of His riches. We may illustrate the fullness by pouring water into a cup. When the water partly fills the cup, we have the riches of the water, but when the water fills the cup to the brim, the overflowing of the water is the fullness, the expression, of the water. In his Epistles Paul speaks of the riches and the fullness. In Ephesians 3:8 he said, "To me, less than the least of all saints, was this grace given to announce to the Gentiles the unsearchable riches of Christ as the gospel." In 1:23 he spoke of "the fullness of the One who fills all in all," and in 3:19 he said, "...that you may be filled unto all the fullness of God."

The riches of Christ are what Christ is. Christ is exceedingly rich. Christ is God (Rom. 9:5); He is man (1 Tim. 2:5); He is the Son (Matt. 16:16), the Spirit (2 Cor. 3:17), and also the Father (Isa. 9:6); and He is the body of all the shadows (Col. 2:16-17). The sun, the air, and water are all shadows. Even our eating and drinking and the feasts, new moons, and Sabbaths are shadows. Eating and drinking refer to our daily experience; the Sabbath refers to our weekly completion and rest; new moons refer to monthly new beginnings, with light in the darkness; and feasts refer to our yearly joy and enjoyment. Whatever we enjoy daily, weekly, monthly, and yearly is a shadow, but Christ is the body, the reality, of all the shadows. This Christ is our allotted portion (1:12). In the whole universe God has allotted Christ to us as our portion, in every way and in everything, as the real sunshine, air, water, food, feast, completion, new beginning, and rest. These are the riches of Christ. When we enjoy all the riches of Christ, we assimilate the riches into the fibers of our being. Then what we assimilate becomes our constitution, and we become the totality of what Christ is. The aggregate of this totality is the Body of Christ, and the Body of Christ is Christ's expression. Americans are the totality and expression of the riches of America that they have eaten and digested, including American beef, pork, and fish. In the same way the expression of the riches of Christ that have been eaten, digested, and assimilated by us is the fullness of Christ, which is the Body of Christ.

The Gospel of John speaks of the fullness of Christ. John 1:14 says that Christ came as the incarnated One, full of grace and reality, and verse 16 says that we have all received of His fullness. This shows us that Christ came in incarnation for one thing: that we may receive Him. God is abstract and mysterious. The mystery of God is Christ (Col. 2:2), and this Christ became incarnated. Colossians 2:9 says, "For in Him dwells all the fullness of the Godhead bodily." All the fullness of the Godhead dwells in Christ as the mystery of God in a bodily way. Christ's coming as the embodiment of God may be compared to serving water in a glass. When the water is in the water pipes, it is not possible to drink it. But when it is served in a glass, it is easy to take it in. Christ came in the way of incarnation in order that we may receive Him. The Word was God, and the Word became flesh and tabernacled among us, full of grace and reality, and of His fullness we have all received, grace upon grace. This is the Gospel of John. The Gospel of John concerns the Triune God, God in His trinity, becoming the riches as the fullness that He may give, impart, and dispense Himself to us on His side, and that we may receive the Triune God on our side. He is dispensing and we are receiving.

Each of the four Gospels presents a particular aspect of Christ. Matthew presents Christ as the King; Mark presents Christ as a Servant; Luke presents Christ as a man; and John presents Christ as God. The Gospel of John tells us that Christ is the way, the reality, and the life (14:6); the light (8:12); the resurrection (11:25); and the great I Am (8:58). None of the other Gospels speaks in such a particular way concerning Christ. Although the Gospel of John is very mysterious, it does contain two definite and solid points: one concerns the Triune God's giving, imparting, and dispensing of Himself into us, and the other concerns our receiving of Him. John 3:16 says, "For God so loved the world that He gave His only begotten Son." Among the four Gospels, only John says that God gave Himself to us. God gives Himself to us in His trinity. He gives Himself to us as the Father, the Son, and the Spirit. God is triune for the purpose of giving Himself to us. The love of God, the grace of Christ, and the fellowship of the Holy Spirit (2 Cor. 13:14) are for God's dispensing, for His giving of Himself to us. If God were not the Father, the Son, and the Spirit, He would have no way to give Himself to us.

The New Testament tells us that we believe into the Son to receive the Son (John 1:12). We receive the Son because through His death and resurrection the Son has become the

Spirit (1 Cor. 15:45b). Therefore, the New Testament also tells us to receive the Spirit. John 20:22 says, "And when He had said this, He breathed into them and said to them, Receive the Holy Spirit." In Galatians 3:2 Paul said, "Did you receive the Spirit out of the works of law or out of the hearing of faith?" The receiving of the Son and the receiving of the Spirit are not two receivings. To receive the Son is to receive the Spirit because the Son today is the Spirit (2 Cor. 3:17). Likewise, to receive the Spirit is to receive the Son because the Spirit today is the Son.

When we receive the Son, we also receive the Father. First John 2:23 says, "Everyone who denies the Son does not have the Father either; he who confesses the Son has the Father also." Jesus said, "I and the Father are one" (John 10:30). Since the Son and the Father are one, when we receive the Son, we also receive the Father. Jesus also said, "Believe Me that I am in the Father and the Father is in Me" (14:11). The Father and the Son coinhere; They cannot be separated. Therefore, when we receive one, we receive the other. The way to receive the Triune God is not to receive the Father directly, but to receive the Son. The receiving of the Son is actually the receiving of the Spirit. When we have the Son and the Spirit, we have the Father.

According to John 3:16, the Son is for the Triune God to give Himself to us. In the Gospel of John the Son is likened to food and water. Jesus said that He is the bread of life (6:35, 48), the bread from heaven (v. 51b), and the living bread (v. 51a). This is marvelous. As the bread of life, He is the living bread. He is fresh and living. Jesus is also the living water (4:10, 14) and the flowing water (7:38). This corresponds to Revelation 22:1-2a, which says, "And he showed me a river of water of life, bright as crystal, proceeding out of the throne of God and of the Lamb in the middle of its street. And on this side and on that side of the river was the tree of life." Out of the throne of God and the Lamb flows the river of the water of life, and in this river the tree of life grows as a spreading vine. The Bible concludes with this river and its tree of life. The river and the tree are Christ given by God for us to receive. When we receive Him, whatever He is, is within us and becomes our constitution. This is the divine economy with the divine dispensing according to God's central thought to mingle Himself with man, to make God and man, man and God, one entity, the New Jerusalem.

The Gospel of John also reveals Christ as the breath. After His consummation through His processes, Christ came to His disciples in resurrection and breathed into them, saying, "Receive the Holy Spirit" (20:22). The word for *Spirit* in this verse can also be translated *breath*. The holy breath is for Christ to breathe out and for us to breathe in. The entire Bible is a record of God breathing out and man breathing in. The Scripture itself is God's breathing (2 Tim. 3:16). Every time we come to the Scripture we should not only read it but breathe it in. This is pray-reading. Pray-reading the Word transforms us because in pray-reading we breathe. In pray-reading we first breathe out our sorrow and sin; then we breathe in God's fullness.

A. B. Simpson, the founder of the Christian and Missionary Alliance, wrote a hymn concerning breathing the Lord (*Hymns,* #255), and the following verse and chorus show how much he enjoyed the Lord by breathing Him in:

> O Lord, breathe Thy Spirit on me,
>   Teach me how to breathe Thee in;
> Help me pour into Thy bosom
>   All my life of self and sin.

> I am breathing out my sorrow,
>   Breathing out my sin;
> I am breathing, breathing, breathing,
>   All Thy fulness in.

A. B. Simpson was one of the most spiritual persons the United States has produced in the past one hundred years. He enjoyed breathing in the Lord's fullness and breathing out all the negative things within him. His mentioning of "fulness" in the chorus was a reference to John 1:16. The way to receive the Lord's fullness is by breathing Him. This renews, sanctifies, transforms, and conforms us. Eventually, this will glorify us.

God gives Himself to us by breathing Himself out, and we receive Him by breathing Him in. Physically, the secret to a long life is proper breathing, eating, and drinking. The One who gives Himself to us is the breath, the food, and the water, and we receive Him by breathing, eating, and drinking. This is the way John shows us to receive the given One, who is the processed Triune God in His trinity, the aggregate of the all-embracing blessing of the full gospel of God. This is the highest understanding of the Gospel of John.

All the churches should learn how to "cook" something of the Triune God for their supply. When we come to the Bible, we must learn to exercise our spirit not only to read but also to pray-read. We may not understand a portion of the Word, but we can eat it. We can pray-read John 1:1, saying, "In the beginning was the Word. Amen! Oh the Word! Hallelujah for the Word! The Word was with God. Hallelujah for the beginning, for the Word, and for God! Although I do not understand these things, I have God, the Word, and the beginning." Pray-reading in this way will be a morning revival and a real "breakfast" to us. Pray-reading will also help us to have the proper understanding of the Word.

In the remainder of this message we shall consider another twelve ways revealed in the Gospel of John to receive, experience, and enjoy the all-inclusive Christ as the all-inclusive life-giving Spirit—the aggregate of the all-embracing blessing of the full gospel of God.

14. By Hating Our Soul-life
That We May Keep It unto Eternal Life

To receive, experience, and enjoy the all-inclusive Christ as the all-inclusive life-giving Spirit, we must hate our soul-life in this world that we may keep it unto eternal life (John 12:25). Our soul-life is our self. Thus, to hate our soul-life in this world is to hate our self in our daily living. If we love our soul-life we will lose it, but if we hate our soul-life we will keep it. The word for *unto* in Greek carries the notions of *for, with a view to,* and *resulting in.* Hence, to keep our soul-life unto eternal life is to keep it for, with a view to, and resulting in eternal life.

We all have three lives. Our physical life is the life in our body. Our psychological life is the life in our soul. This is the natural life. The spiritual *zoe* life is the eternal life, the divine life in our spirit. The way to enjoy the divine life in our spirit is to hate our soul-life. If we hate our soul-life, we will keep it, resulting in the enjoyment of the eternal life. The more we hate our soulish life, the natural life, the more we will keep it, resulting in more enjoyment of the eternal life. This enjoyment will extend for eternity. We have this eternal life, but we often do not have the enjoyment of it because we do not hate our soulish life. If we hate our self, we will keep our soul-life to enjoy and experience the divine life, which is in us from now unto eternity.

15. By Following Him in His Death to Release the Divine Life and to Receive the Father's Honor

Another way to receive, experience, and enjoy Christ is by following Him in His death to release the divine life and to receive the Father's honor (12:24, 26). In John 12:24 the Lord said, "Truly, truly, I say to you, Unless the grain of wheat falls into the ground and dies, it abides alone; but if it dies, it bears much fruit." Here the Lord said that if He as a grain of wheat would fall into the earth and die, the divine life would be released, and He would become many grains and thus would increase and be multiplied. As the grains of wheat today, we must not learn first how to live; we must learn how to die. To die is to live. While Christ was on the earth, He was always being put to death. Now we need to follow Him in His steps of dying. If we learn to die, we will receive the Father's honor. The more one talks, insists on certain things, and expresses himself, the less honorable that one is. Such a one is too active and living. The most honorable person is a dying person. It is not glorious to be living and active in the natural life; the glory is in learning to die. Thus, every Christian should be a dying person.

16. By Keeping His New Commandment to Love One Another for the Expression of His Love

The way to receive, experience, and enjoy Christ is by keeping His new commandment to love one another for the expression of His love that all the people may know that we are His disciples (13:34-35). In the Old Testament there were ten commandments, but in the Gospel of John the Lord gave only one: love one another. If we love one another, we will express His love, and all men will know we are Jesus' disciples.

17. By Taking Him as the Way, the Reality, and the Life to Come to the Father

We receive, experience, and enjoy Christ also by taking Him as the way, the reality, and the life to come to the Father. John 14:6 says, "Jesus said to him, I am the way and the reality and the life; no one comes to the Father except through Me." This is an excellent verse concerning the way to receive and enjoy Christ. Without Jesus as the way, the reality, and the life, no one can come to the Father. This does not mean that no one can come to the place where the Father is, but that no one can come to the Father *Himself.* Some have misunderstood this verse to mean that the Father is in a heavenly mansion and that Jesus is the way for the believers to go to this heavenly mansion. However, since the way is Christ, a living person, so the place to which the Lord brings us must also be a person, God the Father Himself. The Lord Himself is the living way to bring man into God the Father, the living place.

The way refers mainly to the Son. The Son as the way was incarnated to bring God into man. Then He died to accomplish redemption and resurrected to impart the divine life. The reality refers mainly to the Spirit, for the Spirit is the reality and is called "the Spirit of reality" (14:17; 1 John 5:6). The Father is in the Son and the Son is in the Father (John

14:11), and the Spirit comes as the Spirit of reality to be the reality of the Son. If we have the Spirit, we have the Son, who is the way.

The life refers mainly to the Father. We take Christ as the way to come to the Father. The way is the Son, and the destination is the Father as life. First John 1:2 says, "And the life was manifested, and we have seen and testify and report to you the eternal life, which was with the Father and was manifested to us." This verse says that the eternal life was with the Father. The Son is the way, the Spirit is the reality, and the Father is the life as the destination. It is by this way that we come to the Father and enjoy Him as the source with the Son as the course and the Spirit as the reaching, the reality, of the Divine Trinity.

18. By Loving Him and Keeping His Word

The way to receive, experience, and enjoy Christ is by loving Him and keeping His word to gain the Father's love and to have Christ manifest Himself to us and have the Father and Him make Their abode with us (John 14:21, 23). If we love the Lord and keep His word, we will have three results. First, we will gain the Father's love. This is the response of the divine love. Second, we will have the Son's manifestation. Then, third, the loving One and the manifesting One will come to make Their abode with us. Love is from the Father as the source; the manifestation is through the Son; and the making of the abode is by both the Father and the Son. Not only do the Father and the Son make us Their abode, but They also become our abode. We and the Father and the Son become a mutual abode in the Father's love and the Son's manifestation. In this way the Triune God has an abode, and we the believers of Christ also have an abode. His abode is in us, and our abode is in Him.

19. By Abiding in Him
as a Branch Abiding in the Vine
to Enjoy All the Riches of What He Is

The way to receive, experience, and enjoy the all-inclusive

Christ is also to abide in Him as a branch abiding in the vine to enjoy all the riches of what He is (15:4-5). We are not branches of the vine by birth, but we have become the branches of the vine by grafting (Rom. 11:17). If we as a branch abide in Him, we enjoy all the riches of what He is. As the branches of the wild tree that have been grafted into Christ as the true vine, we have the position, the capacity, and the right to enjoy whatever is in Christ. Therefore, this abiding is the way to enjoy the riches of Christ. After breathing, eating, and drinking Christ, we abide in Him as a grafted branch to absorb all His riches.

20. By Going Forth to Bear Remaining Fruit

The way to receive, experience, and enjoy Christ is also by going forth to bear fruit, even remaining fruit, that we may be kept in the enjoyment of His riches (John 15:16, 2). In order to bear fruit, we must go forth. We must go forth from one door to another door, even from one city to another city and from one country to another country. John 15:16 says, "You did not choose Me, but I chose you, and I set you that you should go forth and bear fruit and that your fruit should remain." Christ set us, as grafted branches, in Himself to be those who go forth to bear fruit. If we do not go forth, we cannot bear fruit. We should go forth to contact people every day. We can at least go forth by contacting someone on the telephone. Moreover, to bear remaining fruit implies feeding. Fruit cannot remain without being fed. It must be watered and fertilized and have adequate sunshine and air. The reason that some of our fruit does not remain is that we have not cared for them adequately.

Going forth to bear fruit and helping the fruit to remain is the way to enjoy the riches of Christ. If we do not bear fruit, we will be cut off from the vine (v. 6). To be cut off from the vine is not to perish. It is to lose the enjoyment of the riches of the vine. To enjoy the aggregate of the all-embracing blessing of the full gospel of God, we must abide in the vine, but we cannot abide in the vine without bearing fruit. We must go forth to bear fruit and do something to cause the fruit to remain. Then we will be in the right position and will have the right to enjoy the riches of Christ. Some may claim that they have not been cut off from the vine. They still come to the meetings, pray, and function. However, this does not mean that they are enjoying Christ. If we bear even one remaining fruit, we will be joyful in the enjoyment of Christ. To see one of our fruit remain in the church and begin to serve in the same way that we do causes us to be joyful. This joy indicates that we are enjoying Christ. Without new fruit and without remaining fruit, we do not have such joy. This indicates that we have lost the enjoyment; we have been cut off from the riches of Christ.

21. By Being Convicted by the Comforter, the Spirit of Reality

Another way to receive, experience, and enjoy Christ is by being convicted by the Comforter, the Spirit of reality, concerning sin (from Adam), concerning righteousness (Christ), and concerning judgment (the devil's eternal portion), that we may be justified and regenerated (16:8-11). On the one hand, the Spirit is the Comforter; on the other hand, He is the Convicter, the One who rebukes and reproaches. The best comforter always rebukes. If one always speaks well of you, he is a deceiver and has an evil intention. If one is an honest and faithful comforter, he will rebuke and reproach. He will tell others that as long as they do a certain improper thing, they will suffer and not have any comfort. He will exhort them to have a change and be corrected. The Comforter is the Spirit of reality. He comes to comfort us with convicting. He convicts us of sin, of righteousness, and of judgment. Sin came from Adam, and righteousness is Christ. We must give up Adam, that is, put sin aside, and receive Christ as our righteousness. Otherwise, we will participate in the judgment that is the ultimate portion of the devil. We came from Adam, but if we come to Christ, He will become our righteousness, and we will not suffer the eternal judgment that is the devil's portion. We will be justified to have Christ as our righteousness and be regenerated to have the Spirit as our life.

22. By Receiving the Riches
of the Triune God through the Transmission
of the Divine Trinity

The way to receive, experience, and enjoy the all-inclusive Christ is also by receiving the riches of the Triune God through the transmission of the Divine Trinity that we may partake of all the realities for His glorification. In John 16:13-15a the Lord Jesus said, "But when He, the Spirit of reality, comes, He will guide you into all the reality....He will glorify Me, for He will receive of Mine and will declare it to you. All that the Father has is Mine." Christ has inherited whatever the Father has. The riches of the Father's being are Christ's inheritance; what Christ inherits from the Father is received by the Spirit; and whatever the Spirit receives of Christ He declares to us. This is a transmission. The riches are in the Father as the source; they pass through the Son as the course; and the Spirit is the reaching to us of all the riches of the Triune God. From the Father, through the Son, and by the Spirit, all the riches of the Triune God become our portion. We enjoy this blessing by being one with the Triune God and allowing the transmission from the Triune God to reach us. In this way we have the riches of the Triune God by the divine transmission.

23. By Being One with the Believers
to Partake of the Oneness
of the Divine Trinity

The way to receive, experience, and enjoy Christ is also by being one with the believers to partake of the oneness of the Divine Trinity that the people of the world may believe in Him (17:21). Oneness is a particular attribute of the Divine Trinity. The three of the Trinity are one, and we can participate in this oneness by being one. The more we are one with the believers, the more we are in the oneness of the Trinity. This is a corporate blessing. When we are not one with the brothers and sisters, we suffer. When we are one, we enjoy the riches of the Triune God. This is the participation in the Divine Trinity in Their oneness. Their oneness becomes our oneness, and as They coinhere, we coinhere with Them. Ephesians 4:4-6 speaks of one Body, one Spirit, one Lord, and one God and Father. These four coinhere together in oneness. The New Testament speaks strongly against division. Romans 16:17 says, "Now I exhort you, brothers, to mark those who make divisions and causes of stumbling contrary to the teaching which you have learned, and turn away from them." Division diminishes our enjoyment of the Triune God in Their triune oneness. To have such an enjoyment is a great blessing.

24. By Receiving His Breathing to Enjoy Him as the Pneumatic Christ

We receive, experience, and enjoy Christ also by receiving His breathing to enjoy Him as the pneumatic Christ (John 20:22). The Lord is breathing Himself out, and we are receiving not simply His breath but His breathing, which includes His person. This is our enjoyment.

25. By Loving Him in Feeding His Lambs and Shepherding His Sheep for His Flock—the Church

The last way revealed in the Gospel of John to receive, experience, and enjoy the all-inclusive Christ as the all-inclusive life-giving Spirit is by loving Him in feeding His lambs and shepherding His sheep for His flock—the church (21:15-17). Feeding the lambs, the young ones, takes place in the home meetings, and shepherding the sheep takes place in the group meetings. Feeding Christ's lambs and shepherding His sheep are for His flock, the church, which is His heart's desire and God's good pleasure (Eph. 1:9). This is also the way for us to enjoy the Triune God.

By all the preceding points we can see that the Gospel of John is a book on the dispensing of the Triune God and the receiving of this dispensing by the believers through their breathing, eating, and drinking of Him and their abiding in Him.

The Central Line of the Divine Revelation

THE DIVINE ECONOMY
AND THE DIVINE DISPENSING

MESSAGE SEVENTEEN

THE AGGREGATE OF THE ALL-EMBRACING BLESSING OF THE FULL GOSPEL OF GOD IN CHRIST FOR THE DIVINE DISPENSING ACCORDING TO THE DIVINE ECONOMY

(8)

Scripture Reading: Rom. 8:3-6; 12:2-5; 1 Cor. 1:2b, 9; 6:17; 12:13; 15:45b; 2 Cor. 13:14

Prayer: Lord, we worship and praise You that You are the One who operates among us in everything. We trust in You and believe that You are with us. We also have the confidence and assurance that we are under Your care. Lord, we are nothing, we have nothing, and we can do nothing. But praise You that we have You as the all-inclusive Christ. Today we are coming to Your Word to learn of You and to learn how to experience and enjoy You. Lord, do open Yourself to us. We trust in You for Your move and Your work. Lord, we remember those saints who are now moving and working in Moscow. Lord, do remember them. We thank You for this moment, for Your presence, and for all things. Amen.

II. THE WAY TO RECEIVE, EXPERIENCE, AND ENJOY THE ALL-INCLUSIVE CHRIST AS THE ALL-INCLUSIVE LIFE-GIVING SPIRIT— THE AGGREGATE OF THE ALL-EMBRACING BLESSING OF THE FULL GOSPEL OF GOD

C. The Way in the Rest of the Books of the New Testament

In the previous messages we have seen the way to receive, experience, and enjoy the all-inclusive Christ as the all-inclusive life-giving Spirit in the book of Galatians and the Gospel of John. In this message we will begin to see the way to receive, experience, and enjoy Christ in the rest of the books of the New Testament.

First, we will consider sixteen items related to the way in Romans, 1 Corinthians, and 2 Corinthians. The way to receive, experience, and enjoy Christ as the aggregate of the all-embracing blessing of the full gospel of God in these books is related to the Spirit. The blessing is the Spirit, and the way to experience and enjoy such a Spirit is also the Spirit. On the one hand, the Spirit is the blessing, and on the other hand, the Spirit is the way for us to participate in the blessing. Both the blessing and the way are the all-inclusive Spirit, and this Spirit is the consummation of the processed Triune God.

1. By Walking according to the Spirit

The first item in Romans concerning the way to receive, experience, and enjoy the all-inclusive Christ as the all-inclusive Spirit is to walk according to the spirit (Rom. 8:3-4). The word *walk* in Greek means to have one's being, to move, and to act. It denotes the general walk in our living. To walk according to the spirit is to have one's being not merely by or through the spirit, but according to the spirit.

Strictly speaking, we should not express anything that is not according to the spirit. If we are asked whether something is right or wrong, we should not answer yes or no. We should answer according to the spirit. Naturally, I am a quick and frank person, especially with my wife. But I have learned the lesson that I should not answer my wife according to yes or no, but according to the Lord.

We must do everything according to the spirit. We must comb our hair not according to our barber's instructions but according to the spirit. Everything we say and do must be according to the spirit. We might pray in a very spiritual way and might be able to speak very well, using many spiritual terms, but our appearance might be according to the modern fashion of this age, not according to the spirit. To do something according to another person's instructions is very difficult. A person may be a very good child or student, but it is difficult for a child to do everything *according to* his parents or for a student to do everything *according to* his teacher. It is easy to do things according to our own opinion. We should have our being not just by Christ but also according to Christ.

In Romans 8:3-4 Paul said, "For that which the law could not do, in that it was weak through the flesh, God, sending His own Son in the likeness of the flesh of sin and concerning sin, condemned sin in the flesh, that the righteous requirement of the law might be fulfilled in us, who do not walk according to the flesh but according to the spirit." The law was ineffective because it was weak through the flesh. Because of this, God sent His Son in the likeness of the flesh of sin. The phrase *the flesh of sin* in this verse and the word *flesh* in John 1:14 are negative terms. The flesh that Christ, as the Word of God, became is the flesh of sin, but this does not mean that Christ had any sin within His flesh. In Romans 8:3 Paul said that Christ was "in the likeness of the flesh of sin," implying that Christ had the likeness, the form, of the flesh of sin, but He did not have the reality of the sin of the flesh. God condemned sin in the flesh through Christ's death on the cross in the likeness of the flesh of sin, that the righteous requirement of the law might be fulfilled in us, who walk according to the spirit.

To have our being merely according to the written word of the Bible is inadequate. If we had ten times as many words as are presently in the Bible, it would still be inadequate. But just the single phrase *according to the spirit* encompasses everything. There is not a verse in the Bible that tells us how to comb our hair. But if we walk according to the spirit, the Holy Spirit not only will bother us about the way we comb our hair but also will touch our attitude and intention. By walking according to the spirit, we enjoy Christ as the all-inclusive life-giving Spirit, who is the blessing of the gospel. Thus, the Spirit is not only the blessing but also the way.

2. By Setting Our Mind on the Spirit

We receive, experience, and enjoy Christ also by setting

our mind on the spirit (Rom. 8:5-6). Romans 8:4 tells us to walk according to the spirit, and verse 5 tells us to set our mind on the spirit. We should not do anything that is not according to the spirit, and we should not think anything without our mind being set on the spirit. Every person, even a little child, is controlled by his mind. Whenever we begin to think about something, we as seeking Christians should always check whether or not our mind is set on the spirit. If our mind is not set on the spirit, the source of our thinking is wrong. If our mind is not set on the spirit, it is surely set on the flesh. The flesh is contrary to the Spirit (Gal. 5:17). Because our mind is fallen, whatever we think when our mind is set on the flesh is an offense to God (Rom. 8:7).

The spirit mentioned in Romans 8:4-6 refers to the regenerated spirit, which is indwelt by and mingled with the Holy Spirit. In his New Translation, John Nelson Darby said that in many verses in the New Testament one cannot discern whether the spirit refers to the human spirit or the Holy Spirit. He then said that the spirit in verses such as Romans 8:4-6 refers to both the human spirit and the divine Spirit. In addition to this, I would say that the spirit in these verses refers to the mingled spirit, the divine Spirit mingled with the human spirit.

Today, we no longer have a single, independent spirit; we have a mingled spirit. Such a mingled spirit is troublesome to us. Very often we are troubled by the mingled spirit. At certain times I would like to say something unpleasant to my wife, but as I am about to speak, something bothers me within, and I have to stop without finishing my statement. Instead of saying something unpleasant, I change my tone and begin to praise the Lord. Because of this behavior, I may seem to be mysterious. Actually, I have such behavior because I have a mingled spirit. Every proper Christian is a mystery, and within every proper Christian there is a mystery—the mingled spirit. We must learn to walk according to the spirit and to set our mind on this spirit. When we set our mind on the spirit, we have life and peace (v. 6). These are signs of our enjoyment of Christ.

3. By the Renewing of Our Mind for the Transformation of Our Soul That We May Know the Will of God concerning the Body Life

The way to receive, experience, and enjoy Christ in the book of Romans includes three things: first, walking according to the spirit, second, setting our mind on the spirit, and third, the renewing of our mind. The renewing of our mind is for the transformation of our soul that we may know the will of God concerning the Body life (Rom. 12:2-5). The mind is the leading part of the soul. When the leading part of the soul is renewed, the entire soul will be transformed. The purpose of transformation is that we may know the will of God. The will of God in Romans 12:2 is not His will related to our daily affairs, but His will concerning the Body life, the church life.

The book of Romans, which is the gospel of God (1:1), has four sections. The first section is on justification (chs. 1—4); the second section is on the full realization of being in Christ (chs. 5—8); the third section is on God's selection (chs. 9—11); and the fourth section is on the Body life, issuing in local churches (chs. 12—16). First, we must experience justification, both objectively and subjectively. Then we must have the full realization of being in Christ. Today we are no longer in Adam; we are now in Christ. With this realization, we then need to experience the Body life and live a proper local church life.

Romans 12 is on the Body life. Verse 5 says, "So we who are many are one body in Christ, and individually members one of another." We need to live the Body life. In order to live such a life, all the members must have their minds renewed. This renewing will cause us to be persons who know God's will concerning the Body life, the church life.

The Lord's recovery has stressed the Body life since 1939. In 1934 Brother Nee held a conference concerning Christ as God's centrality and universality. At that time my eyes were opened, and my Christian life took a big turn from doctrines and knowledge to a living person, Christ, who is God's centrality and universality. Five years later, after his return from Europe, Brother Nee called a conference and began to give messages on knowing the Body of Christ. These messages caused me to have another turn. My first turn was to know Christ, and my second turn was to know His Body. To know Christ is only half of what we need. We also must know the Body of Christ. Christ is the Head (Eph. 1:22), and He is also the Body (1 Cor. 12:12).

4. By Participating in the Fellowship of Christ as Our Portion

The way to enjoy Christ is by participating in the fellowship of Christ as our portion (1 Cor. 1:2b, 9). First Corinthians 1:2b says, "...to those who have been sanctified in Christ Jesus, the called saints, with all those who call upon the name of our Lord Jesus Christ in every place, who is theirs and ours." The meaning of the phrase *who is theirs and ours* is that Christ is the portion of both the saints in Corinth and the saints who "call upon the name of our Lord Jesus Christ in every place." If I say that a certain thing is mine, I indicate that it is my possession. In the same way, the phrase *who is theirs and ours* indicates that Christ is the portion possessed by all the saints.

First Corinthians 1:9 says, "God is faithful, through whom you were called into the fellowship of His Son, Jesus Christ our Lord." The fellowship of Christ is the participation in Christ, the enjoyment of Christ. Today, we are participating in Christ. Every day we enjoy Him as our portion. We enjoy the all-inclusive Spirit as the aggregate of the all-embracing blessing of the full gospel of God by participating in the fellowship of Christ as our portion.

5. By Partaking of Christ as Power and Wisdom to Us from God

The way to enjoy Christ is also by partaking of Christ as power and wisdom to us from God (1 Cor. 1:24, 30). In order to achieve anything, we need power and wisdom. Power is the ability and wisdom is the way. According to 1 Corinthians 1:30, Christ is wisdom to us from God as righteousness for our past, as sanctification for our present, and as redemption for our future. Christ is first our power, and then He is our wisdom, that is, our way. His being power to us from God means that there is now a transmission taking place from God to us (Eph. 1:19-22). The electricity that flows from the power plant to a building illustrates how power and wisdom are transmitted to us from God.

Without the transmission of power and wisdom to us from God, we do not have any power or wisdom. Every day the power and wisdom of God are being transmitted from God the Giver to us the enjoyers. In the morning I may be in the transmission, but at noon I may be out of the transmission. We must learn to remain in this transmission hour after hour, day by day, all the time. Power and wisdom are continually being given to us from God. It is not a once and for all matter. Our enjoyment of this continual transmission is the way to enjoy Christ.

6. By Partaking of Christ as the Lamb of the Passover and the Unleavened Bread That We May Become a New Lump

We enjoy Christ also by partaking of Christ as the Lamb of the Passover and the unleavened bread that we may become a new lump (1 Cor. 5:7-8). The Passover lamb was for redemption and initial feeding. The Israelites took the lamb, slew it, shed its blood, and cut the meat of the lamb into pieces. The blood of the lamb was for the redemption of the Israelites, and the meat of the lamb was their food. After the Passover, they had to immediately walk out of Egypt. In order to walk out of Egypt they needed strength, and their eating of the lamb supplied them with the needed strength.

The Passover lamb was eaten with unleavened bread (Exo. 12:8). According to their constitution, the children of Israel were completely leavened; that is, they were constituted sinners (Rom. 5:19a). But after their eating of the Passover lamb with the unleavened bread, they were cleansed and began to have an unleavened constitution. This change in constitution came about because of the change in their diet.

From the time of our regeneration we began to have a

new constitution. Christ as the unleavened bread became our unleavened food to reconstitute us, so that we may become a new lump. Before regeneration, we were the old lump, full of leaven. But now we have become a new lump, because we are becoming unleavened. This new lump is the church.

In Leviticus 23 two loaves of bread baked with leaven were presented to the Lord on the day of Pentecost (vv. 15-17). These two loaves signify the church in two sections, one section being of the Jews, represented by the Jews at Pentecost (Acts 2:1-4), and the other section being of the Gentiles, represented by the house of Cornelius (10:24, 44). The two loaves included leaven because both the Jewish and Gentile believers still have sin. By eating Christ as the unleavened bread, we become unleavened. We must eat Christ as the Lamb and as the unleavened bread. As the Lamb He is for our strengthening and support. As the unleavened bread He causes us to be unleavened constitutionally, making us a new lump.

7. By Being Joined to the Lord as One Spirit

We enjoy Christ also by being joined to the Lord as one spirit (1 Cor. 6:17). First Corinthians 6:17 is one of the highest verses in the entire Bible. Today we as fallen human beings can become one spirit with the Lord. Although this may seem difficult to believe, it is nevertheless a fact. Because Paul wrote such a word in his Epistle, we must believe that we are one spirit with the Lord, who is the all-inclusive, life-giving, compound, indwelling, processed, and consummated Spirit. Because we are one spirit with Him, we experience His crucifixion, resurrection, and ascension. This is the way to enjoy Christ.

8. By Eating the Spiritual Food
and Drinking the Spiritual Drink

We enjoy the all-inclusive Christ also by eating the spiritual food and drinking the spiritual drink (1 Cor. 10:3-4). The spiritual food is typified by the manna (Exo. 16:4, 14-15, 35), and the spiritual drink is typified by the water that flowed out of the cleft rock (Exo. 17:6; Num. 20:10-11). Today we have Christ as our manna, and we have the Holy Spirit out of the crucified Christ as our drink. To eat and drink in this way is to enjoy the all-inclusive Christ.

9. By Drinking the Spirit

Another way to receive, experience, and enjoy the all-inclusive Christ is by drinking the Spirit. First Corinthians 12:13 says, "For also in one Spirit we were all baptized into one body, whether Jews or Greeks, whether slaves or free, and were all given to drink one Spirit." This verse says that we are one Body because we all were baptized in the one Spirit. The Spirit was first the means through which we were baptized into the one Body. Now that we have been baptized into the Body through the one Spirit, we should continually drink the same Spirit. We have been given by Christ to drink the one Spirit, in whom we have all been baptized. The Spirit in whom we have been baptized and whom we are now drinking has two aspects, the outward and the inward. The Spirit in the outward aspect is the economical Spirit, and the Spirit in the inward aspect is the essential Spirit. We are baptized in the economical Spirit, and we drink the essential Spirit. Thus, baptism is economical, and drinking is essential.

10. By Partaking of Christ as the Life-giving Spirit

We enjoy the aggregate of the all-embracing blessing of the full gospel of God also by partaking of Christ as the life-giving Spirit (1 Cor. 15:45b). The incarnated, crucified, and resurrected Christ has become the life-giving Spirit. We must partake of Him as the life-giving Spirit every day.

11. By the Anointing, Sealing, and Pledging of the Spirit

We enjoy the all-inclusive Christ also by the anointing, sealing, and pledging of the Spirit (2 Cor. 1:21-22). Anointing is horizontal, but sealing is vertical. The anointing of the Spirit permeates us horizontally, and the sealing of the Spirit saturates us vertically by reaching deeply into our being. The pledging of the Spirit is the first taste, a sample, of the

Spirit. The anointing, sealing, and pledging reveal three aspects of the one Spirit today. The Spirit is on us as the anointing Spirit; He is within us as the sealing Spirit; and He is with us as the pledging Spirit. The anointing Spirit is permeating us, the sealing Spirit is saturating us, and the pledging Spirit is the guarantee, the first taste, the sample, given to us for our enjoyment. This anointing, sealing, and pledging is the way for us to enjoy the all-inclusive Christ.

12. By the Life-giving Spirit
as the Writing Ink in Our Ministry

The way to enjoy Christ is also by the life-giving Spirit as the writing ink in our ministry (2 Cor. 3:6b, 3). Second Corinthians 3:3 says, "Since you are being manifested that you are a letter of Christ ministered by us, inscribed not with ink but with the Spirit of the living God; not in tablets of stone but in tablets of hearts of flesh." This verse refers not only to the believers who receive the apostles' ministry but also to the ministers who minister the word of God to others. Both the believers and the ministers should be written on by Christ with the life-giving Spirit as the writing ink. Today we are under the writing of the life-giving Spirit. The more Christ writes upon us with the inking Spirit, the more we enjoy the aggregate of the all-embracing blessing of the gospel.

I can surely testify that the more I speak, the more I am written upon. Today there is writing going on within me. When I began to write the outlines for these messages concerning the way to enjoy Christ, a great deal of writing took place within me. The more I wrote, the more writing took place within me. It is in this way that we become ministers of the word. The ministry comes out of the inward writing of Christ with the Spirit as the writing ink. This writing Spirit is the life-giving Spirit.

13. By Beholding the Glory of the Lord
for Our Transformation from the Lord Spirit
with the Element of the Lord

We enjoy the all-inclusive Christ also by beholding the

glory of the Lord for our transformation from the Lord
Spirit with the element of the Lord into His image from
glory to glory (2 Cor. 3:18). Today we all need to have an
unveiled face, a face not covered by any veil. With such
an unveiled face we can behold the glory of the Lord. The
more we behold the glory of the Lord in this way, the more
we are transformed from the Lord Spirit. The phrase
from the Lord Spirit indicates a transmission. As we are
beholding the Lord, a transmission takes place. This transmission is from the Lord Spirit with the element of the Lord.
Transformation requires the addition of another element;
without such an addition, transformation cannot take place.
Through the transmission from the Lord Spirit, within
whom is the element of the Lord, we are transformed from
glory to glory.

We are all busy in the morning, but we must do our best
to save ten or fifteen minutes each day to behold the Lord. To
do this is not a waste of time. If possible, we should reduce
our time for sleep. If we normally rise at six o'clock in the
morning, we can gain fifteen minutes by rising fifteen
minutes earlier. If we take another ten minutes from the
time given to our business, we can have a total of twenty-five
minutes for beholding the Lord each day. By beholding Him
we will receive an element from the Lord that will transform
us into the glorious image of Christ, even from glory to glory.
This is the way to enjoy Christ.

14. By Being Renewed
in Our Inner Man Day by Day

Another way to enjoy the all-inclusive Christ is by being
renewed in our inner man day by day (2 Cor. 4:16). Today we
stress the matters of being revived every morning and of
overcoming every day. However, Paul's word is that we must
be "renewed day by day." We must not merely overcome; we
must also be renewed. Daily our outer man is decaying, is
being consumed, and our inner man is being renewed. This
renewing of our inner man is of the Spirit within our spirit.
This also is a way to enjoy Christ.

15. By Being Renewed as the New Creation in Christ

Another way for us to enjoy Christ is by being renewed as the new creation in Christ (2 Cor. 5:17). Formerly we were the old creation in Adam. Because we have been transferred out of Adam into Christ, we are now a new creation in Christ. This transfer is not only outward but also inward. The inward transfer is the renewing. We are being renewed from the old creation into the new creation. The New Testament uses the word renew quite often (Rom. 12:2; Eph. 4:23; Col. 3:10; Titus 3:5). If we are to experience the renewing of the mind, the renewing in the spirit of our mind, the renewing of the new man, and the renewing of the Holy Spirit, we must be renewed in our inner man day by day. All these aspects of renewing are for us to enjoy Christ as the Spirit.

16. By the Fellowship of the Spirit in the Enjoyment of the Divine Trinity

We can enjoy Christ as the Spirit also by the fellowship of the Spirit in the enjoyment of the Divine Trinity. Second Corinthians 13:14 says, "The grace of the Lord Jesus Christ and the love of God and the fellowship of the Holy Spirit be with you all." The grace of Christ, the love of God, and the fellowship of the Spirit are all for our enjoyment. God's love is embodied in Christ's grace, and Christ's grace is dispensed by the fellowship of the Spirit. Today as we are in the fellowship of the Spirit, we participate in the grace of Christ and enjoy the love of God. This enjoyment of the Divine Trinity is altogether in the fellowship of the Spirit, which is in our spirit. Therefore, we must learn the lesson either to remain in our spirit or to come back to our spirit. We must learn not to be absent from our spirit. If we find ourselves away from the spirit, we should do our best to come back to the spirit. In our spirit we meet the Spirit of fellowship. By the fellowship of this Spirit we participate in the enjoyment of the Triune God in every way. This enjoyment is the aggregate of the all-embracing blessing of the full gospel of God.

The Central Line of the Divine Revelation

THE DIVINE ECONOMY
AND THE DIVINE DISPENSING

MESSAGE EIGHTEEN

THE AGGREGATE OF THE ALL-EMBRACING BLESSING
OF THE FULL GOSPEL OF GOD IN CHRIST
FOR THE DIVINE DISPENSING
ACCORDING TO THE DIVINE ECONOMY

(9)

Scripture Reading: Eph. 3:2, 8, 16-19; Phil. 1:19b-21a; 4:13; Col. 1:12; 2:6; 3:4; Rev. 2:6-7, 17a; 21:6b; 22:1-2, 14, 17

II. THE WAY TO RECEIVE, EXPERIENCE,
AND ENJOY THE ALL-INCLUSIVE CHRIST
AS THE ALL-INCLUSIVE LIFE-GIVING SPIRIT—
THE AGGREGATE OF THE ALL-EMBRACING BLESSING
OF THE FULL GOSPEL OF GOD

C. The Way in the Rest of the Books
of the New Testament

In this message we will fellowship concerning the way to receive, experience, and enjoy the all-inclusive Christ as the all-inclusive life-giving Spirit—the aggregate of the all-embracing blessing of the full gospel of God—in Ephesians through Revelation.

17. By the Dispensing of the Riches of Christ
through the Ministers' Stewardship

The way to receive, experience, and enjoy Christ as the all-inclusive life supply is by the dispensing of the riches of Christ through the ministers' stewardship (Eph. 3:2, 8). Ephesians is a book on the church as the counterpart of Christ, which receives, experiences, and enjoys the rich supply of Christ through the stewardship of the apostles. The word *stewardship* in Greek is *oikonomia.* This word in Ephesians 3:9 is translated *economy* in reference to the preaching of the unsearchable riches of Christ. Such a preaching of the riches of Christ is a dispensing according to God's economy. The same word in verse 2 is translated *stewardship,* referring to the stewardship of the apostles as the ministers. God has a plan to dispense Himself in His divine trinity into man, and this dispensing is carried out by the stewardship of the apostles as the ministers.

The stewardship of the ministers is necessary for us to understand the Bible. Paul did not teach us to read the Bible without interpretation. Rather, the book of Hebrews is his exposition of Leviticus. Without Hebrews no one can understand Leviticus. In the same way, we need the exposition of the New Testament. It is not easy to understand the pure word of the New Testament. In Hebrews, Paul spoke of the word of righteousness, which is the solid food, and the good word of God, which is the milk (5:12-14; 6:5). Without the proper exposition we cannot understand what these two kinds of words are. Our understanding of the Word today is built on the stewardship of the ministers, beginning from the church fathers in the second century and consummating in this century with Watchman Nee. These ministers include Martin Luther, the mystics, such as Madam Guyon, Father Fenelon, and Brother Lawrence, and the inner life believers, such as William Law, Andrew Murray, and the speakers at the Keswick conventions. They also include G. H. Pember, D. M. Panton, and Robert Govett, as well as A. B. Simpson, Mrs. McDonough, and Ruth Paxson. All of these were ministers of the Word, from whom we have received much help.

As the ministers who speak the Word of God, we all need to learn how to make our stewardship a dispensing ministry. In our ministry we must dispense Christ, the Spirit, life, and the church. Paul did this very much in his dispensing ministry. He spoke concerning Christ and concerning the church as the Body of Christ, His counterpart.

18. By the Strengthening of the Spirit
That Christ May Make His Home in Our Hearts
That We May Be Filled unto All the Fullness of God

The way to receive, experience, and enjoy Christ is also by the strengthening of the Spirit that Christ may make His home in our hearts that we may be filled unto all the fullness of God (Eph. 3:16-19). The indwelling Spirit is always within us to strengthen us that Christ may make His home in our hearts that we may be filled unto all the fullness of God. Many Christians know nothing concerning Christ's making His home in our hearts, but I am confident that most of the saints in the Lord's recovery do know something concerning this matter. Therefore, we should take the opportunity to speak to others concerning this truth.

19. By Holding the Head
That We May Grow into Him in Everything
for the Building Up of His Body

We receive, experience, and enjoy Christ also by holding the Head that we may grow into Him in everything for the building up of His Body (Eph. 4:15-16). To understand any portion of the Bible we must take care of its context. The meaning of holding the Head in Ephesians 4:15 is found in verses 13 through 16. We need to read these verses again and again. One item mentioned in these verses is the winds of teaching (v. 14). While we are in the recovery growing in Christ, the winds of teaching often come. In the past several years the winds came a number of times, and some of the weaker ones have been blown away; that is, they have left the Head. To hold the Head is to hold on to Christ as our centrality, universality, and everything and not listen to the heretical, distracting teachings.

20. By Being Renewed in the Spirit of the Mind
for the Putting On of the New Man

The way to receive, experience, and enjoy Christ is also by being renewed in the spirit of the mind for the putting on of the new man (Eph. 4:23-24). As a faculty of our being, our mind can be empty or it can be filled with the spirit. If our spirit is strong, it will invade and occupy our mind, causing our mind to be full of our spirit. Our mind must be under the control of our spirit, and our spirit must be in our mind. The spirit that is in our mind renews us. This is one of the ways to experience Christ as revealed in Ephesians.

Being renewed in the spirit of the mind is for the putting on of the new man. We are in the process of putting off the old man as our old "garment" and putting on the new man, the church life. Many Christians today are "naked" because they do not have the church life. For many saints, talking too long on the telephone is the old garment, the old man. We must put off the old garment, the old daily habits, and endeavor to put on more of the new man every day. By being renewed in this way we enjoy Christ.

21. By Being Nourished and Cherished as a Member of the Body of Christ by Christ as the Head

To be nourished and cherished as a member of the Body of Christ by Christ as the Head (Eph. 5:29) is also a way to receive, experience, and enjoy Christ. To be nourished is to be fed, whereas to be cherished is to be made happy. Being cherished includes being warmed up. As ministers who serve the Lord, we all need to learn how to make people happy. Those whom we go to visit need our cherishing. Our coming to someone with a cold face may cause him to feel threatened. When we go to visit people, our face, especially our eyes, must be pleasant. To visit people in this way is to cherish them. Mothers know how to nourish and cherish their children. If a mother spanks a naughty child who does not want to eat, the child will become more naughty. However, if the mother picks up and embraces the child, the child will be warmed up. Then he will behave properly and will pleasantly receive his mother's feeding. The elders must learn how to cherish the saints. A stern face may frustrate the elders' ministering to the saints.

Very often Christ not only nourishes us but also cherishes us. Throughout the years I have been cherished many times by the Lord. He did not come to rebuke, condemn, or reprove me. Rather, He said, "I love you." This touched me and caused me to confess and repent of my mistakes, sometimes with tears. One experience of such cherishing builds us up more than hearing ten messages. By being nourished and cherished in this way by our Head, we enjoy Him.

22. By Being Empowered in the Lord to Put On the Whole Armor of God

The way to receive, experience, and enjoy Christ is also by being empowered in the Lord to put on the whole armor of God (Eph. 6:10-11). To be empowered in the Lord is to arm ourselves for fighting. In Ephesians 5 the church as the bride of Christ is a female; as such, she should not be too bold. But in Ephesians 6 the church is a corporate warrior to fight for God; as such, the church must be bold. We should not be timid or afraid; we should be bold. God's grace makes us His horses of majesty in battle (Zech. 10:3). We are fighters, not against the churches or against our fellow believers but against the unique enemy, Satan, who is the ruler of the authority of the air (Eph. 2:2). Toward him we must be bold and show no mercy. If we fight for Christ, we will enjoy Him.

23. By Enjoying the Bountiful Supply of the Spirit of Jesus Christ to Magnify Christ by Living Him

Another way to receive, experience, and enjoy Christ is by enjoying the bountiful supply of the Spirit of Jesus Christ to magnify Christ by living Him (Phil. 1:19b-21a). Today the Spirit is no longer merely the Spirit of God; He is also the Spirit of Jesus Christ. He is the Spirit of Jesus (Acts 16:7), who lived a lowly, humble, and sorrowful life on the earth and who grew up like a tender plant, like a root out of dry ground (Isa. 53:2). The Spirit is the Spirit of such a One. He is also the Spirit of Christ in His glory, resurrection, and ascension (Rom. 8:9). Jesus Christ today is a Spirit (1 Cor. 15:45b; 2 Cor. 3:17), and this Spirit is called the Spirit of Jesus Christ. The Spirit of Jesus Christ is the bountiful supply. The Greek word for *bountiful supply* refers to the supplying of all the needs of the chorus by the choragus, the leader of the chorus. This bountiful supply of the all-inclusive Spirit of Jesus Christ is for us to magnify Jesus Christ by living Him. We live Him that He may be magnified. First we live Christ; then we magnify Him. Paul magnified Christ in this way. While he was in the Roman prison, he did not shame Christ but magnified Christ by his living of Him every day.

24. By Pursuing Christ That We May Gain Him as the Excellent Christ

To pursue Christ that we may gain Him as the excellent Christ (Phil. 3:8-14) is another way to receive, experience, and enjoy Christ. Christ is not only the all-inclusive Christ but also the excellent Christ. Sometimes our living and behavior is good but not excellent. We must be excellent by enjoying the excellent Christ. The way to have the excellent Christ and live the excellent Christ is to pursue Him. Paul said that he pursued Christ (v. 12). The Greek word for *pursue* is the same word as for *persecute*. When he was Saul, Paul persecuted Christ, but after being saved, Paul pursued Christ.

We need to "persecute" Christ, to force Him to do something and not let Him go. Jacob wrestled with God (Gen. 32:24-30). He forced God to bless him, so God did it, and Jacob became Israel, the prince of God. It is true that we must always be submissive, believing that everything is under God's sovereignty and that all things work together for our good. In this sense we do not need to force God to do anything for us. However, every truth has more than one side. This is illustrated by the four Gospels. The four biographies of Christ present Him in four different ways, as the King (Matthew), the Slave (Mark), the man (Luke), and God (John). On the one hand, we need to learn how to be submissive, suffering whatever happens to us and worshipping the sovereign Lord. On the other hand, we must exercise our spirit to command the Lord. We may say, "Lord, we are too barren. We command You to produce some fruit for us." This is one of many ways to experience and enjoy Christ.

25. By Being Empowered in Christ
That We May Be Able to Do All Things

The way to receive, experience, and enjoy Christ is also by being empowered in Christ that we may be able to do all things. In Philippians 4:12-13 Paul said, "I know also how to be abased, and I know how to abound; in everything and in all things I have learned the secret both to be filled and to hunger, both to abound and to lack. I am able to do all things in Him who empowers me." *All things* in verse 13 refers to the six items in verse 8—the things that are true, the things that are dignified, the things that are righteous, the things that are pure, the things that are lovely, and the things that are well spoken of. Paul could carry out the high virtues in human life not merely by the One who empowered him but in the One who empowered him. To do all things in Christ is to enjoy Christ and experience the dispensing of Christ into us.

26. By Partaking of Christ
as the God-allotted Portion of the Saints

To partake of Christ as the God-allotted portion of the saints (Col. 1:12) is a rich way to receive, experience, and enjoy Christ. Colossians tells us that Christ is our God-allotted portion. When the Israelites entered the good land, each family was allotted a portion of the land. We, the New Testament Israelites, have all received the all-inclusive Christ as an allotted portion from God. This portion is the image of God, the Firstborn of all creation, the One in whom, through whom, and unto whom all things were created, and the One in whom all things cohere (vv. 15-17). He is also the Head of the Body, the beginning, Firstborn from the dead, and the One in whom all the fullness was pleased to dwell (vv. 18-19). Such a One is our portion. Like the Colossian believers, we must learn to forget about the angels and all the "isms," such as Judaism, Gnosticism, and asceticism, and partake of the central and universal Christ as our portion.

27. By Receiving Christ and Walking in Him as Living in the God-given Good Land

To receive Christ and walk in Him as those living in the God-given good land (Col. 2:6) should also be considered as a way to experience and enjoy Christ. First we receive Christ as a portion of the good land, and then we walk in Him. We live, move, act, and have our being in Him as those living in the God-given good land. The children of Israel enjoyed the good land by tilling, sowing, watering, and harvesting the land. This is a type of the way to enjoy Christ.

28. By Partaking of Christ as the Body of the Shadows of All Our Necessities

To partake of Christ as the body of the shadows of all our necessities (Col. 2:16-17) is also a way to receive, experience, and enjoy Christ. Our necessities include eating, drinking, a weekly rest, a monthly new beginning with light in the darkness, and yearly feasts. The Jews had a daily enjoyment in eating and drinking, a weekly enjoyment (the Sabbath) in being completed and resting, a monthly enjoyment (the new moon) with a new beginning with light in the darkness, and a yearly enjoyment with the annual feasts. Today Christ is our daily supply, our weekly rest, our monthly new beginning, and our yearly satisfaction. Christ is every kind of enjoyment to us. The enjoyments in the Jewish religion are merely shadows, but Christ is the body of all the shadows.

29. By Taking Christ as Our Life and Living by Him That We May Be Glorified at His Manifestation

Another way to receive, experience, and enjoy Christ is by taking Christ as our life and living by Him that we may be glorified at His manifestation (Col. 3:4). Today we have Christ within us, and in the future we will be manifested with Christ in His glorification. We receive Him as our life and live by Him. While we are living by Him as our life, this life is saturating our being. This saturation will continue until our body will be redeemed and glorified. That will be our manifestation with Christ in glory. Every day, especially every morning, we need to pray, "Lord, today is another day for me to take You as my life and to live by You." This is one of the ways for us to enjoy and experience Christ.

30. By Rejoicing Always, Praying Unceasingly, Giving Thanks to God in Everything, Not Quenching the Spirit, and Not Despising the Prophesyings

Another practical way to receive, experience, and enjoy Christ is to rejoice always, pray unceasingly, give thanks to God in everything, not quench the Spirit, and not despise the prophesyings, that we may be wholly sanctified and saturated with the element of God's holy nature in our spirit, soul, and body (1 Thes. 5:16-20, 23).

Such a practical way to enjoy Christ includes not despising the prophesyings. Every Lord's Day morning we practice the prophesying. Some of the prophecies may not seem to be very high. However, we must be careful not to despise them. If we despise them, we will suffer the loss of enjoying Christ's dispensing. We must not despise any prophecy. To prophesy in 1 Thessalonians 5:20 refers not mainly to predicting but to speaking for the Lord. It is good for the new ones to speak a word for the Lord, even if their speaking is broken or very brief. It is very pleasant for them simply to say, "I love the Lord because He is good." If we despise such a prophecy, we will offend the Lord. Even such a short speaking is out of the Spirit's inspiration. Before the new ones were saved, they never said this, but now they can speak in this way with joy. We must also regard such speakings and not despise them.

The practice of rejoicing always, praying unceasingly, giving thanks to God in everything, not quenching the Spirit, and not despising the prophesyings results in our being wholly sanctified and saturated with the element of God's holy nature in our spirit, soul, and body. If we despise the prophesying of the new ones and criticize the prophesying meetings, we will miss the mark of sanctification and even suffer the loss of the dispensing for our constitution with the holy nature of God. However, if we say, "Praise the Lord! So many are speaking for the Lord," we will receive Christ as our supply.

31. By Calling on the Lord out of a Pure Heart for the Pursuing of His Virtues

To call on the Lord out of a pure heart for the pursuing of His virtues (2 Tim. 2:22b) is also a way to receive, experience, and enjoy Christ. We need to call continually, "O Lord Jesus!" out of a pure heart. This is for the pursuing of righteousness, faith, love, peace, and all the virtues of Christ.

32. By the Renewing of the Spirit, Whom God Pours Out upon Us Richly

Another way to receive, experience, and enjoy Christ is by the renewing of the Spirit, whom God pours out upon us richly (Titus 3:5-6). God's pouring out of His Spirit is not once for all; it is continuous. Every day and every hour God's pouring out of His Spirit continues. This outpoured Spirit renews us. We need to contact the Lord in order to keep receiving the outpouring of the Spirit, who renews us every moment and every day for our enjoyment of Christ.

33. By Eating the Word of Righteousness as the Solid Food

To eat the word of righteousness as the solid food (Heb. 5:13-14) is a strong way to receive, experience, and enjoy Christ. The word of righteousness is the solid food. Hebrews is divided into five sections, and each section ends with a warning concerning the coming kingdom (2:1-4; 3:7—4:13; 5:11—6:20; 10:19-39; 12:1-29). If we do not heed the warnings, we will suffer punishment and lose the kingdom in the millennium. Many in today's Christianity not only do not understand this word but even oppose it. Some say that since the redemption accomplished by the blood of Jesus is perfect and complete and we have been washed by Him, we cannot be punished when Christ comes again. They say that if Christ can punish His redeemed ones, then His redemption is not complete. It is true that Christ's redemption is complete, but Hebrews tells us that God chastises those whom He receives (12:6). God's chastisement is not against Christ's redemption. Moreover, there is no word in the New Testament that says that God chastises His people only in this age and not in the next. In nearly every book of the New Testament we are warned concerning the possibility of being chastened by God in the coming age. We must live a life of the highest righteousness. If we do, we will enter into the kingdom of the heavens and enjoy it as a reward (Matt. 5:20). Otherwise, according to the Lord's word in the Gospels, we will be cast into outer darkness, where there will be the weeping and the gnashing of teeth, as a kind of chastisement (25:30).

Many Christians will lose the kingdom as a reward, but they will still enjoy eternal redemption. The word concerning the kingdom is not "the good word of God" (Heb. 6:5); it is the word of righteousness. The good word of God is like milk. It is easy to receive, but it does not sustain long. Paul told the Hebrews that they had tasted of the heavenly gift, had become partakers of the Holy Spirit, and had tasted the good word of God and the powers of the coming age (vv. 4-5). However, he also told them that he had deeper things to say to them that they were not able to understand (5:10-12). The word of righteousness, on the other hand, is solid food. It is difficult to take, but it is solid and it sustains long.

34. By Taking the Milk of the Word as Newborn Babes for the Growth in Life unto Salvation

Another way to receive, experience, and enjoy Christ is by taking the milk of the word as newborn babes for the growth in life unto salvation (1 Pet. 2:2). Experiencing Christ in this way is proper while we are still babes. After a certain period of time, however, we should not remain babes. We need to advance beyond 1 Peter 2:2 and proceed to Hebrews 5:13-14 to eat the word of righteousness.

35. By Abiding in the Lord according to the Teaching of the Divine Anointing

Another wonderful way to receive, experience, and enjoy Christ is by abiding in the Lord according to the teaching of the divine anointing (1 John 2:27). There is a teaching within us that is not by man's speaking but by the inward anointing. The Spirit who indwells us today is moving, acting, working, and operating in us as an anointing. The anointing is the action of the Spirit's operation. In Philippians 2:13 Paul said that God operates in us both the willing and the working for His good pleasure. This operating within us is an anointing, and this anointing is a teaching. While we are combing our hair, the inner moving may teach us how to do it. This is the inner teaching that is not by a spoken word but by the operation of the anointing. In order to enjoy Christ, we must abide in Him according to the inward teaching of the anointing.

36. By Overcoming the Things That the Lord Hates through the Hearing of the Speaking of the Spirit and the Enjoyment of Christ as the Tree of Life and the Hidden Manna

Another way, which is the overcoming way, to receive, experience, and enjoy Christ is by overcoming the things that the Lord hates through the hearing of the speaking of the Spirit and the enjoyment of Christ as the tree of life and the hidden manna (Rev. 2—3). In Revelation 2:6 the Lord said, "But this you have, that you hate the works of the Nicolaitans, which I also hate." The Lord hates the clergy-laity system, which includes the system of one man speaking that annuls the functions of the other members of the Body of Christ. The things that the Lord hates also include even the Jewish and Christian religions. Both Judaism and organized Christianity are hateful in the eyes of Christ, and we must overcome them through the hearing of the speaking of the Spirit and the enjoyment of Christ as the tree of life and as the hidden manna. Seven times in Revelation 2—3 (2:7, 11, 17, 26; 3:5, 12, 21) the speaking One, the Lord Jesus, called for His overcomers to overcome all the negative things mentioned there, especially these two kinds of religions.

It is difficult for the members of a denomination to leave their denomination. It requires all their strength to overcome in this way. Even after leaving the denominations, to overcome the denominational things is still difficult. Some among us may still desire to keep the Lord's Day morning meetings with one speaker. They may prefer this to a meeting where many prophesy. This desire is the tendency to go back to one item of today's organized Christianity. If our eyes are opened, we will see that this is a hateful and abominable thing. It rejects the Head, kills the Body, and annuls all the functioning members. This is not a small matter.

We must overcome every item of every "ism" and every "anity." If we do, we will be qualified to eat Christ as the tree of life and the hidden manna. Christ as both the tree of life and the hidden manna is the top portion for God's elect to eat. However, many among God's elect are not overcoming. The small remnant who do overcome will enjoy this particular portion given by God.

37. By Drinking the Spirit
as the Flowing Living Water and Eating Christ
as the Supplying Tree of Life

The ever-sustaining and satisfying way to receive, experience, and enjoy Christ is by drinking the Spirit as the flowing living water and eating Christ as the supplying tree of life (Rev. 21:6b; 22:1-2, 14, 17). At the end of the Bible there is a river flowing out of the Triune God, and in this river the tree of life grows. The river signifies the Spirit of God, and the tree of life signifies Christ growing along the flow of the Spirit. These are two items of God's supply. The river is to satisfy us and quench our thirst, and the tree of life is to fill us and strengthen us constantly. The river of life is the drink, and the tree of life is the food. This is our eternal enjoyment. For eternity we will be drinking of the living water and eating of the tree of life for our eternal enjoyment of Christ.

THE DIVINE ECONOMY
AND THE DIVINE DISPENSING

MESSAGE NINETEEN

IN THE PROMISES AND TYPES
OF
GOD'S ANTICIPATED REDEMPTION AND SALVATION

(2)

Scripture Reading: Exo. 12:1-10; 1 Cor. 5:7b; Matt. 15:32; Exo.
12:11; 14:22; 15:13, 22; Heb. 12:1b; 2 Tim. 4:7b; 1 Cor. 5:7a, 8;
Exo. 13:6-7; 16:13b-15; Num. 11:7-9; 1 Cor. 10:3; John 6:35,
50, 57b; Exo. 17:5-6; 1 Cor. 10:4; John 7:37-39; 1 Cor. 2:12

The three promises of the seed of the woman (Gen. 3:15;
Isa. 7:14), the seed of Abraham (Gen. 17:8; Gal. 3:16;
Matt. 1:1-2a), and the seed of David (2 Sam. 7:12-14a; Matt.
1:1, 6; 22:42-45; Rom. 1:3; Rev. 22:16) were covered in earlier
messages concerning the promises of God's anticipated
redemption and salvation. In this message we come to the
types of God's anticipated redemption and salvation. In
the types the dispensing of Christ as the embodiment of the
Triune God is revealed very clearly.

THE PASSOVER BEING A COMPLETE PICTURE
OF GOD'S FULL SALVATION

God's salvation is based on His redemption. Without
redemption, God's salvation has no foundation. However,
God's salvation is not that simple; it includes many more
items than redemption. How we thank the Lord that in the
Passover we have a complete picture of God's full salvation.
Adam and Eve, the first generation of mankind, enjoyed
God's salvation to a small degree before the Passover. They

were the first generation to enjoy God's salvation. Then Abel enjoyed more of God's salvation than his father and mother did. Many generations passed, including Abraham, Isaac, and Jacob, but no one experienced God's complete salvation until the Passover. It was not until the time of the exodus that God ordained the Passover.

TEN ASPECTS OF GOD'S FULL SALVATION EXPERIENCED BY THE CHILDREN OF ISRAEL

God's full salvation typified by the experience of the children of Israel includes ten aspects: the blood of the lamb, the flesh of the lamb, the unleavened bread, the bitter herbs, the arm of Jehovah, the Angel of Jehovah, the cloud, the manna, the water, and the healing of the Physician.

The Passover clearly typifies the redemptive aspect of God's salvation. In the Passover the first striking thing is the blood shed by the Passover lamb (Exo. 12:7). The blood is stressed very much by many Christians. However, the Passover includes not only the blood of the lamb; it also includes the flesh of the lamb, the unleavened bread, and the bitter herbs (v. 8). The blood of the lamb was applied outwardly, being sprinkled on the doorposts of the houses. But the flesh of the lamb, the unleavened bread, and the bitter herbs were taken inwardly because they were eaten by the children of Israel.

The blood on the doorposts and lintel was a sign to the smiting angel (v. 23). On the night of the Passover, God judged the firstborn throughout the land of Egypt. The firstborn signifies the first man, Adam (1 Cor. 15:45a). According to God's judgment, all the firstborn should die. God's judgment included not only the Egyptians but also the Israelites, who were just as sinful as the Egyptians. They were all condemned by God in His righteousness. But on the night of the Passover, all the Israelites had the blood as a sign upon their houses. By the blood upon their houses, the firstborn of the children of Israel were redeemed. God's redemption took care of their problem directly with God, the problem of God's condemnation because of their sins. The blood of the lamb dealt with this problem, but it was the flesh of the lamb, the unleavened bread, and the bitter herbs that saved the children of Israel from Pharaoh, Egypt, and the tyranny of Egyptian slavery.

God's full salvation experienced by the children of Israel also included the miraculous acts of God. These miraculous acts, such as the opening of the Red Sea, were related to the arm of Jehovah (Exo. 15:16) in the Old Testament. The arm of Jehovah, referring to the power, the miraculous strength, of Jehovah, acted to save the children of Israel. In addition to this, Christ as the Angel of Jehovah led the army of Israel as their invisible Commander. When the children of Israel fled Egypt, before they crossed the Red Sea, the Egyptian army pursued them. The Angel of Jehovah then turned from the front of the camp to the rear in order to protect them (14:19-20).

The children of Israel also enjoyed the pillar of cloud in the daytime and the pillar of fire in the nighttime. These became a covering, a canopy, to the children of Israel (Isa. 4:5). In God's full salvation, the children of Israel enjoyed such a canopy all the time.

God's salvation included not only the escape of the children of Israel from Egypt but also their supply while they journeyed through the wilderness. After the children of Israel left Egypt and entered into the wilderness, they did not have a sea in which to gain fish or land on which to farm in order to gain a harvest of grain and cereals. In the wilderness there was nothing to eat. So part of God's salvation was to give them manna from the heavens (Exo. 16:14-22). They could not get food from any other source. God gave them manna, not from the water or from the land but from the heavens above.

In the wilderness the children of Israel also had a problem concerning water. God gave them water out of the cleft rock (17:1-6). According to Paul in 1 Corinthians 10:4, the rock followed them through the wilderness. The rock was struck by the lawgiver, Moses, and out of the cleft rock living water flowed to quench their thirst.

In addition to the foregoing items, God's full salvation included the matter of healing. At Marah God as their Physician healed them by changing the bitter water into sweet water (Exo. 15:23-25).

Of the above ten aspects of God's full salvation, the first aspect that indicates something of God's dispensing Himself into His redeemed is the flesh of the Passover lamb. On the night of the Passover, the lamb had to be slain. According to history, the Israelites placed the lamb on two pieces of wood put together in the form of a cross, with one vertical stake and one horizontal crossbar. They tied the forefeet of the lamb on the horizontal crossbar and the hind legs to the vertical stake. They then slew the lamb, shedding its blood, and took the blood and applied it on the lintel and the two doorposts of their houses for their redemption. By applying the blood in this way, they were saved. They knew that the angel would smite the firstborn in all of the land of Egypt, but because they were under the covering of the blood, their firstborn would not be killed. Then, in their homes they roasted the lamb that they might eat it.

God's full salvation involved something on God's side and something on the children of Israel's side. God's side involved the above-mentioned ten items. On their side, the children of Israel ate the lamb with their staffs in their hands, with their shoes on their feet, and with their loins girded (Exo. 12:11). This was their preparation to leave Egypt. After the people ate the flesh of the lamb, the lamb was dispensed into them, and by this dispensing they were strengthened.

In God's full salvation as typified by the experience of the children of Israel, in addition to the flesh of the lamb, the unleavened bread, the manna, and the water also indicate something of God's dispensing of Himself into His redeemed people. It is the same with us today. In God's full salvation today, we enjoy God's dispensing by Christ being our Lamb, our unleavened bread, our manna, and our spiritual water.

II. IN THE TYPES

A. In the Enjoyment of the Items of the Passover

The divine economy and the divine dispensing are shown in the types of God's anticipated redemption and salvation in the enjoyment of the items of the Passover (Exo. 12:1-10).

1. The Flesh of the Lamb to Be Eaten by God's Redeemed, Signifying the Redeeming Christ to Be Dispensed into His Believers as the Life Supply

First, the flesh of the lamb was to be eaten by God's redeemed people (v. 8a). This signifies that the redeeming Christ is to be dispensed into His believers as the life supply (1 Cor. 5:7b). The Lamb, which is the redeeming Christ, is dispensed into His believers in order to give them the strength and energy to go the way ordained by God.

The flesh of the lamb was eaten by God's redeemed people to satisfy them (Exo. 12:4; Matt. 15:32) and to strengthen them to run God's way (Exo. 12:11; 14:22; 15:13, 22; Heb. 12:1b; 2 Tim. 4:7b). First, the meat of the lamb was for their satisfaction. Then, once they were satisfied, the meat of the lamb strengthened them and gave them the energy to run God's way. The children of Israel would not have been able to take the way that God had ordained for them if they had not eaten the flesh of the lamb on the night of the Passover. The dispensing of the flesh of the lamb as their life supply gave them the strength and energy to walk the long way ordained by God in order to reach God's goal. By this strength they journeyed from Egypt to Mount Sinai, and there they were trained and built up by God.

2. The Unleavened Bread to Be Eaten by God's Redeemed, Signifying the Sinless Christ to Be Dispensed into His Believers as the Unleavened Element

The unleavened bread was to be eaten by God's redeemed (Exo. 12:8b), signifying that the sinless Christ is to be dispensed into His believers as the unleavened element

(1 Cor. 5:8). The lamb signifies the redeeming Christ; the unleavened bread signifies the sinless Christ. Bread was used as a meal offering (Lev. 2). The meal offering signifies Christ in His humanity. All men have the element of sin in their flesh, but Christ as a man had no sin in His flesh (2 Cor. 5:21). Romans 8:3 tells us that Christ came in "the likeness of the flesh of sin." He was in the likeness of the flesh of sin, but He had no reality of the sin of the flesh. He had no substance of sin within Him. Christ had no sin and committed no sins (1 Pet. 2:22a); He had nothing to do with sin. Apparently, He was in sinful flesh. Actually, there was no reality of any sin in the flesh of Christ, because He was not born of Adam. He was born of a virgin through the Holy Spirit (Matt. 1:20, 23). As a result, He took on flesh, but His flesh had no sinful element. Christ is sinless. This sinless Christ is to be dispensed into His believers as the unleavened (sinless) element.

a. To Cause God's Redeemed People to Live an Unleavened Life

The element in our nature is altogether sinful. But Christ has come into us to be another element within us, a sinless element. This other element causes God's redeemed people to live an unleavened life (Exo. 13:7; 1 Cor. 5:7a). First Corinthians 5:7 says, "Purge out the old leaven that you may be a new lump." A new lump is a lump without leaven. This means that we become a new creation (2 Cor. 5:17) without sin.

b. To Make the Course of Life of God's Redeemed People a Feasting One

The unleavened bread eaten by God's redeemed makes the course of life of God's redeemed people a feasting one (Exo. 13:6; 1 Cor. 5:8). Because we are God's redeemed, our life should always be a happy, feasting life. Throughout the course of our life, we should always be pleasant. We should be pleasant all our days, weeks, months, and years. However, we often are not like this because we eat leavened bread. Leaven signifies the sinful element. Whenever we eat leavened bread, we become unhappy people. We become unpleasant whenever sin has come in. When we are unleavened, we are happy and everything is pleasant with us. This is the function of the unleavened bread within us.

We have one Christ with two aspects, the redeeming aspect and the unleavened aspect. In the redeeming aspect, He becomes our food to satisfy us and to strengthen us to run the course God has set before us. In the unleavened aspect, He is the unleavened bread to supply us with the unleavened element so that we can live an unleavened life. In this way we can live a life without sin in following the Lord through the entire course of our life. Living such a life, we become happy. Every day, every week, every month, and every year is a feast, and we are feasting all the time.

B. In the Enjoyment
of the Heavenly and Spiritual Supply

As the children of Israel journeyed in the wilderness, they needed more than just the Passover with the lamb, the unleavened bread, and the bitter herbs. So God opened the heavens to give them manna. The Hebrew word for *manna* means, "What is it?" Even today no one knows what manna was. Yet we do know that manna came from the Lord. Every day for forty years the children of Israel saw one of the greatest miracles in the universe. Each morning, wherever they journeyed, manna was outside their tents. Yet the children of Israel were stubborn and still could not believe. Actually, we are the same as they. The Lord still does such a miracle every day. Whenever we wake up, we should say, "O Lord!" To say "O Lord" in the morning and to have morning revival is to gather manna.

1. Manna to Be Eaten by God's Elect
Signifying Christ as the Heavenly Food
to Be Dispensed into Us for Our Nourishment
to Constitute Us a Heavenly People

Manna was to be eaten by God's elect, signifying that

Christ as the heavenly food is to be dispensed into us for our nourishment to constitute us a heavenly people (Exo. 16:13b-15; Num. 11:7-9; 1 Cor. 10:3; John 6:35, 50, 57b). Every human being is a constitution of the food he has eaten. Before their exodus the children of Israel were in Egypt. They had an Egyptian constitution. The book of Numbers tells us that while the children of Israel journeyed in the wilderness, they remembered the fish, cucumbers, melons, leeks, onions, and garlic that they had eaten freely in Egypt (11:5). This diet made the children of Israel Egyptian in their constitution.

a. To Change the Diet of God's Redeemed People from the Earthly to the Heavenly

God gave the children of Israel manna to eat to change their diet from the earthly to the heavenly (Num. 11:5-6; John 6:57b). For forty years in the wilderness God's diet replaced the Egyptian diet. Through the change of diet, every one of the children of Israel became a constitution of the heavenly diet. Thus they became no longer an Egyptian people but a heavenly people. According to John 6, manna typifies Christ (vv. 35, 50, 57b). He is our heavenly food, our food of life, and our living food. If we eat Him, we become Him; then we live Him. Today we are still being constituted with Christ as our diet, so that we may become a heavenly people. Christians are not "Egyptians." Christians are a heavenly people with a new diet. This is very meaningful.

b. To Replace God's Redeemed People's Earthly Constitution with the Heavenly One

The reason for the change of diet was to replace God's redeemed people's earthly constitution with the heavenly one. Christ not only redeemed us from the outward, sinful things, but He also entered into us. However, His entering into us was not once for all. From the day He first entered into us, every day we should take Him as our daily food, our daily meat. As we take Him day by day and time after time, He is constituting us to change our inward constitution.

2. The Water out of the Cleft Rock to Be Drunk by God's Elect, Signifying the Spirit of Christ as the Spiritual Drink to Be Dispensed into Us for Our Watering to Make Us Spiritual Persons

The water out of the cleft rock drunk by God's elect signifies the Spirit of Christ as the spiritual drink dispensed into us for our watering to make us spiritual persons (Exo. 17:5-6; 1 Cor. 10:4; John 7:37-39). The water out of the cleft rock is to saturate God's redeemed people with the Spirit of Christ instead of with the spirit of the world (1 Cor. 2:12) and to constitute God's redeemed people to be spiritual rather than worldly. When the children of Israel were in Egypt, they bore a particular spiritual flavor. That flavor was the Egyptian flavor. This flavor was also a spirit, an Egyptian spirit. It is the same with us today. If we are Chinese, we may bear a Chinese flavor, a Chinese spirit. If we are Japanese, we may bear a Japanese flavor, a Japanese spirit.

Today as Christians we no longer drink Egyptian water. We drink the water that comes out of the cleft rock, that is, the wounded Christ. As the cleft rock, Christ streams out His Spirit to be the living water for us to drink. As we drink the Spirit as the living water, we receive an element in the water. Then after a long period of drinking such a Spirit, we bear a divine, heavenly spirit as a particular flavor. Others will realize that we have a certain taste. This taste is the Spirit of Christ.

The Central Line of the Divine Revelation

THE DIVINE ECONOMY
AND THE DIVINE DISPENSING

MESSAGE TWENTY

IN THE PROMISES AND TYPES
OF
GOD'S ANTICIPATED REDEMPTION AND SALVATION

(3)

Scripture Reading: Lev. 2:1-3; 6:14-18; 7:9-10; 6:26, 29-30; 7:5-7, 15-21, 28-36; 23:4-21, 23-43; 1 Cor. 5:7, 8; 15:12-20; Acts 2:1-4, 32-33; Matt. 24:31; Zech. 12:10—13:1; 14:16-21; John 20:16-17; Rom. 4:25b; Phil. 3:10a, 11b

Prayer: O Lord Jesus, we worship You for what You are and for Your moving. Lord, we look to You for Your speaking. Thank You, Lord, that You are so eatable. You are dispensing Yourself through all the Scriptures, from Genesis to Revelation. Lord, open Yourself to us, and open our eyes to see what is on Your heart. We want to see Your good pleasure, Your desire, concerning us. Lord, do cover us once again, and anoint us with Yourself with the living utterance. Amen.

In this series of messages we are emphasizing the all-inclusive Christ whom we are eating, rather than the way to eat Him. Some expositors have emphasized the details of the way to eat the Passover lamb in Exodus 12:1-10, but they have missed the central issue of eating. The way in which we eat is not as important as what we eat. The Lord Jesus whom we are eating is rich in many items. We need to see the riches of Christ whom we have eaten and will be eating for eternity in the New Jerusalem. However, when we come to the Scriptures, we are often distracted by our preoccupations and prior knowledge. Today there are few who stress the enjoyment of Christ. We ourselves did not speak of the enjoyment of Christ and eating Christ before 1958. John 6:57 says, "He who eats Me, he also shall live because of Me." We all need to see that God is good for food; He is eatable.

In the preceding messages we have seen the promises and types concerning God's redemption and salvation in the Old Testament, especially related to the eating of Christ as the threefold seed in humanity. We should stress this, rather than the way to eat Him. In John 14 one of the Lord's disciples asked Him to show him the way, and in verse 6 the Lord said, "I am the way and the reality and the life." Thus, the way to eat the Lord is the Lord Himself. The way is a person, the very One whom we eat.

II. IN THE TYPES

The types in the Old Testament show us how to enjoy God as our life supply that He may dispense Himself into us. The best way to educate someone is to use types or pictures. A type or a picture is better than a thousand words. For this reason, teachers in elementary schools often use pictures to illustrate their subjects. The things in the Scriptures concerning Christ are all mysterious, divine, spiritual, and invisible. They are too difficult for people to apprehend. As the best Educator, God used types to illustrate these matters, that His people would know His intention to dispense Himself as the nourishing, constituting element into them. God is waiting to dispense Himself into us. If we simply read the New Testament without the Old Testament, these matters will not be clear to us. However, without the New Testament we cannot understand the types in the Old Testament. We need both the Old Testament and the New Testament. When we put both together in our understanding, we enjoy God, and He has more opportunities to dispense Himself into us.

In the previous message we considered God's dispensing in the children of Israel's enjoyment of the items of the Passover, mainly by the eating of the flesh of the lamb and the unleavened bread, and in their enjoyment of the heavenly and spiritual supply in the wilderness by eating the manna

and drinking the living water from the cleft rock. In this
message we come to the second part concerning the matter of
eating for the Lord to dispense Himself into us—the enjoyment of all the offerings. Before the decree of the law at
Mount Sinai, Abel, Noah, and Abraham made offerings to
God. Abraham's living was to set up a tent and an altar
to offer something to God (Gen. 12:7-8; 13:18). The descendants of Abraham, the children of Israel, also practiced
something similar, but in an untrained way. At Mount Sinai,
however, God trained the children of Israel concerning how
to eat Him through the offerings in a regulated way. The
regulation concerning the offerings was in two sections. The
first section concerned the continual offerings, that is, the
daily, weekly, and monthly offerings. The second section concerned the annual offerings at the annual feasts. This shows
us that in our daily, weekly, monthly, and yearly living, and
even eternally, we need to receive God's dispensing of Himself into us, not merely by God's giving but even the more by
our eating. God's part is to dispense; our part is to eat. We
must eat what God dispenses.

C. In the Enjoyment of the Continual Offerings

The divine economy and the divine dispensing are shown
in the types in the enjoyment of the continual offerings
(Lev. 1—7). The enjoyment of the continual offerings typifies
our enjoyment of God as our life supply to dispense Himself
into us in a continual way. The continual offerings typify the
very Christ whom we enjoy daily in a regular way. The times
of the offerings were regulated because they are like our
meals. Almost everyone on earth eats three meals each
day—breakfast, lunch, and dinner. Our eating of meals is
regulated by the experience of human kind for the past six
thousand years. This regulated eating results in the best
dispensing. Every day whatever we have eaten is dispensed
into us and is assimilated to become us through the dispensing. In God's economy the most important matter is His
dispensing.

1. The Meal Offering
to Be Eaten by the Priests

The meal offering to be eaten by the priests signifies
Christ in His humanity to be dispensed into us for us to live
a priestly life (Lev. 2:1-3; 6:14-18; 7:9-10). The meal offering
was a piece of bread, or a cake (2:4-5). These cakes entered
into the priests by the priests' eating, and the element of
these cakes was dispensed into the priests. Since the meal
offering was a type of Jesus, the eating of the meal offering
by the priests indicates that we must eat Jesus. However, the
Jesus whom we eat is not a cake. According to the New Testament, today this Jesus in His resurrection is a Spirit
(1 Cor. 15:45b). The cake that we eat is a spiritual cake,
which is just the Spirit Himself. Christ is the cake and the
bread of the meal offering, and this Christ is the Spirit
(2 Cor. 3:17). We eat physical bread with our hands and
mouth and receive it into our stomach. But today the spiritual bread, the spiritual cake, is Christ Himself as the Spirit.
We eat this spiritual bread not with our physical organs but
with our spiritual organ, our spirit. This shows us clearly
that the way to eat Jesus is to exercise our spirit to contact
Him and to dwell on Him. Hence, through our spirit we can
take Christ the Spirit as our spiritual cake.

2. The Sin Offering and Trespass Offering
to Be Eaten by the Offering Priests

The sin offering and trespass offering to be eaten by the
offering priests signify Christ in His redemption from sin
and sins to be dispensed into us that we may enjoy Him with
others as the Redeemer from sin and sins (Lev. 6:26, 29-30;
7:5-7). The sin offering and the trespass offering are two
offerings, and they are also one offering. In Leviticus 5 these
offerings are referred to interchangeably (vv. 7-12). All the
priests were qualified to eat the meal offering (2:3, 10; 6:16, 18;
7:10); however, only the serving priests, the offering priests,
had the right to enjoy the sin offering (6:26; 7:7).

Christ as the Spirit is the meal offering, and He is also
the offering for sin and trespasses. When we exercise our

spirit to enjoy, dwell upon, and receive Christ as the sin offering and the trespass offering, we are filled with Christ as the Spirit, and we sense that all our sins are gone. We no longer have sins or sin; we have only Christ as the Spirit. Then, as the serving priests we offer to God the Christ whom we have enjoyed as the sin and trespass offering. However, we do not offer Him for ourselves but for others. After enjoying Christ for ourselves, we need to come to God to offer Him for others. This is to contact sinners to minister to them the Christ whom we have received and enjoyed. In this way we enjoy Christ even more as our sin and trespass offering. In our ministering of Him to others as the sin and trespass offering, we enjoy Him as these offerings for ourselves. This is the meaning of the type of the sin and trespass offering.

The sin offering from which any blood was brought into the tent of meeting to make propitiation in the holy place was not to be eaten by anyone; it was to be burned with fire (6:30). However, the offering whose blood was sprinkled at the altar could be enjoyed not by the sinner but by the offering priests. The sinner brought an offering for sin, and a priest offered this sin offering for the sinner. The offering priests then had the right to enjoy what the sinner had offered to God. The enjoyment of Christ as the sin and trespass offering is very subjective and particular. We must first enjoy Christ as the sin and trespass offering in our spirit and be filled with Him as the Spirit. Then we can help others by ministering Christ as such an offering to them, that is, by offering Christ as the sin and trespass offering for them. Then both we and they will receive the benefit of Christ as our sin offering. On our side, we will enjoy Him, while on His side, He will have more opportunity to dispense Himself into us as the sinless element, the element for overcoming sin. Then this sinless, sin-overcoming element will be dispensed into us to constitute our being, and we will overcome sin.

It is easy for us to lose our temper. This is one of many of our sins, and we cannot overcome it in ourselves. However, every morning we can spend a time to exercise our spirit to look on Him, to dwell on Him, as the Spirit. This is to eat

Him, enjoy Him, and absorb Him as the very element that is sinless and overcomes sin. His element is dispensed into us and constitutes our being. In this way our constitution will change. When the occasions for sin come, we will have a constitution within that is more than able to overcome sin. This is what it means to live by the Spirit. To live by the Spirit is not merely to reckon that we have died with Christ; it is to live by a positive element that constitutes us continually. This element is the offering that we eat.

3. The Peace Offering
to Be Eaten by the Clean Persons

The peace offering to be eaten by the clean persons signifies Christ, who is our peace, to be dispensed into us, who are clean, for our spiritual enjoyment in the fellowship with God (Lev. 7:15-21). All the people of God, as long as they were clean, were allowed to eat the peace offering. To offer the peace offering to God is higher than to offer the sin and trespass offering. To help others to overcome sin and sins is not as high as bringing others into fellowship with God and with His saints.

4. The Wave Offering
of the Breast of the Peace Offering
and the Heave Offering
of the Right Thigh of the Peace Offering
to Be Eaten by the Offering Priests

The wave offering of the breast of the peace offering and the heave offering of the right thigh of the peace offering were to be eaten by the offering priests, signifying that the Christ of love and the Christ of strength are to be dispensed into us as the offering priests for our enjoyment of Christ in His love and in His strength (Lev. 7:28-36). The peace offering could be eaten by all God's people who were clean. However, the breast and the right thigh were particular parts of the peace offering that only the offering priests could eat. If we are God's children and are cleansed by His blood, we have the right to eat Christ as the peace offering for our enjoyment in the fellowship with God and the fellowship with all His dear saints. However, we do not have the right to eat the breast, signifying the Christ of love, and the right thigh, signifying the Christ of strength. These particular parts are only for the serving priests. For the Triune God, who is embodied in Christ, to dispense Himself into us, we need to be the right persons. First, we need to be God's people; second, we need to be God's cleansed people; third, we need to be God's priests; and fourth, we need to be God's serving priests, ministering to others what we have enjoyed of Christ. If we are merely cleansed, redeemed persons, we have the right to enjoy only the peace offering. We do not have the right to enjoy Christ as the meal offering, the sin offering for others, or the breast and right thigh of the peace offering.

Many believers today are going on in a general way. They are saved, and whenever they sin, they confess their sin, and the Lord's blood cleanses them. However, most are not priests, but if they are priests, they are not offering priests. They do not offer the sin and trespass offering for others, or even if they do, they may not offer the peace offering for others. When we offer Christ to God for others, we have a particular right to enjoy Him. If we are such ones, we can enjoy Christ as the meal offering, the sin and trespass offering, the peace offering, and the two particular parts of the peace offering—the loving breast and the strengthening thigh. In this way we have more and more enjoyment of God, and God has more and more opportunities to dispense Himself into us. We have four levels of the enjoyment of God, and God dispenses Himself into us in four levels. He dispenses Himself into us as His cleansed and redeemed people in a general way, as priests in a higher way, as priests who offer Christ as the sin and trespass offering in an even higher way, and as the priests who offer Christ as the peace offering for others to have fellowship with God and His people in the highest way.

When we preach the gospel to a sinner, we offer Christ as the sin and trespass offering. The one whom we contact may be an unsaved sinner or a fallen believer. We contact such a one with a burden and with Christ in our spirit to bring him Christ as his sin offering and trespass offering. This is to offer Christ to others. To contact others in this way will make us stronger and stronger in the preaching of the gospel. Many times we may come to a sinner not knowing what to say or having nothing to minister. If we enjoy Christ as the sin offering, we will have a strong word to speak about Christ being the offering for our sin. When we speak in such a way, we enjoy Christ. In the same way, if we do not have much fellowship with God in the enjoyment of Christ as the peace offering, we will not have much to minister to the saints to help them to enter into the fellowship with God by enjoying Christ as the peace offering. If we have the experience of the riches of Christ, we will be able to help others. We will be able to minister Christ to others as their peace offering, and we will also enjoy what we minister. This will afford God the opportunities to dispense Himself into us.

D. In the Enjoyment of the Offerings at the Annual Feasts

God's dispensing is typified by the enjoyment of the offerings at the annual feasts (Lev. 23).

1. Seven Annual Feasts Being Appointed by God to the Children of Israel

Seven annual feasts were appointed by God to the children of Israel. God ordered His peoples' lives in such a way that they were to have festivals, and every festival was a time for God's people to enjoy Him as a feast. The feasts afforded Him the opportunity to dispense Himself into His people.

a. The Feast of the Passover

The Feast of the Passover signifies the salvation of the New Testament believers (vv. 4-5; 1 Cor. 5:7b). When children are learning something new, they prefer to hear a story rather than an instruction or a charge. We should learn to preach the gospel to people by using the pictures of the Old Testament. We should present the New Testament salvation using the picture of the Passover to teach people that God's salvation is based first on redemption by His blood and then on the life supply. If we present salvation in this way, we will stir up peoples' interest, and they will pay attention to us.

b. The Feast of Unleavened Bread

The Feast of Unleavened Bread signifies the sinless living of the New Testament believers for the whole course of their Christian life (Lev. 23:6-8; 1 Cor. 5:7a, 8). The Passover took place on a single evening, but the Feast of Unleavened Bread lasted seven days. In the Bible seven days always denotes a full course of time. Thus, the seven days of the Feast of Unleavened Bread denotes the full course of our Christian life, from the first day we were saved to the day when we will be raptured to meet the Lord or will rest by sleeping. The whole course of our Christian life should be unleavened, without sin.

c. The Feast of the Firstfruits

The Feast of the Firstfruits signifies the New Testament believers' enjoyment of the resurrected Christ (Lev. 23:9-14; 1 Cor. 15:12-20). The firstfruits signify Christ as the produce of the land.

d. The Feast of Pentecost

The Feast of Pentecost signifies the New Testament believers' enjoyment of the outpoured Spirit as the aggregate of the rich produce of the resurrected Christ (Lev. 23:15-21; Acts 2:1-4, 32-33). The Feast of Pentecost came fifty days after the Feast of the Firstfruits, indicating that the outpoured Spirit is the aggregate of the rich produce of the resurrected Christ. The rich produce of Christ's resurrection includes the firstborn Son of God (Rom. 8:29; Heb. 1:6), the life-giving Spirit (1 Cor. 15:45b), the many sons of God (Rom. 8:29), and the new creation of God (2 Cor. 5:17). Christ was not the firstborn Son of God until He was resurrected. In resurrection He became the firstborn Son of God. Likewise, before the resurrection the life-giving Spirit was not yet (John 7:39); Christ produced the life-giving Spirit through His resurrection. Before the resurrection God did not have any sons besides His only begotten Son, but through Christ's resurrection we were all begotten of God to be His many sons (1 Pet. 1:3). These many sons became the many grains (John 12:24), who are the members of Christ, the brothers of Christ to constitute His Body (1 Cor. 10:17). All these items are in the aggregate of the rich produce of the resurrected Christ. The Feast of Pentecost is the totality of the produce of the Spirit through Christ's resurrection.

On the day of resurrection Christ was produced as the firstborn Son of God, the life-giving Spirit was produced, the many sons of God were produced, and the new creation was produced. However, the church was not yet produced. The church came into being on the day of Pentecost. This was the last item of all the produce of the resurrected Christ as the firstfruits offered to God. The totality, the aggregate, of these firstfruits is the outpoured Spirit.

e. The Feast of the Blowing of Trumpets

The first four feasts are for the New Testament believers. The Feast of the Blowing of Trumpets, however, signifies God's calling together of Israel, His scattered, dispersed elect (Lev. 23:23-25; Matt. 24:31). This feast is for the coming Jews. The day of this feast has not yet come. It will come in the future. When Christ comes back, the angels will trumpet a call to gather His scattered people.

f. The Feast of Propitiation

The Feast of Propitiation signifies God's propitiation for the repentant Israel (Lev. 23:26-32; Zech. 12:10—13:1). At the time Zechariah 12:10—13:1 is fulfilled, all the remnant of Israel will repent with weeping. A fountain of cleansing will be opened for them, and they will all be forgiven. That will be their Feast of Propitiation.

g. The Feast of Tabernacles

The Feast of Tabernacles signifies Israel's full enjoyment of the restored old creation in the millennium (Lev. 23:33-43; Zech. 14:16-21). This feast will usher in the new heavens and the new earth.

2. The Firstfruits of the Feast of the Firstfruits, after Being Offered to God for His Enjoyment, to Be Eaten by the People of Israel

The firstfruits of the Feast of the Firstfruits, after being offered to God for His enjoyment, were to be eaten by the people of Israel. This signifies that the resurrected Christ, after being presented to God in His freshness (John 20:16-17), is to be dispensed, with all the riches of His resurrection, into us for our enjoyment (Lev. 23:14; 1 Cor. 15:14, 17; Rom. 4:25b; Phil. 3:10a, 11b). According to the record of Leviticus 23, the offering of only one of the seven feasts, the Feast of the Firstfruits, was to be eaten. As we have seen, the firstfruits refer to Christ in His resurrection. The firstfruits were not to be eaten immediately after being reaped. This signifies that after the reaping we must first offer Christ to God in His freshness. This is unveiled in John 20. On the morning of the resurrection Mary saw the Lord Jesus. When she tried to touch Him, the Lord said, "Do not touch Me, for I have not yet ascended to the Father; but go to My brothers and say to them, I ascend to My Father and your Father, and My God and your God" (v. 17). Christ became our portion only after His freshness in resurrection had first been offered to the Father.

Whatever Christ is as our portion to be eaten is related to His resurrection. The blood of the Passover lamb signifies the crucified Christ, but the meat of the lamb signifies the resurrected Christ. The blood was from the crucified Christ, but the meat refers to the Christ who is in resurrection. If Christ were not the Spirit in resurrection, we could not take Him in. The crucified Christ alone is not our life supply; only Christ in resurrection can be our life supply. The unleavened bread of the Passover was made of grain that had been ground and blended to be one loaf, signifying death and resurrection. Therefore, both the meat of the lamb and the unleavened bread signify Christ as the Spirit in His resurrection. It is Christ in His resurrection who dispenses Himself into us as many items. This is why the offering of only one of the seven feasts, the Feast of the Firstfruits, was to be eaten.

According to the type of the feasts, what we enjoy and what is being dispensed into us is the resurrected Christ. The resurrected Christ is the consummated Triune God. In eternity past God was not yet consummated, but after He passed through the processes of incarnation, crucifixion, and resurrection, the Triune God was consummated. Now He possesses the divine nature and a human nature with incarnation, crucifixion, and resurrection. Now He is the processed, consummated, and compound God. It is such a One who is good for us to eat and who, in His resurrection and consummation, dispenses Himself into us.

The Central Line of the Divine Revelation

THE DIVINE ECONOMY
AND THE DIVINE DISPENSING

MESSAGE TWENTY-ONE

IN THE ACCOMPLISHMENT OF
GOD'S FULL REDEMPTION AND SALVATION
IN CHRIST

(1)

Scripture Reading: John 1:14; Luke 1:35; Matt. 1:20; John 1:17, 16; 12:24; 1 Pet. 1:3; 1 Cor. 15:45b

In this message we will consider the divine economy and the divine dispensing in the initiation of the New Testament. In the New Testament the first two things that carry out God's dispensing are the incarnation and resurrection of Christ. Our God went through a process; the beginning of this process was incarnation, and the end of this process was resurrection. Both the beginning and the end of God's process depend on God's dispensing. Between the incarnation and resurrection are the steps of Christ's human living and Christ's all-inclusive death. It is very difficult to find any indication that God's dispensing was involved in either of these two steps.

Christ's incarnation was a great step for God to dispense Himself into humanity. The crucial point concerning the Lord's birth is the matter of dispensing, but this thought is missed by most Christians today. Most Christians are veiled from seeing this matter because of all the outward things in the celebration of Christmas. As those who are living in the environment of Christianity, we must drop all our former knowledge derived from the celebration of Christmas, because that knowledge has become a thick veil preventing us from seeing the mystery in the Lord's incarnation. In a similar way, most Christians are veiled concerning the mystery in the Lord's resurrection. The Lord's incarnation and resurrection are the two basic steps of God's dispensing of Himself into His chosen people.

As I pointed out in earlier messages, the matter of the divine dispensing can be seen in the promises, prophecies, and types in the Old Testament, but the fact and the fulfillment of the dispensing did not take place in the Old Testament. In the first four thousand years of man's six-thousand-year history, strictly speaking, there was no dispensing. During this period of time, God always kept Himself separate from man. At most, He only came to man or upon man. Thus, it is very difficult to find a verse in the Old Testament that says that Jehovah God was in man or entered into man.

In the New Testament, especially in the Epistles, many verses use the preposition *in* to form phrases such as *in Christ* (2 Cor. 5:17), *in Him* (Eph. 1:4, 10; 3:12), *in the Lord Jesus Christ* (2 Thes. 3:12), *in Christ Jesus* (Rom. 6:23b; 8:2; 1 Cor. 1:30), *in God* (1 Thes. 1:1), and *in the Spirit* (Col. 1:8). In the Old Testament age God purposely did not join Himself with man; God was God and man was man. But today we cannot say that God and man are separate, because we have been regenerated of God. Therefore, it is impossible for us to be separated from God. Even if we go downward in our Christian life, He goes with us. In Luke 24, after the Lord's resurrection, the Lord took a journey with two of His disciples as they were going away from Jerusalem to Emmaus (vv. 13-35). They were going downward, yet the Lord went with them and walked with them. The two disciples talked about the Lord and even rebuked the Lord (v. 18), but the Lord pretended not to know anything. Their eyes were kept from recognizing Him (v. 16). Eventually, however, He opened their eyes and they recognized Him (v. 31). As soon as they recognized Him, He disappeared from them. This shows that we can never be separated from the Lord.

Today the age of grace is the age of God's dispensing. He

is dispensing to such an extent that He and we, we and He, are mingled as one (John 17:21; 1 Cor. 6:17). Jesus was the first One to be mingled with God, the first God-man. Before Him, God was God and man was man. But beginning with Him, God and man became one. In the whole universe, a little man named Jesus is both God and man. He is man and God. God and man are not only united but mingled. This mingling depends altogether on dispensing. As a God-man, Jesus is a compound person, a person compounded with God and man.

Before His death Jesus was a person compounded with God and man, with divinity and humanity. But after He went through death and resurrection, He picked up the elements of death and resurrection. These elements were compounded into Him. Today He is not merely God and man; He also comprises death and resurrection. He is a God-man with death and resurrection. He is such a compound. This compound is the issue of God's dispensing. If dispensing were subtracted from incarnation, there would be no incarnation. Likewise, if dispensing were subtracted from the resurrection, there would be no resurrection.

I. IN THE INCARNATION OF CHRIST

Incarnation is the top, universal conception. Matthew 1:20 says, "But while he pondered these things, behold, an angel of the Lord appeared to him in a dream, saying, Joseph, son of David, do not be afraid to take Mary your wife, for that which has been begotten in her is of the Holy Spirit." Joseph and Mary had not come together as man and wife, yet Mary was pregnant. This caused Joseph to doubt concerning their marriage. At this juncture an angel of the Lord appeared to him in a dream and told him not to be afraid to take Mary as his wife, because "that which has been begotten [born] in her is of the Holy Spirit." The One who was born in the womb of Mary was not man but the very God. At the beginning of Mary's conception, God was born into Mary. At the end of that conception, nine months later, God came out with humanity. This is Jesus, the God-man. Before this conception, Mary did not have God in her. But at the conception God came into her by dispensing Himself into her.

A. The Incarnation of Christ Being through the Conception by the Holy Spirit in a Human Virgin, Dispensing the Holy Nature of God into Humanity

The first step in the accomplishment of God's full redemption and salvation in Christ was the incarnation of Christ. The incarnation of Christ was through the conception by the Holy Spirit in a human virgin, dispensing the holy nature of God into humanity (Luke 1:35).

1. What Was Born of This Conception Being a Holy Thing Bearing the Holy Nature of Divinity

From the first day of Mary's conception, God was dispensed into humanity. God was in Mary's womb for nine months. God's divinity and Mary's humanity came together and were mingled together for nine months. During those nine months, the divine dispensing increased. This increase of the dispensing of divinity into humanity caused the growth of that conception. Thus, the entire process of Mary's conception was a process of the divine dispensing into humanity. When this divine dispensing was "ripe," when nine months were consummated, a child came out. That child was the mingling, the blending, of the divine dispensing into humanity. His name was called Emmanuel—God with us (Matt. 1:23). He was a little child, yet He was God with man. On the one hand, He was the complete God, and on the other hand, He was a perfect man. He was the complete God mingled with a perfect man. In human history, there had never been such a One. He is wonderful! He was a child who possessed skin and bones and blood and flesh. He was a real man. Yet within Him was the complete Triune God (Col. 1:19; 2:9). He was not merely the Son of God, but the Triune

God—the Father, the Son, and the Spirit (Isa. 9:6; Luke 1:35; Matt. 1:20).

As such a One, He eventually became *the* Christ. Acts 2:34-36 indicates that in Christ's ascension, He was made both Lord and Christ. At the time of His birth He was called Christ (Matt. 1:16-18); but thirty-three and a half years later, when He ascended to the heavens, He was made Christ. Through resurrection Christ was consummated to be the perfect, complete Christ, the One who is the mingling of divinity with humanity.

Today there are thousands of "Christs." These Christs are called Christians. The word *Christian* means "a person who belongs to Christ." As Christians, we belong to Christ and are His counterpart. As those who belong to Christ, we are Christ (1 Cor. 12:12). He is the mingling of divinity with humanity, and we are too. We are exactly the same as He is in life and nature. We are copies of Christ, and these copies are the mingling of the Trinity with humanity. He is the model, the mold, and we are His mass production. The second and fourth stanzas of *Hymns,* #203 express the thought that we are Christ's duplication and reproduction:

By Thy death and resurrection,
　Thou wast made God's firstborn Son;
By Thy life to us imparting,
　Was Thy duplication done.
We, in Thee regenerated,
　Many sons to God became;
Truly as Thy many brethren,
　We are as Thyself the same.

We're Thy total reproduction,
　Thy dear Body and Thy Bride,
Thine expression and Thy fulness,
　For Thee ever to abide.
We are Thy continuation,
　Thy life-increase and Thy spread,
Thy full growth and Thy rich surplus,
　One with Thee, our glorious Head.

With the Lord Jesus, the mingling of divinity with humanity began at the time of His incarnation, but with us as His mass production, this mingling began at the time of His resurrection. In resurrection we all were mingled with God and began to have a life of mingling. This was the beginning of the mingling in reality. But this mingling began in a practical way when we were regenerated. At that time God was born into us. Because God has been born into us, we are wonderful people! Every proper Christian is a wonderful person. We are not wonderful in material possessions, but we are wonderful in God. Regardless of who we are, as long as we are a proper Christian, we are a wonderful person. Our being wonderful is in the fact that we are being mingled with the Divine Trinity by His divine dispensing.

The mingling by the divine dispensing at the time of the Lord's incarnation was consummated in nine months. But the Christian life may cover a period of many years; therefore, the divine dispensing in our Christian life continues within us every day, from morning until evening. From the time of our regeneration we have been enjoying the divine dispensing. From that time onward the whole course of our Christian life is a period of God's dispensing. This divine dispensing mingles God with us. If we need sanctification, we need this mingling. If we need victory, we need this mingling. If we need transformation, we need this mingling. Regeneration, renewing, sanctification, transformation, conformation, and glorification are all the issue of the divine dispensing.

Although we have been regenerated, in another sense we have not yet been born. Revelation 12:1-5 reveals that a woman, who signifies the totality of God's people on earth, brings forth a man-child. This man-child is a symbol of the corporate overcomers (Rev. 2:26-27). These overcomers today have been conceived within the woman, but they have not yet been born. Regeneration was the beginning of their conception, but the consummation of this conception will be their birth as the corporate overcomers, the man-child. Today they are still in the process of conception, because there is still the need of more dispensing. We all need much more dispensing.

With more dispensing, we will be matured. Maturity will be the real birth, and this birth will be the result of the divine dispensing.

2. This Holy Thing Being Called the Son of God, Who Was Born of God, Possessing God's Life and Nature through the Dispensing of the Holy Spirit

Luke 1:35 says, "And the angel answered and said to her, The Holy Spirit will come upon you, and the power of the Most High will overshadow you; therefore also the holy thing which is born will be called the Son of God." The holy thing born of Mary was called the Son of God. The holy thing mentioned in this verse is God Himself, that is, Christ as the embodiment of God. He was born of God, possessing God's life and nature through the dispensing of the Holy Spirit. Although Christ was born of Mary (Matt. 1:16), He was a child of the Holy Spirit. The birth of Christ was directly of the Holy Spirit (v. 20). His source was the Holy Spirit, and His element was divine.

B. What Was Conceived in That Virgin Being God Begotten in Her of the Holy Spirit

1. First, God Being Begotten into Mary in Her Conception through the Dispensing of His Nature by His Spirit

Some have the thought that conception cannot be considered a birth. But Matthew 1:20 clearly says that what was begotten in Mary was of the Holy Spirit. From the first day of Mary's conception, God was born in her. God was begotten into Mary by the dispensing of His nature by His Spirit.

2. After the Conception Was Completed, God with the Human Nature Being Born to Be a God-man

First, God was born into Mary through His Spirit; then after the conception was completed, He, with the human nature, was born to be a God-man, possessing both divinity and humanity. This God-man is Jesus, our model.

C. Christ Coming through Incarnation

1. With God as Reality and Grace for His Dispensing into His Believers

Christ came through incarnation with God as reality and grace for His dispensing into His believers. John 1:14 says, "And the Word became flesh and tabernacled among us..., full of grace and reality," and verse 17 says, "For the law was given through Moses; grace and reality came through Jesus Christ." The law could not come, because it had no life; hence, it was given. But because He is a living person, Jesus was not given; He came down to man, and He came with something. Christ came through incarnation with God as reality and as grace.

Reality is God gained by us, and grace is God enjoyed by us. We gain God and we enjoy God. God as grace is God enjoyed by us, and God as reality is God gained by us. By gaining God and enjoying Him, we eventually enjoy all His fullness.

2. Of His Fullness His Believers Having All Received, and Grace upon Grace

Of His fullness His believers have all received, and grace upon grace (John 1:16). Today, the grace upon grace that we are enjoying is a matter of dispensing. We are enjoying and He is dispensing. He is dispensing for our enjoyment. Our enjoyment today is altogether a matter of the dispensing of the Triune God into us.

This dispensing of the Triune God into us can take place only by the Holy Spirit in our spirit. This is the reason that we must remain in our spirit. When we get out of our spirit, we must return quickly and remain there. In our spirit we enjoy the dispensing, and from the dispensing we receive the fullness, all the riches of what the Triune God is.

II. IN THE RESURRECTION OF CHRIST

In incarnation the divine dispensing was mainly for Christ, the Head, but in resurrection the divine dispensing is mainly for us, the Body. The Head and the Body are two marvelous entities in the universe. The dispensing in incarnation for the Head has been completed, but the dispensing in resurrection for the Body is still going on today.

A. Christ as the Grain of Wheat Producing, in His Resurrection, Many Grains for the Dispensing of His Divine Life into His Many Believers That They May Be His Many Members

In His resurrection Christ as the grain of wheat produced many grains for the dispensing of His divine life into His many believers that they may be His many members (John 12:24). Christ was the one grain of wheat. He fell into the earth and died, and then He grew up. By His growing up, a kind of dispensing took place in which the many grains were produced to be the many members of His Body. In the past we realized that the many grains were the fruit of Christ as the one grain of wheat. But we did not realize that the producing of the many grains was altogether a matter of dispensing. Without the dispensing of the divine life, the many grains could not have been produced. We as the many grains are the issue of Christ's dispensing of His divine life into us.

B. God the Father Regenerating Us, the Believers, through Christ's Resurrection for the Dispensing of His Divine Life into Us That We May Be His Many Sons

God the Father regenerated us, the believers, through Christ's resurrection for the dispensing of His divine life into us that we may be His many sons (1 Pet. 1:3). The resurrection of Christ was a dispensing. As the many grains, we were produced to be Christ's many members. As the many believers, we were born to be God's many sons. The producing of the many grains and the regenerating of the many sons was carried out by the same procedure of the divine dispensing.

C. Christ as the Last Adam Becoming, in His Resurrection, the Life-giving Spirit for the Dispensing of the Divine Life to Germinate the New Testament Believers

In His resurrection Christ as the last Adam became the life-giving Spirit for the dispensing of the divine life to germinate the New Testament believers that they may become God's new creation (1 Cor. 15:45b). In Christ's resurrection we sinners have all been made three things: the many grains, the many sons, and the new creation (2 Cor. 5:17). The many grains are the many sons, and the many sons are the new creation. These three things are all due to the dispensing of the divine life and nature into us. By this dispensing we become the members of Christ's Body, the many sons in God's household, and the new creation. In the past, we did see that we are the many members of Christ's Body, the many sons of God's household, and the new creation; but we did not see so clearly that the crucial point concerning these three things is the dispensing of divinity into humanity. Today this dispensing is still going on.

The Central Line of the Divine Revelation

THE DIVINE ECONOMY
AND THE DIVINE DISPENSING

MESSAGE TWENTY-TWO

IN THE ACCOMPLISHMENT OF
GOD'S FULL REDEMPTION AND SALVATION
IN CHRIST

(2)

Scripture Reading: John 20:22; Acts 2:17, 33; 10:45; Titus 3:6;
Acts 2:4; 1:5; 13:52b; 1 Pet. 1:3; John 17:2b; 3:5, 6b; 1:12-13;
Rom. 6:19, 22; 2 Pet. 1:4; 1 Thes. 5:23

In the Old Testament we can see God's dispensing according to His divine economy in the promises and types of God's anticipated redemption and salvation. In the New Testament the divine economy and the divine dispensing are revealed in the accomplishment of God's full redemption and salvation. First, this accomplishment was in Christ's incarnation, and second, it was in Christ's resurrection. We passed over Christ's death because nothing was dispensed in the death of Christ. After Christ's resurrection, the accomplishment of God's full redemption and salvation continued in the breathing of the essential Spirit into the believers and then in the outpouring of the economical Spirit upon the believers.

Many Christians celebrate the outpouring of the economical Spirit that occurred on the day of Pentecost. However, they do not consider the breathing of the essential Spirit into the disciples in John 20 as important as the outpouring of the economical Spirit. The resurrection of Christ, the breathing of the essential Spirit, and the outpouring of the economical Spirit may be compared to the birth of a child. After a child is delivered, he first begins to breathe, and then he is bathed.

The birth of the believers took place at the time of Christ's resurrection (1 Pet. 1:3). After this birth, the disciples began to breathe the Holy Spirit in John 20:22. Then, the Lord Jesus as the Head of the Body "bathed" the Body through the baptism of the Holy Spirit on the day of Pentecost.

THE BIOGRAPHY OF THE DIVINE TRINITY

The Gospel of John may be considered the biography of the Divine Trinity. The Triune God had and still has a biography. The four Gospels are considered by many Christians to be four biographies of the one Savior, the Lord Jesus. The sequence of the arrangement of these four Gospels is very meaningful. Matthew, Mark, and Luke, the synoptic Gospels, mainly concern Christ in His humanity. Christ in His humanity is revealed first as the King-Savior in Matthew, then as the Slave-Savior in Mark, and then as the Man-Savior in Luke. However, what is revealed in the fourth Gospel, the Gospel of John, is Christ's divinity. The Gospel of John, as a biography of our Triune God in His humanity, reveals Christ as the God-man, a person with the divine nature and the human nature. Whereas Matthew and Luke contain a genealogy of the Lord Jesus (Matt. 1:1-17; Luke 3:23-38), John has no genealogy. Rather, John 1:1 says, "In the beginning was the Word, and the Word was with God, and the Word was God." The Word had no beginning in time; therefore, He has no genealogy.

For four thousand years of human history, from the creation of Adam, God was only in His divinity. During that time no one knew the real meaning of the universe and of the human life. God contacted man, and the Spirit of Jehovah even came upon man (Num. 11:25; Judg. 3:10; 6:34; 1 Sam. 16:13), but God was God and man was man. Then one day, almost two thousand years ago, the Word came out of eternity and entered into time. As the threefold seed—the seed of the woman, the seed of Abraham, and the seed of David—He came into mankind. The infinite and eternal Word became flesh (John 1:14). He was conceived in a human womb and was born of a virgin to be a wonderful man with blood and flesh. The Lord's incarnation, as His beginning in His humanity, was a landmark of His biography in His humanity. In His incarnation, the Divine Trinity was imparted into man's being. That was the divine dispensing.

When this wonderful and unique man named Jesus came in His incarnation, He did not come empty-handed. Rather, John 1:14 says, "And the Word became flesh and tabernacled among us (and we beheld His glory, glory as of the only Begotten from the Father), full of grace and reality." His entire being was not full of commandments, ordinances, and regulations but was full of grace and reality.

Few people know what grace and reality are. Many believe that grace is merely unmerited favor. They may even think that having a new home or a new car is God's grace. However, Paul said that he counted such things as refuse (Phil. 3:8). Grace in its highest definition is God in the Son to be enjoyed by us (*Hymns,* #497). Reality is God in His Son to be gained by us. The wise king Solomon said that all things are vanity (Eccl. 1:2); but God in the Son gained by us is reality. Christ came filled in His being as God in the Son to be given to us for our enjoyment and to be gained by us as our reality. When people ask us what we have, we may say, "We do not have material riches. Rather, we have God as our grace, our enjoyment, and as our reality, our gain." Christ did not come with a small amount of grace and reality; on the contrary, He was full of grace and reality. John 1:16 says, "For of His fullness we have all received, and grace upon grace." The Gospel of John as the biography of the Triune God in His humanity begins in this way.

John 1:12-13 says, "But as many as received Him, to them He gave the authority to become children of God, to those who believe into His name, who were begotten not of blood, nor of the will of the flesh, nor of the will of man, but of God." To be born of God to be His children is the dispensing of the Divine Trinity into us that we may enjoy Him as grace and gain Him as reality to such an extent that He becomes our life, our nature, our element, our essence, and our very being. Such a dispensing qualifies us to be His children.

In John 3, Nicodemus, a ruler of the Jews, came to Jesus in

the night to receive some teaching from Him. Jesus said, "Truly, truly, I say to you, Unless one is born anew, he cannot see the kingdom of God" (v. 3). Nicodemus misunderstood the Lord and responded, "How can a man be born when he is old? He cannot enter a second time into his mother's womb and be born, can he?" (v. 4). The Lord Jesus answered, "Truly, truly, I say to you, Unless one is born of water and the Spirit, he cannot enter into the kingdom of God" (v. 5). The Lord told Nicodemus that he needed to be buried through water and have a new birth through the Holy Spirit; then he would be regenerated. As a result, in Nicodemus as well as in many others, the Lord would have His increase, His bride, His counterpart (vv. 29-30). Although the word *dispensing* is not found in the Bible, without dispensing there can be no increase of Christ. The increase comes from the divine dispensing. Every point in the Gospel of John is a matter of the divine dispensing.

In John 3 a moral man came to the Lord Jesus, but in chapter four the Lord went to contact an immoral woman (vv. 3-4). The Lord told her that He had the living water (vv. 10, 14). She said, "Sir, give me this water so that I will not thirst nor come here to draw" (v. 15). He told her, "Go, call your husband and come here" (v. 16). The woman answered, "I do not have a husband," and Jesus said to her, "You have well said, I do not have a husband, for you have had five husbands, and the one you now have is not your husband; this you have said truly" (vv. 17-18). In this way the Lord wisely touched her conscience, and she realized that He knew all her sinful history. Eventually, the Lord Jesus led her to receive the living water by drinking of Him. He told her, "But an hour is coming, and it is now, when the true worshippers will worship the Father in spirit and truthfulness, for the Father also seeks such to worship Him" (v. 23). To receive the Lord Jesus as the living water is to worship God the Father. The real worship of God is not to kneel before Him; it is to receive His dispensing. What pleases God the most is our allowing Him to dispense Himself into our being. To open ourselves and embrace and receive His dispensing is the best worship we can render to our God. God is waiting today to dispense Himself into us, the thirsty ones, as the living water. When we drink and receive His dispensing, God is very happy. This is a pleasure to Him.

John 5 tells us that whether or not we are in the tomb, we all are dead persons; but the Lord comes to us that we may have life. Moreover, His life is transmitted into us by His word. If we receive His word and believe the One who sent Him, we receive Him as life, which transfers us out of death into eternal life (v. 24). Again, this is the transmission, the impartation, the dispensing, of the Triune God as life in the Son into us.

In John 6 the Lord said that He is the bread of life (vv. 35, 48), the bread from heaven, and the living bread (v. 51). If we are thirsty, we must drink of Him, and if we are hungry, we must eat of Him. Those who heard the Lord's word in John 6 did not understand Him (v. 60). Therefore, He said, "It is the Spirit who gives life; the flesh profits nothing; the words which I have spoken to you are spirit and are life" (v. 63). When we hear the Lord's speaking, we spontaneously receive the dispensing of Christ as God into us. After we sit in a meeting that is full of the Lord's speaking, we are filled with this dispensing.

John 7:37-39 says, "Now on the last day, the great day of the feast, Jesus stood and cried out, saying, If anyone thirsts, let him come to Me and drink. He who believes into Me, as the Scripture said, out of his innermost being shall flow rivers of living water. But this He said concerning the Spirit, whom those who believed into Him were about to receive; for the Spirit was not yet, because Jesus had not yet been glorified." The drinking of the living water is God's dispensing.

In John 8:12 Jesus said, "I am the light of the world; he who follows Me shall by no means walk in darkness, but shall have the light of life." Light is for dispensing. Trees that receive adequate sunshine grow and blossom well, but a tree planted in the shade may not grow well because it does not receive the dispensing of the sunshine.

In John 9 a blind man came to the Lord Jesus. The Lord spat on the ground and made clay of the spittle and anointed the eyes of the blind man with the clay (v. 6). The blind man received his sight (v. 7), and through his sight he received light. This was a receiving of the divine dispensing.

In John 10:1-9 the Lord Jesus said that He is the door of the sheepfold. On the positive side, the sheepfold keeps the sheep. It covers them in the winter and protects them at night, and it guards them from wolves. However, the sheepfold also keeps the sheep in a negative way from enjoying the pasture. Christ came to open the fold and call the sheep to follow Him out of the fold to receive sunshine and fresh air and to drink the fresh water and eat the green grass in the pasture. Christ is the real sunshine, air, water, and green grass. He is the pasture. This again is the dispensing of the Divine Trinity into His chosen people.

In John 11 Jesus raised Lazarus from the dead. To be resurrected from the dead is to receive the divine dispensing. In John 12:24 Jesus said, "Truly, truly, I say to you, Unless the grain of wheat falls into the ground and dies, it abides alone; but if it dies, it bears much fruit." If the Lord had not fallen into the earth and died, He would have been one grain alone. By falling into the earth and dying, He sprouted in His resurrection, and the one grain became many grains. This is the dispensing of the life within the one grain into many grains.

We can never exhaust the significance of John 14—16. The first part of chapter fourteen tells us that Christ is the embodiment of God the Father to express Him (vv. 7-11). Verses 16-20 tell us that the Spirit is the reality of Christ to make Him real to us, and that all those who believe in Him will receive the Spirit. When we receive the Spirit, we have the Son, and when we have the Son, we have the Father. In this way we have the Divine Trinity within us dispensing Himself to us continually.

In chapter fifteen there is a vine tree with many branches. Every day and every moment the vine tree dispenses its rich life juice into the branches. In chapter sixteen the Lord likened His coming resurrection to the birth of a child (vv. 16-24). Resurrection is a real dispensing of the Divine Trinity into God's chosen people.

In John 17 Jesus prayed to the Father, saying, "That they all may be one; even as You, Father, are in Me and I in You, that they also may be in Us; that the world may believe that You have sent Me" (v. 21). The oneness for which the Lord prayed here is a coinherence, that is, a mutual dwelling of the Father, the Son, the Spirit, and the believers in one another. The Father is in the Son, the Son is in the Father, and all the believers are in the Father and the Son. In this way the believers share the oneness of the Divine Trinity. This kind of sharing indicates the dispensing of the Divine Trinity. He is dispensing, and we receive and enjoy the oneness that is in and among the Divine Trinity. Now, in addition to the Father, the Son, and the Holy Spirit, we become the fourth party in this oneness. Whether or not we can explain this, it is a fact that the oneness revealed in John 17 is a oneness of four parties. To include the fourth party in this oneness was not easy. The Lord accomplished many things to get into us and bring us into the Triune God, to make us one with the Triune God. This is all due to the divine dispensing.

In John 18 the Lord was arrested, and in John 19 He was crucified. Through His crucifixion, blood and water came out of His side (19:34). The blood is for redemption, and the water is for the imparting of life. This imparting of life is the divine dispensing.

III. IN THE BREATHING OF THE ESSENTIAL SPIRIT INTO THE BELIEVERS

In John 20 the Lord resurrected. After the Lord was crucified, the disciples were frightened and sorrowful. They might not have been able to sleep well, but the Lord rested well in the tomb, and on the day of resurrection He came out of the tomb. When Mary went to the tomb, she saw that the stone had been taken away (v. 1). She then told Peter and John, and when they came and saw the empty tomb and the grave clothes lying in order, they believed that the Lord had resurrected (vv. 2-8). The two then returned to their home, but Mary lingered at the tomb and wept for the Lord (vv. 10-11). At that time Jesus appeared to her and said to

her, "Do not touch Me, for I have not yet ascended to the
Father; but go to My brothers and say to them, I ascend to
My Father and your Father, and My God and your God"
(v. 17). The Lord wanted to present the freshness of His
resurrection to the Father.

In His word to Mary the Lord Jesus referred to the disciples as His brothers, and He referred to God as His Father
and their Father, and His God and their God. It was at that
time that the disciples became the brothers of the firstborn
Son of God. On that morning Jesus, who had been the only
begotten Son of God, became the firstborn Son of God with
many brothers. Mary announced this to the disciples, but
they were not comforted and still shut the doors to the room
where they were for fear of the Jews. All of a sudden Jesus
stood in the midst and said to them, "Peace be to you"
(vv. 18-19). He showed them His hands and side, and they
rejoiced when they saw the Lord (v. 20). Then He breathed
into them and said to them, "Receive the Holy Spirit" (v. 22).

The breathing of the Lord into His disciples was greater
than His incarnation and His resurrection. It was the practical impartation of the resurrected Christ, the pneumatic
Christ as the life-giving Spirit, into His believers. It was also
the breathing of the Holy Spirit as the consummated, processed Triune God into His chosen people. The goal of all the
events in the Gospel of John was the consummation of the
Triune God. In eternity past the Triune God was not consummated. He was only divine, not human; He had only divinity
without humanity. The element of the wonderful all-inclusive death of Christ was not yet in Him, and although He
was resurrection (11:25), He had never had the experience of
resurrection. After going through the processes of incarnation, human living, crucifixion, and resurrection, the Triune
God was consummated as the complete God with divinity,
humanity, human living, the all-inclusive death and its effectiveness, and resurrection with its power. Today our God is
not only divine but also human. In His humanity He passed
through incarnation and human living, He entered into
death and passed through that death, and He then entered

into resurrection and remained in that resurrection. Now He has everything: divinity, humanity, human living, the all-inclusive death, and the powerful, excellent resurrection.

Such a processed and consummated God became the best "dose" in the universe. When we take this dose, His element is dispensed into us, and the "antibiotics" in this dose kill all the "germs" within us. He is everything. He is God, He is man, He is death, He is resurrection, and He is life. He is such a dose to us, the sick ones. When the Lord Jesus came to the disciples on that night, He brought such a consummated dose for them to breathe in. When we receive the processed and consummated Triune God as our dose, we are healed, supplied, and supported by the dispensing of Himself into our being. This is the breathing of the essential Spirit into the believers.

Our heavenly, divine, and spiritual birth took place at Christ's resurrection (1 Pet. 1:3), and we began to breathe when Christ breathed Himself as the life-giving Spirit into His disciples. This is true even though we were not present physically at the time that these things took place. When a doctor gives us an injection in the arm, the injection is for our entire body. We do not need to receive the injection in every part of our body, because after a few minutes the injection we received in our arm spreads to the rest of our body. When Christ breathed the Holy Spirit into the disciples, this breathing was an injection of the Holy Spirit into His entire Body, of which we are members. Just as there is no element of time with God, there is also no element of separation with the members of the Body. What God does is for every part of the Body. We were born again in Christ's resurrection, and we began to breathe at His breathing of the consummated Triune God into His believers. This is the divine dispensing.

Our God's eternal intention is to transmit, infuse, impart, dispense, and work Himself into us. Before His incarnation, God did not dispense Himself into man, but from the time of His incarnation, human living, all-inclusive death, and resurrection until today, His dispensing has been taking place. His breathing never stops. This is for His continuous, unceasing dispensing within us that we may be one with our Triune God. Ephesians 4:4-6 says that we—the one Body—and the one Spirit, the one Lord, and the one God and Father are mingled together. There is such a mingling in this universe, and this mingling is the church. The church is the dispensing of the Triune God into the called and chosen people to make them one with God.

IV. IN THE OUTPOURING OF THE ECONOMICAL SPIRIT UPON THE BELIEVERS

The accomplishment of God's full redemption and salvation in Christ was also in the outpouring of the economical Spirit upon the believers (Acts 2:17, 33; 10:45; Titus 3:5-6). After the delivery of the believers in the Lord's resurrection, there was a need to bathe the believers as a newborn child. Hence, on the day of Pentecost the believers were baptized in the Spirit.

The outpouring of the economical Spirit is the outward filling of the Spirit of power and the baptism in the Holy Spirit (Acts 2:4; 1:5). The outpouring of the economical Spirit goes with the inward filling of the essential Spirit, and the infilling of the essential Spirit is the dispensing of the processed Triune God as life into the believers (Acts 13:52b). The baptism in the Spirit was not a direct dispensing into the believers, but the baptism in the Holy Spirit, the outward filling of the Spirit, always goes together with the inward filling. The outward filling of the Spirit may be compared to bathing in water, while the inward filling of the Spirit may be compared to drinking water. According to the natural laws of God's creation, if we take a bath every day and drink some water after our bath, we will be very healthy. The water for drinking follows the water for bathing. One water is within for the inward filling, and the other water is without for the outward filling.

V. IN THE REGENERATION OF THE BELIEVERS

The accomplishment of God's full redemption and salvation in Christ is also in the regeneration of the believers

(1 Pet. 1:3). The regeneration of the believers is the reality, the fact, of the impartation of the resurrected Christ into His believers, whom God the Father has given to Him (John 17:2b). It is also the dispensing of the Spirit, the divine life, and the processed Triune God into the believers (John 3:5, 6b; 1:12-13).

We were born again in Christ's resurrection, but before a certain time this was not yet our experience. As we have seen, Christ's resurrection was a great delivery. In resurrection Christ was delivered to be the firstborn Son of God. He took the lead, and we all followed Him to be delivered also. That was the accomplishing of the reality, the fact, that God brought forth many children through Christ's resurrection. However, we still need the practical, personal experience of regeneration.

Our need for a personal experience of regeneration can be illustrated by the exodus of the children of Israel out of Egypt. The exodus of the children of Israel was a corporate matter, but each Israelite needed to experience the exodus personally. The experience of walking out of Egypt was the personal exodus of each Israelite. The fact was corporate, but the experience was personal. We were born in Christ's resurrection, but at that time we were not yet born physically. After our physical birth, God set a time for us to experience what He accomplished. What He accomplished was a reality, a fact; what we experience is the practicality of the fact.

Both the corporate and the personal experience of regeneration are for God's dispensing. When we were regenerated, we experienced the dispensing. We might not have understood all the doctrines concerning regeneration, but at the time of our regeneration something very strong came into us to revolutionize our entire human life. That was the divine dispensing in our regeneration.

VI. IN THE SUBJECTIVE SANCTIFICATION
OF THE SAINTS

The accomplishment of God's full redemption and salvation in Christ progresses in the subjective sanctification of the saints (Rom. 6:19, 22). After our regeneration, we need to be sanctified subjectively. Subjective sanctification is the dispensing of the holy nature of God into the saints, separating the saints unto God by the saturation of God's holy nature into the saints' being (2 Pet. 1:4; 1 Thes. 5:23).

When we were regenerated, a great change occurred in our life. However, at that time we were still common and worldly, both within and without. The applying of the blood of Christ to separate us from the world (Heb. 13:12) is an outward, positional matter, not a dispositional matter. We still need a dispositional sanctification by the inner life, by the indwelling Spirit, by the very God who is within our spirit. Every day the divine life as the Holy Spirit, who is God Himself, is operating, moving, working, saturating, and anointing us little by little. Today we may be much holier than we were when we were regenerated. After we were regenerated, we might have enjoyed certain worldly entertainments, but today we would not do those things. When we do those things, we do not feel right in our spirit. Because we are being sanctified subjectively, we prefer to meet with the saints to enjoy and praise the Lord.

We need sanctification to follow our regeneration. Regeneration is a beginning, a renewing, but sanctification is a continuation, a constant renewing day by day. By such a sanctification we will not be fashioned according to this age but will be transformed by the renewing of our mind (Rom. 12:2).

Both regeneration and sanctification are a dispensing of God into us. God's intention is to work Himself into our being. He does this little by little, saturating us vertically and permeating us horizontally in every part of our being until our body is redeemed (Rom. 8:23). The redemption of our body is the transfiguration of our body (Phil. 3:21). This is to have our entire being saturated and permeated with the glorious element of the divine God. When we are saturated to this degree, we will be glorified. All this is the dispensing of the Divine Trinity, from regeneration to glorification. This is the accomplishment and experience of God's full redemption and salvation in Christ.

The Central Line of the Divine Revelation

THE DIVINE ECONOMY
AND THE DIVINE DISPENSING

MESSAGE TWENTY-THREE

IN THE ACCOMPLISHMENT OF
GOD'S FULL REDEMPTION AND SALVATION
IN CHRIST

(3)

Scripture Reading: Titus 3:5b; Rom. 12:2b; Eph. 4:23; Rom. 6:4; 7:6b; 2 Cor. 4:16; 5:17; Gal. 6:15; Rev. 21:2; 2 Cor. 3:18; Rom. 8:29-30; Phil. 3:21; Rom. 8:23; Eph. 1:14; 4:30; Heb. 2:10; 1 Pet. 5:10a

FIVE GREAT REVELATIONS IN THE NEW TESTAMENT

The New Testament contains some great revelations, mainly through the apostle Paul. These include the economy of God, Christ, the Spirit, the transformation of the believers, and the Body of Christ. God's dispensing is involved in each of these great revelations. Without knowing these five revelations, it is impossible to know the dispensing of the Triune God.

God's Economy

The first of the five great revelations in the New Testament is God's economy (1 Tim. 1:4; Eph. 1:10; 3:9). The Greek word *oikonomia,* translated *economy,* means "household administration" or "household economy." In the entire Bible, this word is used in reference to God's economy only by the apostle Paul. Even the Lord Jesus in the four Gospels did not use this word. The word *oikonomia* is great in significance because it refers to God's eternal purpose according to His heart's desire.

Some have said that the apostles' teaching, mentioned in Acts 2:42, includes only the teachings that the Lord Jesus gave to the twelve apostles while He was on this earth. However, in John 16 the Lord told His disciples clearly that He had many things to say to them, but they could not bear them at that time (v. 12). Then He told them to wait until the coming of the Comforter, the Spirit of reality, who would receive the things of the Lord Jesus and declare them to the disciples (vv. 13-15). According to my study of the Bible, the Lord's word here was fulfilled mainly with the apostle Paul. He was nearly the unique one who received the Lord's further revelation concerning the economy of God. In Paul's fourteen Epistles, the first great revelation concerns not God alone but God in His economy. God's economy, God's eternal plan, is revealed especially in the four books of Galatians, Ephesians, Philippians, and Colossians. In the ministry in recent years, we have paid particular attention to the matter of God's economy.

Christ in His All-inclusiveness

The second great revelation in the New Testament is Christ in His all-inclusiveness. The knowledge concerning Christ and the apprehension concerning Christ were released to a surpassing degree in the writings of Paul. The apostle Paul used the dimensions of the universe—the breadth, length, height, and depth—in order to show the dimensions of Christ (Eph. 3:18). The breadth, length, height, and depth are all Christ. No one except Christ knows how broad is the breadth, how long is the length, how high is the height, or how deep is the depth of the universe. Christ Himself is the breadth, the length, the height, and the depth of the entire universe. He is all-inclusive and all-extensive. Such a Christ first came down from the heavens to the earth; then He descended into Hades, the lower parts of the earth. After that, He ascended to the earth, and then He ascended far above all the heavens that He might fill all things (4:8-10).

The Spirit

The third great revelation in the New Testament is the Spirit. The Spirit is the reaching of the Triune God to us. Not only so; He is the consummation of the processed Triune God. The Triune God, after being processed through incarnation, human living, crucifixion, resurrection, and ascension, has become the Spirit. Eventually, the Bible ends with the divine title *the Spirit*. Revelation 22:17 says, "The Spirit and the bride say, Come!" The Spirit as the consummation of the Triune God and the bride as the consummation of the chosen, redeemed, regenerated, transformed, and glorified mankind become a universal couple. This couple is the New Jerusalem.

The revelation concerning the Spirit was shown mainly to the apostle Paul. John in his Gospel had some revelation concerning the Spirit, but his writing is only a record of what he saw; it is not his teaching. However, Paul's writing in his Epistles is his teaching.

The Transformation of the Believers

The fourth great revelation in the New Testament is the transformation of the believers. Regeneration, subjective sanctification, renewing, conformation, and glorification are also included in this revelation. As a young man I searched for a proper definition of regeneration, until one day when I read a sentence in one of T. Austin-Sparks's books saying that regeneration is to receive another life in addition to our natural life. When I read this sentence, I was very excited. This is a wonderful definition of regeneration. In addition to understanding regeneration, we also need to understand what sanctification, renewing, transformation, conformation, and glorification are. The Bible says that in glorification we will be exactly the same as Christ in every respect (1 John 3:2). This is a great revelation concerning the transformation of the believers.

The Body of Christ

The fifth great revelation in the New Testament is the

Body of Christ (Eph 1:22-23). The Body is not mentioned in the thirty-nine books of the Old Testament. The first mentioning of the Body in the New Testament is in Romans 12:5. According to Romans 12, we must present our physical bodies (v. 1) for the mystical Body of Christ (v. 5). When we present our bodies and are renewed in our mind, we see, discern, and prove by testing that the will of God is to obtain a Body for Christ to be His fullness and expression (v. 2).

God's economy and His dispensing are intimately involved with these five great revelations. If we desire to know the dispensing of the Triune God, we must know God in His economy, Christ in His all-inclusiveness, the Spirit as the consummation of the Triune God, the spiritual and divine transformation of the believers, and the Body of Christ.

RENEWING IN THE NEW TESTAMENT

In this message we will consider the main verses in the New Testament that deal with the matter of renewing.

The Newness of Life and the Newness of Spirit

Romans 6:4 says, "We have been buried therefore with Him through baptism into His death, in order that just as Christ was raised from the dead through the glory of the Father, so also we might walk in newness of life." Then, Romans 7:6 says, "But now we have been discharged from the law, having died to that in which we were held, so that we serve in newness of spirit and not in oldness of letter." The spirit here is our regenerated spirit, in which the Lord as the Spirit dwells (2 Tim. 4:22). The newness of life is for our daily walk, and the newness of spirit is for our service. We may know the term *the newness of life,* but we may know very little of the reality. In our gospel service, we need to preach the gospel in the newness of spirit, not in the oldness of a certain way or a certain formula.

The New Creation

In the New Testament the believers are a new creation. Second Corinthians 5:17 says, "So then if anyone is in Christ,

he is a new creation. The old things have passed away;
behold, they have become new." In the Bible the word *creation* refers to something created out of nothing. In Genesis 1
God did not need any material in order to create. God said,
"Let there be light: and there was light" (v. 3). He is the One
who calls the things not being as being (Rom. 4:17). The for-
mation of Adam, however, was different; it was not called a
creation. Genesis 2:7 says that "God *formed* man...." God
used the dust of the ground as the material to form the first
man, Adam.

God created His new creation without any physical material. The new creation was created by God with Christ as the
embodiment of the divine life. Hence, the material for
the new creation is the divine life. Anyone who is in Christ is
a new creation because God's life has entered into him.
Before our regeneration, we did not have the divine life, but
through regeneration, God imparted Himself into us and
became our life. Thus, we became the embodiment of Christ.
He has been born into us as our life. In this way we have
become a new creation.

Neither Circumcision nor Uncircumcision
but a New Creation

Galatians 6:15 says, "For neither is circumcision anything
nor uncircumcision, but a new creation is what matters."
The term *circumcision* refers to being religious, and *uncircumcision* refers to being unreligious. Neither of these means
anything as far as the new creation is concerned. Only the
new creation is what matters. God has no intention of
gaining a group of circumcised people or a group of uncir-
cumcised people. He desires to gain a group of regenerated
people as His new creation created by Him with His divine
life embodied in Christ.

We were a part of the old creation, but through regeneration we have become a new creation. Although we are a new
creation, we are still old in our mind, emotion, and will. We
still love and hate in the old creation. Therefore, we need to
be renewed. Our entire being, including our physical body,

needs to be renewed. The redemption of our body (1 Cor. 1:30; Rom. 8:23) is the renewing of every part of our body. This will be the consummation of the renewing of our entire being.

We are tripartite men composed of spirit, soul, and body (1 Thes. 5:23). At the time of our regeneration, God entered into our spirit, and immediately our spirit was renewed. Now our soul also needs to be renewed in every part. Titus 3:5 says, "Not out of works in righteousness which we did but according to His mercy He saved us, through the washing of regeneration and the renewing of the Holy Spirit." Through regeneration our spirit was renewed, but our soul was not renewed by regeneration. Thus, after regeneration the Spirit continues to renew us by saturating our soul.

According to Ephesians 1:13, we were sealed with the Holy Spirit as the sealing ink. When a seal that is wet with ink is placed on a piece of paper, the wet ink saturates the paper. In the same way the Holy Spirit as the sealing ink saturates and permeates our soul. To saturate is to fill or soak deeply, and to permeate is to spread throughout a certain thing. Saturation is vertical, and permeation is horizontal. From the day we were regenerated God imparted Himself into us as life embodied in Christ. At the same time, He put His Spirit within us as a living seal. From that day the sealing Spirit has been saturating and permeating. First, the Spirit saturates and permeates our soul, including our mind, emotion, and will. Eventually, this saturating Spirit of life will reach our mortal body that our body may have life (Rom. 8:11). This saturation and permeation will continue within us "unto the redemption of the acquired possession" (Eph. 1:14), that is, until the redemption of our body (Rom. 8:23).

The sealing of the Spirit first enters into us in our spirit. From there it spreads by saturating vertically and permeating horizontally through every part of our soul to reach our body. Then it goes on to saturate and permeate our body until one day our body will be fully saturated and permeated, that is, fully redeemed. Our body will be redeemed not by the blood of Christ but by the indwelling Christ as our life. Hence, Paul said that Christ within us is our life today (Col.

3:4) and our hope of glory in the future (1:27). The redemption of our body is the glorification of our body (Rom. 8:30; Phil. 3:21). When our body is redeemed, we will be wholly, entirely, and completely in glory. At that time we will be thoroughly permeated and saturated with the spreading and permeating Triune God.

The foregoing aspects of regeneration, sanctification, transformation, conformation, and glorification are the totality of the process of renewing. A white cotton ball that becomes saturated with red ink is an example of the process of renewing. If I inject red ink into the center of a cotton ball for a period of time, the entire cotton ball will become red. If the injection is slow, it may take a longer period of time for the ball to become red. But eventually, the cotton ball will be completely red. That is the "glorification" of the cotton ball.

Today we are in the process of being renewed. Through many years of experience I have learned that the things that happen to me are all part of the renewing process. At first I did not understand why certain things happened to me; but after considering these things for some time, my eyes were opened to see that they were all part of the process of renewing. Second Corinthians 4:16 says, "Though our outer man is decaying, yet our inner man is being renewed day by day." An alternate rendering of this verse is, "Though our outer man is being consumed..." Day by day we are being renewed by being consumed. The reason certain things happen to us is that we need to be consumed. When we are consumed, we are renewed. Through the consuming of our environment, we are renewed. Our relatives are a part of this consuming environment. Our being married or being single also is a part of God's environment to consume us.

If we were soft like a cotton ball, we could easily receive the injection of the Spirit. But because we may be hard like marble, the "ink" of the Spirit may be unable to penetrate us. Thus, we need the hammering and grinding of our environment in order to soften us. God may first hammer us and then grind us to powder. Once we have become powder, we can easily receive the injection of the Spirit. Actually, we all

are somewhat hard. Some of us are like soft stones, while
others are harder than steel. Whether we are hard or soft,
the Lord has a way to work on us. He may use hammers,
grinding stones, water, or fire to deal with us. The Lord uses
different means in our environment to consume us so that
we can be renewed. No matter who we are, the Lord has a
way to renew us through the consuming of our environment.

The New Jerusalem Being
the Consummation of Newness

In the Bible the New Jerusalem is the consummation of
newness (Rev. 21:2). The New Jerusalem is a living composition of all the renewed believers. No unrenewed person is
qualified to be there. Adam was made of clay, the dust of the
ground (Gen. 2:7). But the New Jerusalem is not a composition of clay; it is a composition of gold, pearl, and precious
stones (Rev. 21:18-21). Every part of the New Jerusalem is
transformed and renewed. Today I do not have the confidence that I have been thoroughly renewed. But when we
enter into the New Jerusalem, all our clay and dust will be
gone. Only gold, pearl, and precious stones will remain.
Everything will be renewed; thus, the city is called the *New*
Jerusalem.

Renewing by the Dispensing
of the Processed Triune God

Renewing is a matter of the dispensing of the processed
Triune God. The God whom we have received is the God who
has passed through a process. In eternity He was only God,
but through incarnation He became a man named Jesus.
This Jesus is God with the human nature. We are not able to
receive the God who was before incarnation, but we are able
to receive the God who has become a man, who has passed
through human living on this earth, who has entered into
death by crucifixion, and who has entered into resurrection.
He is no longer merely God alone; He is God plus humanity,
human living, crucifixion, and resurrection.

Experiencing the Renewing

The processed Triune God who has passed through incarnation, human living, death, and resurrection is for our experience. As we experience Him, we are renewed. He renews us by touching us in all the details of our human living. He is concerned about what kind of shoes or necktie we wear. He is also concerned about the way we comb our hair and even about what kind of buttons we have on our clothing. If you wear a certain kind of button on your clothing, you may not have the peace to eat or sleep. You may say, "Lord Jesus, I do not believe that You are concerned about such details of my human living." But the more you say this, the more the Lord Jesus will touch you until you lose your freedom and your peace to do many things. The younger a person is, the freer he can be. But the more the young people grow in the Lord, the more the Lord will touch them. Eventually, their freedom will be greatly reduced.

One time I purchased a necktie. There was nothing wrong with the necktie, but every time I put it on, I did not have peace and I could not pray freely. When I took off the necktie, I had peace and I could pray in an unhindered way. This is the experience of renewing.

TRANSFORMATION BY RENEWING

Christ as the embodiment of God is very real; He is the reality (John 14:6). The Spirit also is real and is called the Spirit of reality (v. 17; 16:13). He is invisible, but He is real. When we touch Him, we touch something real. Anything real has substance, and any substance has an element. Within the element is the essence. When we eat food, we take in some substance. In that substance there is an element, and within that element there is an essence. Upon entering our body, the essence renews and transforms our body into another form. This renewing is transformation.

In the early part of my ministry in this country, I borrowed terms such as *metabolic* and *organic* from biology and chemistry in order to describe the work of transformation in our Christian life. I told the saints that transformation is not only organic but also organically metabolic. I have never studied chemistry, but I understand that chemistry is a study of elements and compounds. In order to have a chemical compound, there must be more than one element. When different elements are put together, a kind of transformation takes place.

A mortician may beautify a dead person's face by adding color outwardly. However, that is not transformation. Transformation is metabolic. In contrast, my face may be changed from a pale complexion to a pink one through eating rich and nourishing food for a period of time. This kind of change is transformation. That transformation of my face is by renewing. Such renewing is a metabolic change; hence, it is something of life.

Transformation does not take place by teaching. If we merely hear a word of teaching, nothing will take place within us. However, when we open to the word that we have heard and pray, something takes place. We may pray, "Lord, I take what You have spoken to me. I love it and I take it. I want to taste it and enjoy it. Lord, I even want to dwell upon it." As such a prayer is offered, the divine element with the divine essence is dispensed into our being. This divine element and essence are invisible yet very real. This dispensing renews us and changes us. Renewing is not a matter merely of teaching. We may understand the teaching concerning the Body of Christ and yet not have the element or essence of the Body. In order to have the element and essence, again and again, time after time, we must open ourselves to what we have heard and pray. If we open to the Lord and pray in this way every morning, it may seem that our prayer is the same day after day. However, this can be compared to our eating the same nourishing breakfast morning after morning. We do not need to change our "diet" from day to day. Just as the children of Israel ate manna every day for forty years in the wilderness, with no change in their diet, we should daily eat Christ in this way, with no change in our spiritual diet. Such a practice will produce a change in our constitution, and that change is the renewing.

The real significance of being renewed is not in merely reading messages. You may read concerning the secret of renewing in this message, but the actual renewing does not take place until you apply what you have read to your experience by going to the Lord, touching Him, and lingering in His presence for a period of time. In this way you will receive His element, which will renew and transform you metabolically. This will not only make you organic, but it will also bring about a metabolic change within you, a change from one form to another form. Your Christian life will grow, and you will be under the sealing, which will result in the glorification of your body. On God's side, this is His dispensing, and on our side, it is our receiving. As we receive God's dispensing, the transformation by renewing takes place.

The Central Line of the Divine Revelation

THE DIVINE ECONOMY
AND THE DIVINE DISPENSING

MESSAGE TWENTY-FOUR

IN THE ACCOMPLISHMENT OF
GOD'S FULL REDEMPTION AND SALVATION
IN CHRIST

(4)

Scripture Reading: Titus 3:5b; Rom. 6:4; 8:2a, 6b, 9-11; 12:2b; Eph. 4:23; 2 Cor. 4:16; 5:17; Gal. 6:15; Rev. 21:2, 9-11

This series of messages concerns the divine economy and the divine dispensing in the accomplishment of God's full redemption and salvation in Christ. Redemption is different from salvation; it is one aspect of God's salvation. In Exodus 12 the Passover typified God's salvation. The Passover was based on God's redemption and carried out His salvation. In 1 Corinthians 5:7 Paul said that the Lord Jesus is our Passover. In the Chinese Union version of the New Testament, the translators added the word *lamb* to the word *Passover,* which causes the verse to read, "For our Passover lamb, Christ, also has been sacrificed." Actually, the word *lamb* should not have been added. Christ is not only the Lamb; He is the entire Passover. Of course, the main item of the Passover is the lamb. Hence, without the lamb there would be no Passover.

The lamb of the Passover consisted mainly of two parts: the blood and the meat, or flesh. The Israelites first enjoyed the covering of the blood of the lamb. That covering was their redemption. In the eyes of God, the Israelites were as sinful as the Egyptians. Hence, the firstborn, representing all the families of both the Egyptians and the Israelites, were to be killed by God. On the night of the first Passover, God intended to kill all the firstborn throughout all the land of Egypt, and He also intended to rescue His people out of Egypt. In order to deliver His people out of Egypt, God told the Israelites to take a lamb for every household and to put its blood upon the doorposts and the lintel (Exo. 12:3-7). When the death angel went to slaughter all the firstborn throughout the land of Egypt, he saw the sprinkled blood upon the doors of the Israelites and passed over their houses (vv. 12-13, 23). This aspect of the Passover typifies redemption. The blood shed by the lamb was the redeeming blood, which redeemed all the firstborn of Israel from the sentence of death. Since the firstborn represented all the Israelites, the redemption of all the firstborn signifies that the whole race of Israel was redeemed by God. This redemption was accomplished by the blood, not the flesh, of the lamb.

God charged the children of Israel to eat the meat, the flesh, of the lamb while they were inside their houses under the sprinkled blood. They were to eat it roasted with fire, and they also were to eat unleavened bread and bitter herbs (v. 8). God prescribed such a healthy diet for them, which included meat (the animal life), bread (the plant life), and herbs (a salad). None of these items was related to redemption, because the children of Israel had already been redeemed by the blood. The meat of the lamb, the unleavened bread, and the bitter herbs were given to them in order to strengthen, satisfy, and fill them so that they would have the energy to flee out of Egypt. Hence, these things were for their salvation.

The salvation experienced by the children of Israel also included all the miracles performed by the Lord. In these miracles God exercised His arm of power to destroy Egypt by smiting Pharaoh, his country, and his army. These miracles were not redemption but were God's salvation. This salvation also included Christ as the Angel of Jehovah, who led the children of Israel out of Egypt and turned to the rear to protect them from the pursuing Egyptian army (14:10, 19). In addition, it included the pillar of fire by night and the pillar of cloud by day. The meat of the Passover lamb, the unleavened bread, the bitter herbs, the miracles, the Angel of Jehovah, the pillar of fire, and the pillar of cloud were the items that constituted God's salvation for the children of Israel.

God's salvation as a whole includes redemption. The rescuing of Israel out of Egypt on the day of the Passover implies both God's salvation and God's redemption. On the one hand, redemption saved them from death under God's judgment. On the other hand, the miracles performed by God in Egypt, the meat of the lamb, the unleavened bread with the bitter herbs, the Angel of Jehovah, the pillar of fire, and the pillar of cloud saved them from Egyptian slavery. When these are added together, they equal God's salvation.

Redemption and salvation are often confused by many Christians. Regeneration by the Holy Spirit is salvation, but it is based on redemption. Regeneration must have a base. God is holy, righteous, and pure, but we are dirty, worldly, and unrighteous. God can regenerate such persons only through His redemption. Thus, before God regenerated us, Christ died on the cross and shed His blood to wash and cleanse us from our sins. We were not only washed and cleansed but also forgiven and justified. Through redemption we were right in the eyes of God, so He could come in to regenerate us. Hence, regeneration was accomplished based on God's redemption. The regeneration of salvation is based on the blood of redemption.

VII. IN THE RENEWING OF THE BELIEVERS BY THE HOLY SPIRIT

In previous messages we have covered six items of the divine economy and the divine dispensing in the accomplishment of God's full redemption and salvation in Christ. These items include the incarnation of Christ (John 1:14), the resurrection of Christ (John 12:24; 1 Pet. 1:3), the breathing of the essential Spirit into the believers (John 20:22), the outpouring of the economical Spirit upon the believers (Acts 2:17, 33; 10:45; Titus 3:6), the regeneration of the believers

(1 Pet. 1:3), and the subjective sanctification of the saints (Rom. 6:19, 22). Of these six items, four are on God's side and two are on the believers' side. On God's side are Christ's incarnation, Christ's resurrection, the breathing of the essential Spirit into the believers, and the outpouring of the economical Spirit upon the believers. On the believers' side are the regeneration of the believers and the subjective sanctification of the saints.

On the believers' side, the first step for God's dispensing is regeneration. God regenerated us because He wanted us to have His life. The way that we could have His life is by God's dispensing. When we called on the name of the Lord, we believed in the Lord Jesus. Immediately, our sins were washed away, we were forgiven, and we were justified in the eyes of God. At the same time, God as the Spirit came into us to impart His life into our being. To impart is to dispense. God imparted Himself into us by dispensing Himself into us as the divine life. Hence, regeneration is the first experience of God's dispensing.

After regeneration, we all need to be sanctified, not objectively but subjectively, in our disposition. In this dispositional sanctification God dispenses His holy nature as an element into our being. When this element is added into our being, it becomes our holiness. God does not need to work very much on us. He simply puts His nature into our being as the divine element, and this nature works within us. By God's holy nature being dispensed into us, we are sanctified. This is the second step on the believers' side in the accomplishment of God's full redemption and salvation in Christ.

The renewing of the believers by the Holy Spirit (Titus 3:5b) is the third step of the divine economy and the divine dispensing in the accomplishment of God's full redemption and salvation in Christ on the believers' side. God created man in a pure way for the purpose of entering into him as His vessel so that man could contain Him. But before God could come into man, Satan came in to damage man with sin. Thus, man became dirty, and immediately he became old.

Man's oldness was not due to his being ancient. Man became old because of the dirtiness of sin.

In Genesis 4 Cain murdered his brother Abel (v. 8). Today murder and robbery are very common. This does not seem strange today because man has been on the earth for several thousand years, and his condition is growing worse and worse. But Cain, being the second generation of mankind, was not old with respect to time. He became old because of sin.

All mothers love their babies, but eventually every lovable infant becomes somewhat unlovable. No mother teaches her child to lie, but after some time, every child lies. He did not learn to lie; rather, he was born that way. Every child is "dirty" from birth. Thus, even a newborn baby is old. To be old is to be sinful. Everyone on this earth is sinful and is therefore old. Thus, we all need to be regenerated to receive another life in order to have a new beginning.

Then, we need to be sanctified. We all are wrapped up with the world. I have discovered through my travels that all young people are the same in loving the world, regardless of their race or nationality. They were never taught to love the world, but spontaneously they know how to love the world. Because of this, all the young people are old. They all need to be subjectively sanctified.

However, sanctification is still inadequate. After being sanctified, we need to be renewed. In the biblical sense, to be renewed is to have a new element added into our being to replace and discharge our old element. This is the process of metabolism. In order to have such a metabolic renewing, another element must be added to our being. In the whole universe only God could be a new element that can be added into our being to replace our old element. Thus, we need to receive God into our being that we may be renewed.

Every part of our being is old, dirty, and sinful. Because our mind is old, dirty, and sinful, we have many thoughts during the day that we dare not tell others. Every part of our being needs to be renewed. We not only need to be washed; we need to be renewed. Washing only takes away the dirt, but it does not bring a new element into us. Only the renewing carried out by God brings in a new element.

Some of the ethical teachers and philosophers, such as Confucius, taught their followers that they must be renewed. However, the people who received their teaching had to renew themselves by themselves. These people received many teachings concerning renewing, but they did not receive an element that could renew them. The New Testament teaching concerning renewing, however, stresses that the Holy Spirit accomplishes the renewing. This renewing is not carried out by the Holy Spirit's working on us—this is the natural, human concept. The Holy Spirit renews us by infusion and by dispensing.

In my youth I learned the Chinese ethical teachings. Eventually, I came to the Bible. While studying the Bible, the thoughts of Chinese ethics troubled me. I found out that ethics does not work. Only the Spirit works. Actually, He does not work; He simply adds Himself as an element into our being.

The renewing that is according to the New Testament is accomplished by adding a new element into the believers' being. Chemistry is mainly a work of combining different elements together in order to obtain a certain compound. Hence, chemistry depends on elements. When two elements are added together, a certain reaction takes place. This is the work of chemistry, and this is also a picture of renewing by the Spirit.

God is wise. He did not do a lot of work; rather, He simply put His divine element as life into our inner being. This divine element is God Himself consummated to be the life-giving, indwelling Spirit. As the Spirit, He gives life to us. This life is a strong divine element. God's element, the strongest element, is the element of life. For God to put His life into us is not a small thing.

The Bible uses grafting to illustrate the organic process of renewing. When a branch from one tree is grafted to another tree, one life is put into another life. These two lives are two elements. When these two elements are put together, a biochemical reaction takes place. This is something organic; it is not a matter of work.

In John 15 the Lord Jesus said that He is the vine and we are the branches (vv. 1, 5). In Romans 11 Paul said that we, the Gentiles, are not the natural branches of the vine (v. 24), but we were wild olive branches (v. 17). One day God's mercy reached us and transferred us into Christ, and we were grafted into Christ. Through such a grafting another element entered into us.

I look to the Lord that in His church we will all learn to teach these things. To teach husbands to love their wives and wives to submit to their husbands does not work. We need to teach others the way to have God as the divine element dispensed into them. When husbands have more of God dispensed into them, they will surely love their wives. They will even love their enemies. This is renewing. Day by day we not only need cleansing, washing, and purging; we also need renewing by the dispensing of the Holy Spirit.

A. The Spirit of God

The Holy Spirit is the Spirit of God (Rom. 8:9a). When He comes in, God comes in. The Holy Spirit dispenses God as the very element into us.

B. The Spirit of Christ

The Holy Spirit is also the Spirit of Christ (Rom. 8:9b). If Christ were not the Spirit, He could not come into us. According to Romans 8:9, the Spirit of God is the Spirit of Christ. Thus, when the Spirit of Christ comes into us, Christ Himself comes in. When we have Christ, we have God as the element.

C. The Spirit of Life

The Holy Spirit is also the Spirit of life (Rom. 8:2a). God, Christ, and life are one. They are three in one. God is Christ, and Christ is life (John 11:25; 14:6). This life is just the Spirit. Thus, the Spirit is called "the Spirit of life."

D. The Indwelling Spirit

The Holy Spirit is also the indwelling Spirit (Rom. 8:11a). How wonderful this is! Do not say that because you are a bad person you are unqualified to have the Spirit indwelling you. No one is good (Rom. 3:12) except God (Matt. 19:17). We all are bad; therefore, we all are qualified to receive God. We need God, we need Christ, and we need life. Now, the Spirit who is God, Christ, and life is indwelling us. He is the indwelling Spirit who gives life. His giving of life is His dispensing of life. I can testify that every day, nearly every moment, the indwelling Spirit is within me dispensing life.

E. The Spirit Who Gives Life

The Holy Spirit as the indwelling Spirit is also the Spirit who gives life.

1. To the Believers' Spirit

The indwelling Spirit gives life first to the believers' spirit (Rom. 8:10). We have three parts: spirit, soul, and body (1 Thes. 5:23). When the Spirit gives life to our spirit, our spirit is regenerated (John 3:6).

2. To the Believers' Mind

The Spirit then gives life to the believers' mind (Rom. 8:6b). In Romans 8 the mind is mentioned instead of the soul because the major part, the leading part, of the soul is the mind. In the New Testament the mind equals the soul. In the renewing of the believers, the first step is to give life to their spirit, and the second step is to give life to their soul.

3. To the Believers' Body

Last of all, the Spirit gives life to our body (Rom. 8:11b). Paul calls our body a mortal body. This means that our body is dying. The more we live, the closer we are to dying. When we live to the end, we die. Today we all are dying persons. We may be dying, but we have the living One—God, Christ, and the Spirit. We are dying, but He is living. As an elderly man, I have often asked the Lord how long He wants me to live. Thus far, I have not received an answer. But regardless of when I will die, I do have God, Christ, and the Spirit as the living factor within me.

Today we have the bountiful supply of the Spirit of Jesus Christ (Phil. 1:19). This bountiful supply of the Spirit of Jesus Christ is our salvation, and He is the source of the dispensing that we enjoy every moment. This supplying Spirit within us is the dispensing One. His supplying is His dispensing. He continually dispenses nothing less than God, Christ, and life into us. This dispensing brings the new element into us to replace our old element and to discharge the old element from us. This makes us not only a new man but a new creation (2 Cor. 5:17). By such a dispensing, we will be made altogether new.

F. In the Believers' Mind

The renewing of the believers by the Holy Spirit is mainly in the believer's mind. Romans 12:2 says, "And do not be fashioned according to this age, but be transformed by the renewing of the mind." Renewing is for transformation. The renewing begins from our mind. The part of us that needs the most renewing is our mind. Our mind directs us. Whatever we think, we do; whatever we think, we say; whatever we think, we express. Our mind is the director. For this reason, God desires to touch our mind. Before touching our mind, He touched our spirit, and we were regenerated; we were made alive in our spirit. But our mind remains a problem, so God continues to touch us in our mind in order to renew it.

G. In the Spirit of the Believers' Mind

The renewing of the believers by the Holy Spirit is also in the spirit of the believers' mind (Eph. 4:23). One day our mind will become the mind of the spirit. This means that, eventually, our spirit will get into our mind. In Romans 8:6 Paul said, "For the mind set on the flesh is death, but the mind set on the spirit is life and peace." A proper Christian life is one in which we always turn our mind to our spirit.

As human beings, we all have relatives—spouses, children, parents, brothers, and sisters. We also have neighbors, friends, classmates, and so forth. Because we have so many relationships, it is easy to get into trouble and to have friction. We may not like some of our relatives, and our relatives may not love us. This causes trouble, and if we are living together, this trouble may cause us to remain in our mind throughout the day. Our mind might be occupied with thoughts about others the entire day. The more we think about others, the poorer they seem to be in our eyes. If you think about your spouse from morning until evening, you will surely quarrel with your spouse. But if you turn your mind to your spirit, after a few minutes you will say, "Praise the Lord!" Before you turned to your spirit, you might have thought that everyone was wrong and that only you were right. But after turning to your spirit, you consider that everyone is right and only you are wrong.

We must set our mind on the spirit (Rom. 8:6). When we set our mind on the flesh, we experience death. Death comprises things such as hatred, darkness, emptiness, weakness, and dissatisfaction. All these are elements of death. To have no peace or to feel dark within is death. These are indications that we have set our mind on the flesh. We must check to see whether we have the feeling of death or the feeling of life. If we sense life, then our mind is set on the spirit. If we sense death, our mind is set on the flesh. If our mind is on the flesh, we will suffer from hatred, dissatisfaction, and a number of other negative things. Hence, we must turn our mind to our spirit.

When we are absent from the spirit, we are absent from the dispensing. When we set our mind on the spirit, our mind and spirit are connected. This is like switching on electricity. Once the electricity is switched on, the current flows. In the same way, when our mind is set on the spirit, the dispensing of the divine element goes on continually. When we remain in our spirit with our mind set on such a spirit, we enjoy the renewing. This renewing will not only keep us clean and purge us, but will also renew us to keep us from being old.

H. The Spirit's Dispensing
of the Newness of Christ's Resurrection
Life into the Believers' Inward Being

The Spirit renews the believers by dispensing the newness of Christ's resurrection life into the believers' inward being (Rom. 6:4). The Spirit's dispensing imparts the life element of Christ's resurrection into our being. This is our need every day. The reason that we pray, read the Word, and pray-read the Word is that we need the continuous dispensing of the Spirit with the resurrection life element of Christ into our being. When we have this dispensing, our need is met in every way.

1. Through the Consuming
of the Believers' Environment

The Spirit dispenses the element of Christ's resurrection life into the believers' inward being through the consuming of the believers' environment (2 Cor. 4:16). Our outer man is decaying, that is, being consumed. The environment around us works to consume us. The husband consumes the wife, the wife consumes the husband, the parents consume the children, and the children consume the parents. The roommates also consume one another. A new pair of shoes, a haircut, or good health also may consume us. Everything in our environment consumes us.

The Lord is sovereign. We do not need to worry. We should simply continue to contact Him and open ourselves to Him. He is within us to dispense God, Christ, life, and the consummated God as the Spirit into us. In this way we are renewed, and we become a new creation. I am glad that I have been under the consuming of my environment for many years. This consuming has caused me to be renewed very much. Through the consuming of our environment, the outer man is decaying, but the inner man is being renewed.

2. Making the Believers Practically
God's New Creation

This renewing makes the believers practically God's new

creation (2 Cor. 5:17; Gal. 6:15). Second Corinthians 5:17 says, "If anyone is in Christ, he is a new creation." This is a declaration, but it is not very practical until we have been consumed. After being consumed to some extent, we become, at least in part, a new creation. The more we remain in the Lord, the more we will be consumed. This consuming helps to make us a new creation in a practical way.

3. Consummating in the New Jerusalem

The renewing of the believers by the Holy Spirit will consummate in the New Jerusalem (Rev. 21:2, 9-11). In the holy city, New Jerusalem, there will be no clay and no dust. The New Jerusalem will be a composition of gold, pearls, and precious stones. These three precious materials are not clay; thus, they do not produce any dust. But today all human beings, including Christians, are still very "dusty." As long as our body has not been transfigured, we are still dusty. Because we are still clay, the longer we remain with one another, the more dust we produce. But when we enter into the New Jerusalem, we will be pearls and precious stones. This will be the result of the renewing of the consummated Spirit of the Triune God.

Today our God is a consummated God, a processed God, as the very Spirit. This Spirit indwells us to dispense God into our being throughout the day. The element that He dispenses into our being replaces our old element and discharges all the old element. In this way we are not only changed but renewed. We are not simply washed and purged; we are renewed. The old things are carried away, and the new element comes in to replace the old element. This is renewing.

The Central Line of the Divine Revelation

THE DIVINE ECONOMY
AND THE DIVINE DISPENSING

MESSAGE TWENTY-FIVE

IN THE ACCOMPLISHMENT OF
GOD'S FULL REDEMPTION AND SALVATION
IN CHRIST

(5)

Scripture Reading: Rom. 12:2b; 2 Cor. 3:16, 18

Prayer: Lord, how we thank You that we can come to You through Your Word and Your Spirit. We thank You that today You are so much to us. You are the Word of life, and You are also the Spirit who gives life. Lord, we do trust in You. You are not only with us; You are now indwelling us as the Word and as the Spirit. This morning we have come to a point that is high and difficult for us to touch. Lord, be our help in this matter, and cover us and cleanse us with Your precious blood that we may enjoy Your anointing. Do anoint us richly that we may have the understanding and may have even the revelation with a vision. Lord, do visit each one of us in this way. Thank You, Lord. Amen.

VIII. IN THE TRANSFORMATION
OF THE RENEWED BELIEVERS

In the previous two messages we covered the renewing of the believers by the Holy Spirit. In this message we will consider the transformation of the renewed believers.

A. Through the Renewing of the Mind
(in the Soul)

The transformation of the renewed believers takes place through the renewing of the mind, that is, in the soul

(Rom. 12:2b). Here again, the matter of renewing is crucial. According to my knowledge, those philosophers, such as Confucius, who stressed human ethics and morality also stressed renewing. However, their renewing is carried out by self-effort. On the contrary, our renewing does not depend on our effort. It depends on the renewing element, that is, the divine element. That element is nothing less than divinity ministered into our being as the very element that renews us. A chemical compound is not formed by man's effort. It is formed by the addition of a new element to another element that is already present. In the same way, renewing is not carried out by our work or effort. Renewing is accomplished by the renewing element.

Actually, renewing is not a work at all. The process of renewing can be illustrated by the digestion of food. Strictly speaking, digestion is not a work. Whenever we take food into us, the food itself works along with our digestion. While the food is being digested within us, the nourishment enters into our blood. Actually, that is not a work; it is the nourishing of the food element. We need to be impressed that in the Bible the God-ordained and God-required renewing is not by our work; neither is it by God's work. In carrying out the renewing, God does everything by dispensing Himself into our being as the divine element. This element within us means everything. The subjective sanctification is by this divine element, which is the holy nature, the holy element, of our Triune God.

Such a thought is divine, spiritual, and abstract; thus, it is not a part of our natural logic. According to our logic, we must work for everything that we want to obtain. Without working, we will get nothing. This is our thought, our logic, and we apply this logic to everything. We would even think, "How can I be regenerated?" That means, "What should I do so that I can be regenerated?" A question often asked by people in the Bible is, "What shall I do?" (Matt. 19:16; Mark 10:17b; Luke 10:25b; John 6:28; Acts 16:30). In the same principle, we may ask, "What shall I do to be holy?" or

"What shall I do to be spiritual?" or "What shall I do to be victorious?" or even "What shall I do to be renewed?"

Recently I received a very brief letter that consisted of only one question: "Dear Brother Lee, Can pray-reading affect our transformation?" My answer is definitely yes. Pray-reading can affect our transformation because pray-reading keeps us in the presence of the divine element. As long as we stay in the presence of the divine element, we will absorb the divine element into us. That element will transform us. The longer we stay in the presence of the Lord, the more we will spontaneously be transformed.

In order to be renewed and transformed, we do not need to do anything; but we do need to absorb the divine element into us. There is no other way to absorb the divine element but to remain in the presence of the Lord. Furthermore, while we are remaining in the presence of the Lord, we need to breathe by calling on the Lord's name. To call on the Lord makes a great difference. If every morning we call "O Lord Jesus" only a few times, we will become a different person. Then, if we would open the Word and pray-read two or three verses, we will taste something in the word. By further masticating the word, we will taste the word even more, and we will receive more of the divine element. This element will enter into us and will be digested and assimilated by us. To say that the word nourishes us in such a way is not a superstition. The word nourishes us in the same way that food nourishes us.

Renewing is the divine element being dispensed into us. As long as this element gets into us, it is organic; it spontaneously enters into a union with us. Before food enters our stomach, the organic process of digestion cannot take place. But after the food enters into our stomach, the organic process of digestion causes the food to have an organic union with our being. This does not mean that our stomach does a work or that the food does a work. Rather, it means that an organic moving occurs in us. This moving is digestion. Although we have a stomach that is organic, if we do not eat any food for three days, there will be no organic moving within us to cause the food to be digested and assimilated.

Especially in the New Testament, our spiritual life is likened to our physical life. In John 6:57 the Lord Jesus said that He is eatable and that whoever eats Him will live because of Him. Moreover, in 7:37 the Lord said that He is drinkable. He said that He is the bread of life and the living bread (6:35, 48, 51), and He also said that He is the living water (4:14; 7:38). When we receive the Lord as the organic foodstuff, this foodstuff comes together with our organic "organs," and an organic moving takes place within us. As a result, we are sanctified, renewed, and transformed.

Concerning our spiritual experience, there are six main items: first, regeneration, and then sanctification, renewing, transformation, conformation, and glorification. It is very difficult to find anything concerning these six items in Christian teaching today. But these items are all part of the apostle Paul's teaching. Paul touched these six items in a very detailed way.

Regeneration is to have the divine life added to our human life. Sanctification is to be separated unto God and for God from anything other than God. This causes us to become holy, not by our doing but by our receiving the holy divine nature. When the holy element enters into us, it sanctifies us. In addition, because of the devastation of Satan and sin, we became old in the three parts of our being—spirit, soul, and body. Thus, we need to be renewed. God's intention is to make us His new creation, beginning from our spirit. At the time of our salvation, the Spirit of God entered into our spirit to regenerate us, to make us new in our spirit (John 3:6). That was a renewing of the Spirit in our spirit. Then, from our spirit this renewing spreads into our mind, that is, into our soul. Finally, from our soul it reaches our body and eventually causes our body to be glorified. These are the steps of renewing to make us God's new creation.

Renewing issues in transformation. Second Corinthians 3:18 says, "We all...are being transformed into the same image from glory to glory." The Greek word for *transformed* in this verse is the same word as in Romans 12:2. This word refers to an inward metabolic change. Such a metabolic change requires a new element to be added into us to replace and discharge the old element. This results in our transformation.

In the word *transformation* the word *form* is included. Genesis 2:7 tells us that God formed man, that is, man's body, out of dust. To form something is to make a new form out of a substance that already exists. Before God created Adam, there was no creature like Adam. There was only dust, which, when mixed with water, produces clay. God used dust plus water to make a new form, that is, Adam's body with all its distinct parts, which did not exist prior to that time. In comparison, to transform is to form something further out of an existing form. Our present form is the form of the old man. Out of this old man's form God is making a further form. This is to transform, to produce another form out of an existing form.

Before we received the Lord Jesus, we had a certain form; but after we received the Lord Jesus, we became another form. This new form came out of the original form. Renewing results in transformation, a change in form. When we are renewed, our form changes, not by our doing but by the organic divine element moving within us organically. The more we are renewed, the more we are transformed into another form.

Before we are transformed, we have a certain kind of form already; however, we need to have another form. To have our present form changed into a new form is to be transformed. Before we experience transformation, we are simply ourselves; what we are is our present form. But God wants to produce another form out of this existing form. He does this by putting Himself as a new element into us, first, to regenerate us, second, to sanctify us, and third, to renew us. The steps of regeneration, sanctification, and renewing result in the changing of our present form into a further form. I am thankful to the Lord that many of the saints, after remaining in the recovery for some time, have experienced a change in form. Some amount of transformation has taken place within them. This transformation is the aggregate of regeneration, sanctification, and renewing. When these three things are added together, the sum is transformation.

Of course, we do not need to be regenerated every day, but we do need to be sanctified and renewed every day. However, sanctification and renewing need a base, and that base is regeneration. From the day of our regeneration we need to be sanctified a little more each day, and we also need to be renewed day by day. I have the assurance that after they remain in the training for two terms, when many of the full-time trainees return to visit their parents, the parents will be surprised and happy to see that something further has been formed in their son or daughter out of what they previously were. In the two terms of training, the trainees do not try to adjust or improve themselves. They simply go along with the atmosphere in the training. When others say, "O Lord," they also say, "O Lord." When others pray-read, they also pray-read. After following such an atmosphere for one year, when they return home, their parents see in them another form.

Transformation takes place when God's divine element is dispensed into our human element. Prior to that time, our human element did bear a certain form. The new divine element, after being added into our old element, participates in an organic moving with our old organic "organs." This produces God's new creation. In God's old creation there is no divine element. After being regenerated, day by day as we are being sanctified and renewed, a kind of organic moving takes place within us by and with the divine element plus something from our old yet regenerated, sanctified, and renewed element. The result of such a moving is something new, a transformed form. This is not by our working; neither is it by God's working. In such a process, God does not do that much. However, as I mentioned previously, we may still pray and even beg the Lord to do something to sanctify us and transform us. In response, the Lord may say, "Do not beg Me to do something. I will simply put Myself into you as an element. I created you in a certain form with all kinds of organic organs. Now I will put Myself into you as another element, a higher element, and this element will touch your organic organs; then an organic moving will take place, and you will be sanctified, renewed, and transformed into something else." This something else is God's new creation, and this new creation is a transformed form.

B. By the Transfusing of the Lord Spirit in Glory into the Believers' Inward Being

The foregoing definition of transformation is based on two verses, Romans 12:2 and 2 Corinthians 3:18. First, in Romans 12:2 Paul said, "And do not be fashioned according to this age, but be transformed by the renewing of the mind." Then, in 2 Corinthians 3:18 Paul said, "But we all with unveiled face, beholding and reflecting like a mirror the glory of the Lord, are being transformed into the same image from glory to glory, even as from the Lord Spirit." Based on these two verses we can see that transformation is to re-form us. By God's creation we were formed already, but that form is too old. With it there is no glory, but only oldness. Yet today God has taken away all the veils from our face. Now we have an unveiled face to behold and reflect the glory of the Lord. Early in the morning, the first thing we need to do is to go to the Lord with an unveiled face to look at Him, to behold Him, and to reflect Him for a period of time. To linger in the presence of the Lord while beholding Him and reflecting Him affords us a real taste, a real enjoyment. During such a time in the Lord's presence, as we behold and reflect the Lord, He transfuses Himself into us, and that transfusing brings into us the divine element. That divine element matches our inward organic "organs." As a result, we are transformed into the image of the Lord from glory to glory. This transformation is from the Lord Spirit, who is the consummated Lord as the life-giving Spirit.

After taking a healthy breakfast in the morning, I feel strong and energetic. But after four hours I am tired and hungry again. Then, after eating lunch, again I am full of energy. However, after another five hours, I need another meal. Do not think that if you have a good morning revival, that will be sufficient. After three or four hours, you need to say, "O Lord, I am empty. Lord, I am hungry now; I am thirsty." To go to the Lord in this way is to contact the very source, which is the processed, consummated Triune God. When we look at Him, lingering in His presence, we behold Him, and He transfuses Himself as the life-giving Spirit into us.

In the Old Testament economy the Angel of Jehovah was with Israel through the forty years of their wandering in the wilderness (Exo. 14:19; 23:20, 23). That Angel was Christ. Even in Zechariah 1, while Israel remained in their captivity in a low condition, at the bottom of the valley, there was One riding on a red horse among the myrtle trees, and that One was called the Angel of Jehovah (vv. 8-12). As the Angel of Jehovah, Christ was among, around, and over the children of Israel, but He never entered into them. But today, after the processes of incarnation, crucifixion, and resurrection, this Angel of Jehovah has become the life-giving Spirit (1 Cor. 15:45b). Furthermore, this New Testament life-giving Spirit is altogether condensed, or embodied, in the living word. Thus, three persons—the Lord Christ (Rom. 8:10a; 2 Cor. 13:5b), the life-giving Spirit (Rom. 8:11), and the personified word of Christ (Col. 3:16)—all dwell in us. Actually, these three—the Lord, the Spirit, and the word— are one. We do have the threefold indwelling of the Lord Jesus Christ, the life-giving Spirit, and the word of life. Every day these three are not only with us but also in us, and They even indwell us. They will never leave us.

The Lord as a person indwells us. Then, His life-giving Spirit indwells us, and His word also indwells us. In His indwelling He does not do something within us, but He is something within us. He is continually dispensing Himself as an element into our being. The food we eat, the water we drink, and the air we breathe are all elements that are dispensed into us every day. We eat three meals daily, drink water even more often, and breathe continually. The dispensing of the elements of food, water, and air accomplishes a great deal in us. The principle is the same with our spiritual life. This is why in John 6 the Lord Jesus likened Himself to food; in John 4 and 7 He likened Himself to water; and in John 20 He likened Himself to air, or breath (v. 22). Eating, drinking, and breathing all bring a solid element into our being. In our spiritual life, this element is the processed and consummated God as a life-giving Spirit, and this consummated Spirit is the all-inclusive dose that nourishes us, heals us, and rescues us. Not only so, He is also present within us. His presence within us means a great deal. This presence is the sanctifying, renewing, and transforming element.

C. To Dispense the Lord's Divine Element in His Resurrection Life into His Believers' Inward Element

The transformation of the renewed believers is by the dispensing of the Lord's divine element in His resurrection life into His believers' inward element. We do have a natural element, and this natural element is not altogether evil. Because Christ's redemption has dealt with the evil element, our natural element is a redeemed element. Into such a redeemed element the divine element is now being dispensed. When the divine element is added into our redeemed and uplifted natural element, we are sanctified and renewed. The result is that we are metabolically transformed, and the image of the resurrected Lord in the glory of His divine life is formed in us.

Christians are not a group of working people but a group of eating and enjoying people. We Christians need to learn to keep ourselves away from work. We should stay away from the "office," the place of work, and come back "home" to eat and enjoy. The teaching in today's Christianity produces a group of working people. Husbands are taught to love their wives, and wives are taught to submit to their husbands. It is possible to pick up hundreds of commandments in both the Old Testament and the New Testament. Brother Nee once said that any teaching that helps us to work is wrong, but any teaching that ushers us into Christ for enjoyment is right. We do not need to work for transformation, but we need to behold and reflect the glory of the Lord in resurrection. Then some element from Him will be dispensed into us and be absorbed by us. He dispenses, and we absorb Him, the very processed and consummated Triune God, as the life-giving, compound, indwelling Spirit into our being. Then, we praise Him with hallelujahs all the day long. If we praise our Lord all day long, we will be blessed; we will be an enjoying people.

The Central Line of the Divine Revelation

THE DIVINE ECONOMY
AND THE DIVINE DISPENSING

MESSAGE TWENTY-SIX

IN THE ACCOMPLISHMENT OF
GOD'S FULL REDEMPTION AND SALVATION
IN CHRIST

(6)

Scripture Reading: Rom. 8:29; Phil. 3:10-11; 4:8

Very few Christians today understand what are the main items of God's full salvation in Christ. God's full salvation does not save us only from eternal perdition. Of course, salvation from eternal perdition is included in God's full salvation. We need to be impressed that God's full salvation in Christ includes six definite items: first, regeneration, that is, to be reborn; second, sanctification, that is, to be sanctified subjectively in our disposition, not just objectively in our position; third, renewing, that is, to be renewed; fourth, transformation, that is, to be transformed; fifth, conformation, that is, to be conformed to the image of the firstborn Son of God; and sixth, glorification, that is, to be glorified.

We need to realize that each of these six items needs God's dispensing. Without God's imparting of Himself into our being as life, we could never be regenerated. In regeneration the main thing is that God gives us an injection to impart, or to dispense, Himself as life into our being to regenerate us, to cause us to be born again. Regeneration is the issue of God's impartation, of God's dispensing. Then, God continues to dispense Himself into us. After regeneration, He sanctifies us by dispensing Himself as the holy nature into our being. Such a dispensing adds a new element into us, just as an element is added into a chemical compound. First, the element of God as life was imparted into our being, causing us to be reborn. After this, God continues to impart Himself into us as the holy nature. In the whole universe only God is holy. God makes us holy by imparting Himself, that is, by dispensing Himself, as the holy element, the holy nature, into our being. This results in a "compound" in which there is an element that is holy.

God also desires to have a new creation. However, we are old, so God has to renew us. The renewing in God's salvation is not like the renewing of a house by putting a coat of paint on it. In God's salvation, we are renewed not by outward "painting" but by an inward renewing through the adding of a further element from God into our being.

The Body of Christ is the mingling of the Triune God with the tripartite man. It is the Triune God mingled with the believers. This simple definition is the conclusion of my study of Paul's writings in his fourteen Epistles. God's new creation work is nothing but to dispense Himself into us, His chosen people, to mingle Himself in His divine element with our human element, making divinity and humanity one. He lived on this earth for thirty-three and a half years as the model, the example, of the divine mingling. The man Jesus was the mingling of God with man. He was God, and He was also man; He was a God-man. Even the term *God-man* does not express the notion of mingling adequately. While Jesus was working and walking on this earth, He was the mingling of the Triune God with the tripartite man. That was Christ; and this Christ today has been enlarged, has been increased. This increase is the church. The church is the mingling of the Triune God with us, the tripartite man. Such a mingling is carried out by dispensing—not a once for all "injection" but a continuous dispensing day by day. Every day God dispenses Himself into us little by little. The issue of this divine dispensing is sanctification.

Because God wants us to be a new creation, He must dispense Himself as the newness into our being to renew us. In the sixty-six books of the Bible, only one verse tells us that

God is always new, like an evergreen. In Hosea 14:8 our God is likened to an evergreen tree, a green fir tree. Because He is evergreen, He Himself becomes the evergreen element. Now He is dispensing Himself into our being as such an element to renew us. I do have the sense that every day I am newer. I am not older; I am newer. I am not old, because I am being renewed. Something of God as the "evergreen tree" is being dispensed into my being.

The next step in God's salvation is transformation. God's salvation not only renews us but also transforms us from one form to another form. Even to transform us from one form to another form is not adequate. We need to be transformed to another definite form. Thus, there is the need of conformation to conform us to the image of the firstborn Son of God.

The last item in God's full salvation is glorification. To be glorified is to be completely conformed to the image of the firstborn Son of God.

IX. IN THE CONFORMATION
OF THE TRANSFORMED BELIEVERS

The accomplishment of God's full redemption and salvation in Christ is in the conformation of the transformed believers. The New Testament directly mentions conformation only once, in Romans 8:29, which says, "Because those whom He foreknew, He also predestinated to be conformed to the image of His Son, that He might be the Firstborn among many brothers." However, in other verses the thought of conformation is implied. Second Corinthians 3:18 says, "But we all with unveiled face, beholding and reflecting like a mirror the glory of the Lord, are being transformed into the same image from glory to glory, even as from the Lord Spirit." This verse says that as we behold and reflect Christ like a mirror, we are being transformed into His image. Although the word *conformed* is not used directly here, the preposition *into* is used, indicating that our being transformed into the image of Christ implies conformation.

First John 3:2 says, "Beloved, now we are children of God, and it has not yet been manifested what we will be. We know that if He is manifested, we will be like Him because we will see Him even as He is." To be made like the Lord in His glory also implies conformation.

A. Conforming the Transformed Believers into the Image of the Firstborn Son of God in Resurrection

The conformation of the transformed believers conforms the transformed believers into the image of the firstborn Son of God in resurrection. There is one verse, Romans 8:29, that clearly and definitely says that the believers will be conformed to the image of the firstborn Son of God. We will be conformed not in a general way but in a specific way to the definite image, the real likeness, of the firstborn Son of God. This verse does not speak of our being conformed to the image of the only begotten Son of God, but of our being conformed to the image of the firstborn Son of God. John 3:16 says that God so loved the world that He gave His only begotten Son. We need to consider why this verse speaks of God's only begotten Son and why Romans 8:29 refers to the firstborn Son of God. It seems that it would be sufficient to say that we will be conformed to the image of the Son of God, without including the adjective *firstborn*. Christ was born in His humanity to be the firstborn Son of God in resurrection (Acts 13:33), and in His resurrection we, His believers, were also born to be the many sons of God, His many brothers (1 Pet. 1:3). Thus, we are to be conformed to the image not of the only Begotten but of the firstborn Son of God.

Now we all are under God's transformation for His conformation. Transformation is for conformation. Transformation merely transforms us from one form to another form. It does not specify into what form we are transformed. But conformation does tell us to what form we are being conformed. We are being conformed to the image, to the form, of the firstborn Son of God.

From my youth I heard Christians stress very much the matter of following Jesus. At that time I did not understand what this meant, so I did not like this term. I said that Jesus was here nineteen hundred years ago, but today He is away. Since He is away and I cannot see Him, how can I follow Him? Then I was told that Jesus is loving; thus, to follow Jesus is to love others. I replied that Confucius taught the same thing: Confucius advised us to love others. Thus, to love others is to follow Confucius. Then what is the difference between following Jesus and following Confucius?

Thank the Lord for Paul. Paul also told us that we must follow the Lord. But he told us in this way: "Be imitators of me, as I also am of Christ" (1 Cor. 11:1). Paul did not use the word *follow;* he used the word *imitate.* He was an imitator of Jesus; thus, he became another Jesus. By imitating Paul, we also become imitators of Jesus. Paul's use of the word *imitate* is an improvement over the term *follow,* but it is still somewhat ambiguous.

As a young person I saw the matter of imitating, but I did not see the matter of being conformed to the image of the firstborn Son of God. It is not a matter of imitating Jesus, but of being conformed to His image. This means that in life, in nature, in appearance, in taste, in everything and in every aspect, we become exactly the same as He is. Eventually, we not only become the same as He is, but He and we, we and He, become one entity. He becomes us and we become Him. The seven lampstands in Revelation 1 are all the same, but they are seven, not one. However, we and Christ are not only the same, but the same one. For this we must be conformed to His image, the image of the firstborn Son of God.

1. Into the Image of the Firstborn Son of God in His Divinity to Express the Attributes of the Processed God in the Resurrected Christ

The transformed believers are conformed into the image of the firstborn Son of God in His divinity to express the attributes of the processed God in the resurrected Christ. The attributes of God are the attributes that belong to God. When Christ was living on this earth, He expressed the attributes of God, which are love, light, holiness, and righteousness. I studied the Ten Commandments item by item. I did my best to find out what the Ten Commandments show us. Eventually, I found out that the Ten Commandments of the law show us a picture of God in four items. The Ten Commandments show us that God is love, God is light, God is holy, and God is righteous. These are the four basic elements—love, light, holiness, and righteousness—with which the Ten Commandments were composed.

When Jesus lived on this earth, He expressed God. First, He expressed God in these four items: in love, in light, in holiness, and in righteousness. By reading the four Gospels, we receive the impression that the One portrayed in the record of the four Gospels is high in love, high in light, high in holiness, and high in righteousness. Eventually, we must conclude that He Himself is love, light, holiness, and righteousness. He loves us; He enlightens us; He is holy, even the embodiment of holiness; and He is righteous, even the very composition of righteousness. When we see Him in such a way, we admire Him, and we also realize that we are very different from Him. We cannot love even our wife, let alone our enemies, but He loved His enemies (Luke 23:34). With Him there was no darkness. Wherever He went, there was light because He is light (Matt. 4:16; John 8:12). Wherever He went, there was holiness, and there was also righteousness. This is the expression of God in Christ's divinity. Christ can be so loving, so enlightening, so holy, and so righteous because He is God. In ourselves, we cannot be like Him; but in Matthew 5:48 He told us that since we are the sons of God, we can be perfect as our heavenly Father is perfect. We can be perfect because the Father has come into us.

2. Into the Image of the Firstborn Son of God in His Resurrected Humanity to Express the Virtues of the Uplifted Man in the Resurrection of Christ

The transformed believers are conformed also into the image of the firstborn Son of God in His resurrected humanity to express the virtues of the uplifted man in the resurrection of Christ. While Christ was on this earth, He expressed God in His divinity—in love, in light, in holiness, and in righteousness. Not only so; He also expressed the human virtues in His uplifted humanity. When Jesus was on the earth, He was very meek, and He was also humble. God does not need to be meek or humble. Meekness and humility are human virtues. Hence, Philippians 2:7 tells us that Christ emptied Himself, taking the form of a slave, becoming in the likeness of men. This is not divine, but human. Thus, on the one hand, Christ expressed God's divine love, divine light, divine holiness, and divine righteousness, while on the other hand, He expressed human virtues such as meekness, humility, obedience, and forbearance.

In 2 Corinthians 10:1 Paul said that he entreated the believers in the meekness and gentleness (or, forbearance) of Christ. Then, in 11:10 he said, "The truthfulness of Christ is in me." Meekness, forbearance, and truthfulness are three human virtues. God does not need to forbear. However, when Christ was on this earth, He lived as a man under all kinds of persecution and trouble. He was very meek, and He was continually forbearing, continually bearing people in a meek way. Moreover, in His dealing with people, He was always full of truthfulness. He did not express any kind of crookedness; rather, He expressed only truthfulness. He said, "Let your word be, Yes, yes; No, no; for anything more than these is of the evil one" (Matt. 5:37). But sometimes He did not answer yes or no. He always answered in a high way, in the way of life, in a way that expressed God (John 4:20-24; 8:3-9; 9:2-3).

While Christ lived on this earth as one person, on the one hand, He expressed God's divine attributes, such as love, light, holiness, and righteousness, and on the other hand, He expressed the human virtues, such as meekness, humility, and forbearance. Today we are His believers, and He is dispensing Himself into us in both His divinity and His humanity. When He was on this earth, He was both divine and human in the way of mingling. The New Testament first tells us that Christ as the Son of God was the only begotten Son of God (John 1:18). Eventually, in His resurrection He was born to be the firstborn Son of God (Col. 1:18; Rom. 1:4; 8:29). In the only begotten Son of God there is only divinity, but in the firstborn Son of God there is both divinity and humanity. Through incarnation God branched Himself out of His divinity into humanity. Thus, as a God-man who walked on the earth, He was both God and man, but His humanity had not yet been brought into divinity. Romans 1:4 tells us that through resurrection He was designated the Son of God according to the Spirit of holiness. In resurrection the humanity of Christ was brought into divinity and was fully "sonized." It is in this way that He could become the First-born among many brothers.

Did we receive Christ while He was the only begotten Son or after He became the firstborn Son? Is the very Christ whom we have received the only begotten Son of God or the firstborn Son of God? The answer is that we all have received a Christ who is no longer the only begotten Son of God, but who has become the firstborn Son of God. In other words, the very Christ whom we have received is both divine and human. In His divinity He expresses God, and in His humanity He expresses man. In His divinity He expresses the divine attributes, such as the divine love, the divine light, the divine holiness, and the divine righteousness, and in His humanity He expresses the human virtues, such as meekness, humility, forbearance, and obedience.

As imitators of Christ, we imitate Him not in His divinity but in His humanity. We all need to be meek, humble, and forbearing. Regardless of how others treat us, we should still be happy; we should not complain but should still love others. Philippians 2:14 tells us to "do all things without murmurings and reasonings." Murmurings and reasonings are related not to divinity but to humanity. If in one day we do not murmur or reason, we are the most holy people. The fact is that we murmur in nearly everything. The husbands murmur to their wives, the wives murmur to their husbands, and the children murmur to their parents. Sometimes we murmur to the windows and even to the bed. Paul said that if we live Christ, we should do all things without murmurings and reasonings. This is the top humanity. When I look at my own experience regarding this matter, I realize that I am the same as others; I cannot do all things without murmurings and reasonings. Only Jesus can do this.

Philippians 1:19 says, "For I know that for me this will turn out to salvation through your petition and the bountiful supply of the Spirit of Jesus Christ." The bountiful supply of the Spirit of Jesus Christ can save us from our murmurings and reasonings. Our married life and our family life are a life of murmurings and reasonings. Only Jesus can live a life without murmurings and reasonings. We cannot do this, because we are not Jesus. This is why we need God's dispensing, little by little, into our being. Those who know me well can testify that my murmuring today has been greatly reduced from what it was twenty years ago. This is because I have received more dispensing from Christ.

To be conformed to the image of the firstborn Son of God is to be conformed to One who is both divine and human. As Christians, we need to express God in His divinity, and at the same time we also need to express man with the proper humanity. We are God-men. As such, we should always be meek and humble. This is not related to God's divinity, because God does not need to be meek and humble. On the other hand, sometimes we need to express God in His divinity. People may offend us to the uttermost, yet we would not hate them but would still love them. This is not human; this is divine. This is not love on the human level but love on the divine level. We can do things and express things that no one else can, because we have God's divine dispensing within us. We can forgive and forget. Only God can forgive by forgetting (Heb. 8:12); human beings cannot do this. When we human beings forgive people, we always remember the offense; we do not forgive by forgetting. However, when God forgives, He forgets. We are those who are under God's divine dispensing. Because of this dispensing, we can forgive as He forgives. When we forgive, we forget. This is not a human virtue; this is a divine attribute.

First, we need to be conformed to the image of the firstborn Son of God in His divinity. Then we need to be conformed to the image of the firstborn Son of God in His resurrected humanity to express the virtues of the uplifted man in the resurrection of Christ. On the one hand, we express the divine attributes, and on the other hand, we also express the human virtues. Both are in resurrection. Christ is the only begotten Son of God and the firstborn Son of God altogether to be our portion in resurrection. After He resurrected, we received a resurrected Christ with His divinity and also with His humanity. Hence, today we can express both His divinity and His humanity in His resurrection.

B. By Dispensing the Element of the Resurrected Christ as the Firstborn Son of God into the Transformed Believers for Their Conformation

God conforms the transformed believers to the image of His firstborn Son by dispensing the element of the resurrected Christ as the firstborn Son of God into the believers for their conformation. We need to realize that all day, from morning until evening, God is working in us to dispense the element of the resurrected Christ into us. Every day the resurrected Christ is being added into our being. This is why He became the life-giving Spirit. As the life-giving Spirit within us, He is continually dispensing Himself in His resurrected element into us.

1. Through the Believers Taking the Resurrected Christ Both in His Divinity and in His Humanity as the Model of a God-man

The element of the resurrected Christ is dispensed into the transformed believers for their conformation through the believers taking the resurrected Christ both in His divinity and in His humanity as the model of a God-man. God is dispensing, and we must respond to His dispensing by taking the resurrected Christ in His divinity and in His humanity as the model of a God-man, that is, of One who is both divine and human.

2. Being Conformed to His Death
in the Power of His Resurrection

Now we are in Christ's resurrection. Resurrection is a power. It empowers us to be conformed to Christ's death (Phil. 3:10). Every day the resurrected Christ dispenses Himself into us to work out one thing, that is, to conform us to His death.

If someone such as our wife, our mother, or our roommate mistreats us, we should react by being conformed to Christ's death. If someone mistreats us and we lose our temper, this is definitely not to be conformed to the death of Christ. Whatever happens to us, we should maintain the attitude that we are dead persons. A dead person does not react to anything. This is to be conformed to the death of Christ.

When Jesus was standing in front of the Jewish rulers and the Roman rulers, He was challenged and accused, but He did not react or speak a word (Matt. 26:59-63a; 27:12-14). That was the image, the form, of His death. We are His imitators, receiving His dispensing. He is now dispensing Himself into our being, yet our environment does not help us. Everything in our environment would irritate us and stir us up to react. At such times we need to be conformed to the death of Christ. No one can do this, but the resurrected Christ can do it. The resurrected Christ is within us, and this resurrected Christ within us is the very resurrection power. He empowers us to be conformed to His death. He lives in us, helping us to be conformed to His death. So, eventually, we have no reaction to anything in our environment. We are conformed to Christ's death not by our capacity, not by our ability, but by Him in resurrection as our capacity.

Paul said that he was able to do all things in Him who empowered him (Phil. 4:13). The "all things" here include whatever is true, whatever is dignified, whatever is righteous, whatever is pure, whatever is lovely, whatever is well spoken of, and whatever is excellent and worthy of praise (v. 8). We are able to do these things not in ourselves but in the One who empowers us. This is to be empowered by the resurrected Christ to be conformed to His death. Eventually, we will be conformed to Him as the firstborn Son of God with two natures—divine and human.

3. Aiming at the Out-resurrection— the Outstanding Resurrection, the Extra-resurrection—as a Prize

In Philippians 3:11 Paul said that he was aiming at the out-resurrection—the outstanding resurrection, the extra-resurrection—as a prize. If we would be conformed to the image of the firstborn Son of God, a reward, a prize, will be given to us—we will participate in the out-resurrection from the dead, which is the extra-resurrection. All believers who are dead in Christ will participate in a general way in the resurrection from the dead at the Lord's coming back (1 Thes. 4:16; 1 Cor. 15:52). But the overcoming saints will enjoy an extra, outstanding portion of that resurrection.

The Central Line of the Divine Revelation

THE DIVINE ECONOMY
AND THE DIVINE DISPENSING

MESSAGE TWENTY-SEVEN

IN THE ACCOMPLISHMENT OF
GOD'S FULL REDEMPTION AND SALVATION
IN CHRIST

(7)

Scripture Reading: Rom. 8:30; 1 Pet. 5:10a; Heb. 2:10; Rom. 8:23; Phil. 3:21; Eph. 1:13-14; 4:30

The divine revelation concerning the divine economy and the divine dispensing is the central line among the many lines in the Bible. The terms *divine economy* and *divine dispensing* are new to most Christians because few know the teaching of God's economy in the New Testament. The word *economy,* the anglicized form of the Greek word *oikonomia,* was stressed very much by the apostle Paul in his Epistles (Eph. 1:10; 3:9; 1 Tim. 1:4). The Greek word *oikonomia* refers to a household administration. Hence, God's economy refers to God's household administration. In this administration there is a marvelous arrangement for God to dispense Himself into His chosen, created, and redeemed people. God's divine economy, His household administration, is carried out by His divine dispensing.

The central thought of God's redemption and salvation is to work Himself into His people. God redeemed us and saved us so that He can work Himself into our being. He also created us with a body, a soul, and a spirit for this purpose (1 Thes. 5:23). Outwardly, we have a body, and inwardly we have a spirit deep within us. Between our spirit and our body is our soul. Many Christians do not know that man has a human spirit. They consider the spirit, the soul, the mind, and the heart as one thing. However, 1 Thessalonians 5:23 definitely mentions the human spirit as one of the three parts of our being, and Hebrews 4:12 even says that man's soul and spirit can be divided.

When I began to minister in the United States thirty years ago, I stressed the matter of the human spirit very much. Wherever I went I spoke on this matter. Many told me that they had never known that they had a human spirit. They had heard only about the Holy Spirit, not the human spirit. Today the life of many Christians is poor because they have missed the organ for the Christian life—the human spirit. In 1 Corinthians 6:17 Paul said, "He who is joined to the Lord is one spirit." This indicates that the Spirit of God can indwell the spirit of man to such an extent that the two spirits become one spirit.

The dispensing of God is very much related to the two spirits. First of all, God Himself is Spirit. In John 4:24 the Lord Jesus said, "God is Spirit, and those who worship Him must worship in spirit and truthfulness." In this verse there is no article between the words *is* and *Spirit*. This indicates that the phrase "God is Spirit" refers to the essence of God. The essence of a gold ring is gold, and the essence of a steel table is steel. In the same way, the essence of God is Spirit. Thus, if we would worship such a God who is Spirit, we must worship Him in our spirit.

Not only so, the Second of the Divine Trinity, after becoming flesh and dying on the cross and entering into resurrection, became a life-giving Spirit (John 1:1, 14; 1 Cor. 15:45b). Thus, the Son also is Spirit. Moreover, the Third of the Divine Trinity, the Holy Spirit, also is Spirit. Hence, the three of the Divine Trinity are Spirit. The essence of the entire God, the complete Triune God, is Spirit. The Father is the source, the Son is the course, and the Holy Spirit is the flowing, the reaching, of the Triune God to us. The three of the Divine Trinity are Spirit for the purpose of dispensing the Triune God into our being.

In the evening on the day of His resurrection, the Lord Jesus came to His disciples, breathed upon them, and said to them, "Receive the Holy Spirit" (John 20:22). This indicates very clearly that God's intention in His redemption and salvation is to make Himself one with His redeemed people by the divine dispensing. God is Spirit, and we have a spirit; therefore, God can make Himself one with us. Only Spirit can touch spirit. Eventually, God as the Spirit touches our spirit. God has regenerated us in our spirit (John 3:6), and He is now dwelling in our spirit to make our spirit one with His Spirit (1 Cor. 6:17)—a mingled spirit. This is the central line of the divine revelation, and this is the divine dispensing of the Divine Being into our being.

X. IN THE GLORIFICATION
OF THE CONFORMED BELIEVERS

In the foregoing messages we have seen that the divine dispensing was prophesied in God's promises to us, was typified in the types of the Old Testament, and is carried out in the accomplishment of God's full redemption and salvation in Christ. In the remainder of this message we will cover the concluding point in the accomplishment of God's full redemption and salvation in Christ—the glorification of the conformed believers.

Romans 8:30 says, "And those whom He predestinated, these He also called; and those whom He called, these He also justified; and those whom He justified, these He also glorified." First, God called us; then He justified us, regenerated us, sanctified us, renewed us, transformed us, and conformed us to the image of the firstborn Son of God. Ultimately, He will glorify us. On the side of redemption, God's salvation consists of forgiveness of sins, the washing away of sins, justification, and reconciliation, whereas on the side of life, God's salvation consists of regeneration, sanctification, renewing, transformation, conformation, and glorification. Glorification is the final step of God's full salvation in Christ.

A. The Destiny of God's Predestinated Sonship Being Glorification

Ephesians 1:5 says that God predestinated us unto

sonship, that is, to be His sons. The destiny of God's predestination is the glorification of His sons (Rom. 8:29-30).

1. The Goal of the Calling
of the God of All Grace Being His Eternal Glory

First Peter 5:10a says that the God of all grace has called us into His eternal glory in Christ. Thus, the goal of the calling of the God of all grace is His eternal glory. God has called us into His eternal glory. This glory involves not just one kind of grace but the "all grace" of God.

John 1:14 and 16 say that Christ as the Word became a man of flesh, full of grace and reality, and of His fullness we have all received, and grace upon grace. The grace that we have received has many different aspects. In 1 Peter 4:10 this grace is called "the varied grace of God." First Peter 3:7 speaks of the grace of life, and Ephesians 1:7 speaks of the grace of forgiveness. These are only two examples of the many kinds of grace in God's salvation. Eventually, God's salvation in its totality is by grace (Eph. 2:8). Everything we enjoy of God is an aspect of grace. God's presence is a grace, His strengthening is a grace, His empowering is a grace, and His sanctifying is a grace. The totality of grace is just God Himself (1 Cor. 15:10; cf. Gal. 2:20). This God of many kinds of grace has called us into His eternal glory.

2. God's Intent in His Salvation
Being to Lead Many Sons into Glory

God's intent in His salvation is to lead many sons into glory (Heb. 2:10). God is leading us onward into glory. He is not leading us into a heavenly mansion or into any kind of blessing for eternity in the physical realm. He is leading His many sons into the eternal glory of God.

B. The Glorification of God's Conformed Sons
Being the Redemption of Their Body

The glorification of God's conformed sons is the redemption of their body (Rom. 8:23). Before we can be glorified by God, we must already be conformed to the image of God's firstborn Son (v. 29). We cannot be infants, children, or even middle-aged; we must be mature sons of God. A mature son of God is one who has been conformed in his maturity of life to the image of the firstborn Son of God.

On the one hand, Jesus Christ as the firstborn Son of God expresses the divine attributes, and on the other hand, He expresses the human virtues. In the four Gospels, Jesus was a pattern, a model, of a person who expressed God's attributes in His divinity and the human virtues in His humanity. As a man, He expressed divinity and humanity. In His divinity, He expressed the attributes of God, such as love, light, holiness, and righteousness. In His humanity, He expressed the human virtues, such as meekness, forbearance, and humility. In His divinity, He was very lofty and high, but in His humanity, He was a lowly person who lived a lowly life.

In the four Gospels we can see Jesus as a person who displayed God's attributes and the human virtues, but in a poor sinner we can see nothing of God or of the human virtues. Instead of the virtues of humanity, we can see all the sinfulness of humanity. After being saved, most Christians do not understand that God's intention is that they express God not only in the human virtues but also in His divine attributes. As a result, they seek only to improve their character and conduct in their human living, not realizing that this kind of seeking is contrary to God's intention.

A Christian should be a God-man with two natures, humanity and divinity. First, we are human; then we are divine. We are divine because we have been born of God (John 1:12). We have received the divine life with the divine nature (2 Pet. 1:4), and the divine essence has entered into our being. We are not merely sons born of Adam; we are also sons born of God. We have had two births, a human birth and a divine birth. Hence, we are God-men, exactly like Jesus. On the one hand, we should live a high human life with all the human virtues, such as meekness, humility, and forbearance. On the other hand, we should express divinity in all the divine attributes, such as love, light, holiness, and righteousness.

We need to realize that glorification will take place on the conformed sons of God, that is, on the mature sons. Today we cannot be glorified because we are not yet mature. We are in the process of becoming mature. When we are fully mature, glorification will come. Glorification may be likened to the blossoming of flowers. When a flower such as a rose blossoms, that is its glorification. A rose cannot blossom unless it has a bud. If there were simply a stump with leaves and branches, the process of blossoming could not take place. But when a bud appears, it grows and grows until it reaches maturity. At that time it blossoms. The blossoming of the bud is its glorification.

As a young believer, I was taught that the glory of God was objective, far away in the heavens. I was told that when the Lord Jesus comes, in the twinkling of an eye He will bring us into the heavens to enter into an objective realm of glory. This teaching was based on Hebrews 2:10, which says, "For it was fitting for Him, for whom are all things and through whom are all things, in leading many sons into glory, to make the Author of their salvation perfect through sufferings." According to this teaching, the destination to which Christ is leading us is the objective glory of God in the heavens. This seems to be confirmed by 2 Timothy 2:10, which says, "Therefore I endure all things for the sake of the chosen ones, that they themselves also may obtain the salvation which is in Christ Jesus with eternal glory." It seems that the eternal glory of God is objective, far away from us, and that we are being led until we reach the destination of glory. However, this teaching is not according to the intrinsic revelation of the Bible.

Adam's fall caused our entire being—spirit, soul, and body—to become fallen. But through Christ's redemption God saves us from this fallen condition. God's salvation begins from our spirit. Our spirit is the innermost part of our being. It is enclosed within our soul, which is within our body. When God came in to save us, He redeemed our spirit by washing away our sins and regenerating our spirit. Regeneration is a matter that took place in our spirit (John

3:6). Before we were saved, we were very active in our soul and very living in our body, but we were dead in our spirit (Eph. 2:1). After forgiving us of our sins (1:7), God came in to touch our spirit and to make us alive in our spirit (2:5). In this way God redeemed our spirit.

God intends to redeem our entire being, including our body, but before He can redeem our body, He must redeem our soul, which is between our spirit and our body. From the time of our regeneration, God has been waiting every day, even every moment, to take every opportunity to spread Himself from our spirit into our soul. We must coordinate with Him by setting our mind on the spirit and not on the flesh (Rom. 8:4b-6). God desires to enter into our mind, emotion, and will, but often He finds the door to the three parts of our soul closed. As a result, God has no way to spread Himself within us. Instead of opening the door of our being to God, we may often try to do good by ourselves. Thus, we must learn to set our mind, the main part of our soul, on the spirit instead of on the flesh. When our mind is set on the flesh, these two work together as "good friends." However, when we turn our mind to our spirit and set our mind on the spirit, our mind will be filled, occupied, and taken over by God. This is the transformation of the soul (Rom. 12:2).

Regeneration and transformation are the redemption of two parts of our being. Our spirit was redeemed when God regenerated our spirit, and our soul is redeemed when our soul is transformed. By regeneration and transformation, we become very spiritual; but our body is still a problem. Sometimes we can sense the lust within our body. Our spirit hates this lust, and our soul abhors the sinfulness of the flesh. Yet there is still something very active in our flesh. This means that although our spirit has been redeemed and our soul is being redeemed, our body has not yet been redeemed. For this reason, we must be strong in our spirit to control our mind, to make our spirit the spirit of our mind (Eph. 4:23), so that we can control our flesh. We will then become a spiritual person and an overcoming saint.

When our mind becomes the spirit of our mind, the divine

life will gradually spread from our spirit through our soul and eventually into our mortal body (Rom. 8:11). This is the genuine divine healing. The reality of divine healing is that our mortal body is saturated with the divine life from our spirit through our soul. Such an experience of the divine life spreading to our body can heal our body and prolong our life.

A careless person, one who behaves, acts, and conducts himself according to the flesh, may die an early death. In principle, no one who lives according to his fleshly lusts will live a long life. Most who live beyond seventy years of age refrain from indulging in the lusts of the flesh. To eat, drink, and live without any self-control is to commit a slow and gradual suicide. If we would learn to control our flesh by controlling our eating, drinking, and sleeping, we will live a longer life.

We not only control the fleshly lusts by exercising self-control, but we also call on the name of the Lord. Calling on the Lord's name also will prolong your life. Whenever you are about to be angry or unhappy with your spouse, the best way to deal with your anger or unhappiness is to call, "O Lord Jesus!" Whenever we call on the Lord, our anger and the damage that it causes to our health is stopped. Not only so, by calling on the name of the Lord, the Holy Spirit, as the embodiment of the divine life, spreads even into our body.

Although the divine life touches our body today, our body will still be a problem until it is redeemed. Therefore, we are waiting for the final redemption of our being, that is, the redemption of our body. This redemption of our body is the full sonship (Rom. 8:23). It will take place when the Spirit with the divine life which fully saturates our spirit, soul, and body soaks our entire being in God's divine life. This soaking is the blossoming of the divine life from within our body.

The glorification of our body is like the blossoming of a rose. When a flower blossoms, the bud cannot be seen any longer. The bud is transfigured into a blossoming flower. Today our body is troublesome to us, but one day our body will be glorified. Every day the sealing Spirit within us is saturating our body. He is saturating vertically, up and down, and He is permeating horizontally, back and forth. This is the process of our glorification. When the process of glorification reaches its climax, we will be fully mature, and this maturity will be our glorification.

1. By Transfiguring Their Body of Humiliation into the Body of Christ's Glory

The redemption of our body is accomplished by the transfiguring of our body of humiliation into the body of Christ's glory (Phil. 3:21). While He was on earth, the Lord Jesus was transfigured in the presence of Peter, James, and John (Matt. 17:1-8). This transfiguration of the Lord Jesus on the mountain was a model of the coming transfiguration of our body. Today our body is a body of humiliation with no glory, honor, or dignity. We are very mean and low, mainly because of our body. However, one day this body of humiliation will be transfigured into the body of Christ's glory. Today our body is like the bud of a flower. But in the day of our transfiguration, our body will be transfigured from a bud to a blossoming flower.

2. Initiated by the Spirit's Sealing unto the Day of the Redemption of the Believers' Body

The glorification of God's conformed sons is initiated by the Spirit's sealing unto the day of the redemption of the believers' body (Eph. 1:13-14; 4:30). Today the Spirit is sealing us, and this sealing is not once for all but will continue for our whole life. From the day of our regeneration, the sealing of the Spirit began to saturate and permeate us. This saturation and permeation will continue unto the day of the redemption of our body, until the sealing reaches its fullness. Even at that time the sealing of the Spirit will not cease. The sealing of the Spirit will go on for eternity, sealing us with the divine essence continually.

3. The Sealing of the Spirit Being
Also for the Redemption of the Believers' Body

The sealing of the Spirit is also for the redemption of the believers' body (Eph. 4:30). The more the Spirit seals us, the more we are redeemed. When the redemption reaches its consummation, we will be glorified. That glorification will be the redemption of our body.

4. The Redemption of the Believers' Body
Being Their Full Sonship

The redemption of the believers' body is their full sonship (Rom. 8:23). Full sonship means that we are of full age. In the United States, a person is not considered to be of full legal age until he is eighteen. Being of full age is a matter of maturity. It is always dangerous for people to do certain things when they are under age. Today some of the young people want to get married as teen-agers. But I have seen that those who married as teen-agers always suffered. The reason they suffered is that they lacked maturity. God predestinated us unto sonship (Eph. 1:5). His intention is to make us His sons, but we need to grow until we reach maturity. When we reach maturity, our sonship will become full. Today God cannot glorify us because we are not yet mature. We cannot blossom because we have not yet grown to maturity. Therefore, we must grow.

5. Through the Spirit as the Firstfruits Dispensing the Divine Essence into the Believers' Entire Being

God's conformed sons are glorified through the Spirit as the firstfruits dispensing the divine essence into the believers' entire being (Rom. 8:23). God has given the Spirit to us as the firstfruits, the foretaste, of our enjoyment of God as our inheritance. Today we are enjoying God as a foretaste, not as a full taste. While we are enjoying the Spirit as our foretaste, He is dispensing the divine essence into our entire being. This dispensing proceeds from the initiation of His sealing to the consummation of the glorification of the believers, which will be their full taste of their enjoyment of God as their inheritance.

6. The Glorification, the Transfiguration, the Redemption of the Believers' Body Being the Maturity of the Divine Dispensing in the Believers

The glorification, the transfiguration, the redemption of the believers' body is the maturity of the divine dispensing in the believers, beginning from their regeneration and proceeding through the entire course of their spiritual life.

C. The Glorification of the Believers Being the Consummation of the Accomplishment of God's Full Redemption and Salvation in Christ

The glorification of the believers is the consummation of the accomplishment of God's full redemption and salvation in Christ and the full qualification for the chosen people of God to be fully mingled with the processed Triune God and to enjoy Him in full for eternity, as signified by the New Jerusalem as the full consummation of God's eternal salvation by the divine dispensing (Rev. 21:1—22:5).

The Central Line of the Divine Revelation

THE DIVINE ECONOMY
AND THE DIVINE DISPENSING

MESSAGE TWENTY-EIGHT

IN THE CONSUMMATION
OF THE FULL ACCOMPLISHMENT
OF GOD'S REDEMPTION AND SALVATION IN CHRIST
AS FULLY SHOWN IN THE NEW JERUSALEM

Scripture Reading: Rev. 21:1—22:5; 1 Cor. 3:9b; 2 Cor. 5:17; Gal. 6:15

Prayer: Lord, we worship You that You have brought us through so many days. Today You have brought us to the end, to the consummation, of the central line of God's revelation. Lord, do cleanse us with Your precious blood, and cover us with Your prevailing blood. We trust in You for this last meeting. Give us a good ending. You are the Alpha, and You are the Omega. We trust in You as our ending. Lord, do cover us that we may be really protected in this hour, listening to Your word. We do not want to merely hear Your word. We also want to see something. We want to enter into the intrinsic revelation of Your Body, the church, which will be consummated in the New Jerusalem. We want to feel the same way that You do, according to Your feeling, and we want to understand the same way that You do, according to Your understanding. Lord, we are the New Jerusalem. We are the Body. We are Your counterpart. Lord, unveil everything that is on Your heart tonight in this meeting. Help us in the speaking. Lord, we realize we are so weak in this matter. Stand with us as one spirit. Amen.

In this message we have come to the end of the Bible. Any good writing always closes with something of the real thing it talks about. If we are going to understand what the Bible talks about, we have to go to the end to see how it concludes.

Most Bible readers appreciate the beginning of the Bible, but they do not pay much attention to the end of the Bible. This is because their understanding deprives them of the preciousness of the ending of the Bible. Their understanding is that the Bible ends merely with a heavenly mansion. This is very objective, having very little to do with us subjectively. According to this natural understanding, God spends many years and does so much just to prepare a mansion for us. This is why not many pay attention to this part of the divine revelation. This shows us that the proper understanding means everything.

Many years ago, I began to realize that the end of the Bible could not be a physical city as a mansion into which we will enter to live for eternity. If the Bible really ended this way, it would be so low. After having studied the Bible for a number of years, I realized to some extent the preciousness of the Bible and the contents of the Bible. Based upon this principle, I realized that the concluding figure shown at the end of the Bible must not be that low or that simple. It must be something very significant, very precious, and very mysterious.

I began to hunt for material and books on the New Jerusalem from past writers. I found something of the truth concerning the holy city in the writings of Tersteegen, a German writer. Tersteegen indicated that the New Jerusalem must be something about the believers in Christ themselves. That opened my eyes a little bit. Brother Austin-Sparks said a little more. He pointed out that the New Jerusalem should be a figure, just as in the beginning of the Bible, God also uses figures such as the tree of life (Gen. 2:9). In the whole universe, there is not such a physical tree—the tree of life. There are apple trees and peach trees. There are many kinds of trees, but who has ever seen or heard of a tree of life? What is life? Life is mysterious. Thus, Brother Austin-Sparks said that this must be a figure of speech. A figure of speech is used to speak of something that is somewhat unseen, somewhat mysterious, and somewhat hidden, concealed. Because something cannot be easily realized or apprehended, it is not possible to express what that thing is in normal terms. This is why figures of speech are used. *The tree of life* is a figure of speech.

Based upon this, I realized something further. Since the tree of life in Genesis 2 is a figure of speech, indicating something mysterious, invisible, and glorious, the same tree of life mentioned in the last chapter of the Bible must also be a figure of speech. The tree of life grows in the New Jerusalem (Rev. 22:2). Furthermore, since one item of the New Jerusalem is a figure of speech, the rest of the items must also be figures of speech. Revelation is a book of signs (1:1) because it unveils to us things which we have never seen and which we cannot understand. Based upon this principle, the New Jerusalem as the conclusion of the book of Revelation should surely be a sign.

We need signs, or figures, to help us see the mysterious things of the new creation. The old creation is altogether visible and physical, and the Bible tells us that God's intention is not to have the old creation as something that remains forever. Instead, God uses the old creation as the means to produce the new creation. The old creation is altogether physical, whereas the new creation is altogether spiritual. Adam was physical, but the second man, the last Adam, is a spiritual person.

Today in the universe there is such a thing that is called, in a figure of speech, the tree of life. We have not seen it, yet it is there. That is actually the very uncreated life, the divine life, the eternal life of God. That life is altogether not physical and altogether invisible. In order to describe it, God in His divine revelation uses a figure of speech. Genesis 1 and 2 speak of how God created the heavens and the earth with billions of items, including man. The created universe is physical and visible. Only one thing mentioned in Genesis 1 and 2 is real yet invisible. That one thing is the tree of life. The tree of life is real but invisible.

The entire book of Revelation shows us invisible things.

Do you believe there are seven physical lampstands? Surely these lampstands are not physical. The seven lampstands signify the seven local churches (Rev. 1:11-12, 20). A local church can be seen since it is physical, but if we are going to see the intrinsic reality of the local church, we need a figure of speech. Thus, the lampstands are not real lampstands. They are figures. They are signs. They signify the local churches, not in the physical sense but in the intrinsic, invisible sense.

In Revelation, the Lord Jesus is described as the Lamb (5:6, 8, 12-13; 6:1, 16; 7:9-10, 14, 17; 12:11; 13:8; 14:1, 4, 10; 15:3; 17:14; 19:7, 9; 21:9, 14, 22-23, 27; 22:1, 3). The Gospel of John also speaks of the Lord Jesus as the Lamb. When John the Baptist saw Jesus, he declared, "Behold, the Lamb of God!" (John 1:36, 29). Of course, the Lord Jesus was not a physical lamb with four legs and a little tail. *The Lamb of God* is a figure of speech indicating a lot. In the book of Revelation, there are the lampstands and the Lamb. There are also many other signs in the book of Revelation. At the end of this book, there is a great sign—the New Jerusalem. This should help us to realize that the New Jerusalem is not something physical. It must be something mysterious, something very intrinsic, something spiritual, and something which can never be apprehended by the human mind and seen by the physical eyes.

I have spent much time to study the last two chapters of Revelation concerning the New Jerusalem. I thank the Lord for this. When I was in mainland China, I understood the New Jerusalem to some extent, but I was not completely clear until after I came to Taiwan in 1949. At the beginning of the 1960s, when we were fixing our hymnals both in Chinese and in English, I wrote some new hymns. Four of these are concerning the New Jerusalem (see *Hymns,* #975, #976, #978, and #979). These hymns express the understanding of the intrinsic reality of the Body of Christ. In the universe there is something called the Body of Christ. The Body of Christ is not something physical like the human body. *The Body of Christ* is a figure of speech to indicate that the church is an organism. This figure of speech must be used because no one can explain it. Things which are mysterious and intrinsic must be described with figures of speech.

The book of Revelation is really a book of revelation, and in this book a great sign is revealed—the New Jerusalem. This great sign signifies the ultimate consummation of God's new creation work. When this new creation work is fully accomplished, the old heaven and old earth will pass away (Rev. 21:1). God's new creation work will take Him at least seven thousand years to complete. Almost six thousand years have passed. God will also use the thousand-year kingdom to complete His new creation work. God's new creation work is not simple. In order to make the old creation, God did not need to become a man. For God to become a man and live on earth for thirty-three and a half years was not a simple thing.

In Revelation 21 and 22 there is a picture of a holy city. This picture must be very significant. Over thirty-five years ago, I received the understanding of the significance, in detail, of every item of this city. Hymns, #979, composed of sixteen verses, gives the details of these items. We need to see what this holy city, the New Jerusalem, is. Many in Christianity say that it is a heavenly mansion, but we need to throw away that inaccurate concept.

I. THE NEW JERUSALEM,
AS GOD'S HOLY CITY, BEING:

A. God's Universal Building
for His New Creation out of His Old Creation

The New Jerusalem as God's holy city is God's universal building for His new creation out of His old creation (1 Cor. 3:9b; 2 Cor. 5:17; Gal. 6:15). The New Jerusalem is the building of God's new creation. God would spend at least seven thousand years to finish this work. How does He carry out this work? First, He became a man. He was begotten in a human virgin's womb and remained there for nine months. Matthew 1 says that God was born into the womb of Mary through His Spirit (vv. 18, 20). It was a great thing for the infinite God, the eternal God, to stay and be confined in the womb of a human virgin for nine months. His being in a virgin's womb could be considered as an imprisonment to Him. Then He came out of that womb to be a God-man. His remaining in humanity in His human living was a longer imprisonment. As the divine person, He was imprisoned in humanity on this earth for thirty-three and a half years. Then He went to the cross and suffered there for six hours until His death (Mark 15:25; Matt. 27:45-46). Afterwards, He went down to Hades and remained there for three days (Matt. 12:40). He was raised from the dead on the third day (16:21). As the resurrected Christ, He has been working in the heavens for almost two thousand years to work out His new creation. This work is not yet finished. I hope we can see how much time, how much energy, and how much wisdom God has put into the work of His new creation. Therefore, the New Jerusalem, as the ultimate consummation of God's new creation work, must be very, very significant.

We have to find out what the New Jerusalem is. The New Jerusalem is a building. First Corinthians 3:9 says that the church is God's cultivated land, God's farm, to grow something, and also God's building. In the whole universe, there is a building, and this building is the building of the new creation. The New Jerusalem is God's universal building.

B. God's Tabernacle, God's Temple, and the Bride, the Wife of Christ

The New Jerusalem is God's tabernacle—God's dwelling in eternity (Rev. 21:3a). It is also God's temple as God's redeemed people's living and serving place (v. 22). In the Old Testament there was first the tabernacle and then the temple. The tabernacle was God's dwelling place, and the temple was the priests' living place. The temple was also God's people's worshipping place, their serving place. We have to realize that even today in the New Testament we are living in the temple as God's new creation. We are living in the temple because the church is the temple (1 Cor. 3:16-17). To us it is the temple; to God it is the tabernacle. The New Jerusalem, as the tabernacle, indicates what God's redeemed people will be to God in eternity, that is, God's eternal dwelling place. And the New Jerusalem, as the temple, indicates what the Triune God will be to His redeemed people in eternity, that is, their eternal dwelling place. In the new heaven and new earth, the New Jerusalem will be a mutual dwelling place for the redeeming God and the redeemed man for eternity.

The tabernacle, as a sign, signifies that the processed and consummated Triune God, after traveling through the wilderness of incarnation, human living, His all-inclusive death, and His life-imparting resurrection, and entering into His surpassing ascension, has secured a redeemed people to be His dwelling in eternity, as in typology after He traveled with the children of Israel through the wilderness and attained to Mount Sinai, He obtained His redeemed people to build Him a tabernacle for His dwelling on the earth. And the temple, as a sign, signifies that the processed and consummated Triune God, after being wrought into His redeemed, regenerated, transformed, and glorified people through His death, resurrection, and ascension in humanity, has been constituted with His redeemed and glorified people to be His organism, which becomes eventually His redeemed people's dwelling in eternity.

The New Jerusalem is also the bride, the wife of Christ as the Lamb (Rev. 21:9). The city becomes a woman, a female. The bride is a virgin, and the wife is a married one. The New Jerusalem is both a virgin and also a married wife. The New Jerusalem is Christ's wife, and Christ is the embodiment of God. Therefore, this New Jerusalem, on the one hand, is God's dwelling and on the other hand, is Christ's counterpart. Christ's counterpart is His Body, the church. For the wife to be the husband's counterpart means that she is a part of him. The New Jerusalem, to God, is the tabernacle; to us, is the temple; and to Christ, is a wife, a counterpart.

C. The Mingling of the Processed and Consummated Triune God with His Redeemed, Regenerated, Transformed, Conformed, and Glorified Tripartite People

The New Jerusalem is the mingling of the processed and consummated Triune God with His redeemed, regenerated, transformed, conformed, and glorified tripartite people. This aspect of the New Jerusalem brings us to the central point of the divine dispensing. In order to be mingled with us, God had to be processed. The processed Triune God is the One who has gone through incarnation, human living, an all-inclusive death, and a wonderful resurrection. These are four steps, four processes. For God to be mingled with us, He also needs to be consummated. He was perfect in eternity, but He was not complete in what He wanted to be. He wanted to be God mingled with man. He wanted to be both divine and human. In eternity past was He complete? He was divine, but not divine and human. Thus, He was perfect and without defect, but not complete. He needed to be completed, to be consummated.

He became consummated by being processed. He became a man, lived a human life, and entered into death. We may think that His entering into death was merely a suffering. It was a suffering, but it was also a marvelous process. The eternal God who is the divine life, the uncreated life, the indestructible life, entered into death. Would you like to travel through death? God desired to do this, and He did it. He traveled through death. He took a tour of Hades. To God this was wonderful because this was His process. Then He entered into resurrection and transcended to the heavens in His ascension. Now He is there as both the perfect and complete God. Today He is not only perfect but also complete. He has been consummated with incarnation, with human living, with a wonderful death, with resurrection, and with ascension. He is completed. He has been consummated.

Such a God, a processed and consummated God, is absolutely qualified and ready to mingle Himself with His people so that they can be redeemed, regenerated, transformed, conformed, and glorified. God today is not so simple and neither are we. God is completed, and we are enjoying Him as the consummated One. One day we will be consummated. That consummation will be the glorification, the redemption, the transfiguration, of our body of humiliation into the body of Christ's glory (Phil. 3:21). We will be the same as He is. He has passed through all the processes, and we will also pass through all the processes of redemption, regeneration, transformation, conformation, and eventually glorification. We have been redeemed and regenerated. Now we are passing through the "tunnel" of transformation. Eventually we will pass through the processes of conformation and glorification. Our God is the processed and consummated Triune God, and we are the redeemed, regenerated, transformed, conformed, glorified tripartite man. He mingles with us, and we mingle with Him to be one. The New Jerusalem is not merely God or merely man. The New Jerusalem is a God-man in the corporate way. The New Jerusalem is a mingling of the processed, consummated Triune God with the redeemed, regenerated, transformed, conformed, and glorified tripartite man. He is triune, we are tripartite, and we are mingled with Him.

D. The Composition of God's Old Testament Saints and Christ's New Testament Believers

The New Jerusalem is a composition of two groups of people—God's Old Testament saints and Christ's New Testament believers. This is signified by the names of the twelve tribes and the names of the twelve apostles (Rev. 21:12b, 14b). The names of the twelve tribes of Israel are inscribed on the twelve gates, the entrance into the holy city. This indicates that the New Jerusalem comprises all the redeemed saints of the Old Testament. The names of the twelve apostles are on the twelve foundations of the holy city. This indicates that the New Jerusalem is also composed of the New Testament saints, represented by the apostles. The Old Testament saints are the entrance, whereas we, the New Testament believers represented by the apostles, are the foundations of the holy city. Without the Old Testament saints, we do not have the entrance, but without us they do not have the foundations. Both the Old and New Testament saints are the composition of the New Jerusalem.

E. A Constitution
with God the Father as the Substance,
God the Son as the Initiation (Entrance),
and God the Spirit as the Building
(the Wall with Its Foundations)

The New Jerusalem is not just a composition but a constitution. Composition is outward, but constitution is inward. Our human body is an example of this. The outward skeleton is a composition of bones, but we also have an inward constitution. The inward constitution of the New Jerusalem is the Triune God, and the outward composition is the redeemed saints and believers. The inward constitution is with God the Father as the substance, signified by the pure gold, with God the Son as the initiation (entrance) through His redemption, signified by the pearls, and with God the Spirit as the building (the wall with its foundations) through His transformation, signified by the precious stones (Rev. 21:18-21).

The New Jerusalem is built of three kinds of precious materials, signifying that she is built with the Triune God. First, the city proper, with its street, is of pure gold (vv. 18, 21). Gold, the symbol of the divine nature of God, signifies the Father as the source, from whom the element for the substantial existence of the city comes.

The twelve gates of the city are twelve pearls. Pearls are produced by oysters in the waters of death. When an oyster is wounded by a grain of sand, it secretes its life-juice around the grain of sand and makes it into a precious pearl. This is a picture of Christ's redeeming and overcoming death and of His life-imparting and producing resurrection with the secretion of His life around us to make us pearls. Christ as the living One came into the death waters, was wounded by

us, and secreted His life over us to make us into precious
pearls for the building of God's eternal expression.

The holy city is also a constitution of precious stones. The
Spirit works to transform the redeemed and regenerated
saints into precious stones. The work of Christ is redemption; the work of the Holy Spirit is transformation. Precious
stones are transformed items. Transformation involves burning and pressing. A piece of coal can be transformed into a
precious stone by tremendous heat and pressure. We may
not want to be burned or pressed. But if we are not burned
and pressed, we will remain pieces of coal, and we cannot be
built up together into the New Jerusalem. There is no coal in
the New Jerusalem.

Some in the church life become dropouts because they
do not like to be transformed. They do not like the elders
because they feel that the elders are too strict. They do not
like the old sisters or the young ones. Actually, they do
not like anybody. They only like themselves. They do not
want to be burned or pressed by anybody. They want to
remain in themselves, and they want their freedom. They
may say that the United States is a country of freedom and
that the elders are controlling them. In recent years, some
tried to bring democracy into the church life. Where are
these ones today? They are pieces of coal outside of the
church life.

In order to be transformed from pieces of coal into precious stones, we must be pressed and burned. I have been
pressed and burned for over sixty years. I have been burned
by the elders, by the young brothers and sisters, by my wife,
by my children, and by my grandchildren. They are the coals
to burn me. When I was young, I tried to press others. Today,
though, I have learned that it is better to be pressed. The
wives are big pieces of coal to burn the husbands, and every
elder is a burning coal to transform us. I believe that I have
received much transformation through this burning.

This is the sovereign arrangement of the Lord, and we
cannot stay away from it. A husband cannot stay away from
his wife because divorce is not allowed by the Lord. We have

to stay under the Lord's sovereign arrangement to be burned every day. In this sense, we should feel happy to be with all the saints, with our spouse, and with our children. We cannot avoid the heat and pressure because this is the age of transformation. We need to be transformed by burning and by pressure to become the precious stones in the New Jerusalem.

II. THE CONTENTS OF THE NEW JERUSALEM

A. God's Glory as the Uncreated Light and the Lamb as the Lamp

Now we want to see the contents of the New Jerusalem. First, the New Jerusalem has God's glory as the uncreated light and the Lamb as the lamp to shine forth the divine brightness through the entire city (Rev. 21:23, 11; 22:5b). In the New Jerusalem, there will be no man-made or God-created light, because God's glory is the light. Within the lamp, Christ, is the light, God. By this way God shines through the entire city. God is the light; Christ is the lamp; and the church, the New Jerusalem, is the lamp container. The New Jerusalem is the lamp container, the container that contains the lamp with God as the shining light.

B. The Throne of God and of the Lamb

The throne of God and of the Lamb is also in the New Jerusalem. This is the throne of the redeeming God, for God's administration in His eternal kingdom for eternity (Rev. 22:1b, 3b). This throne of authority for God's administration in the whole universe is also the throne of grace. We know that it is the throne of grace because out of it flows the river of water of life with the tree of life growing in it. These are not indications of authority but of grace. The river of water of life is grace. The tree of life with its twelve fruits is also grace. The throne is of God and of the Lamb. God and the Lamb are not separate. They are one. Our God is the Lamb-God, the redeeming God, for God's administration in His eternal kingdom for eternity.

C. A Street from the Throne of God and of the Lamb

The New Jerusalem has a street from the throne of God and of the Lamb spiraling through the entire city to reach the twelve gates of the city on its four sides, for communication (Rev. 22:1c). The New Jerusalem has only one street. This street is not straight but a spiral. It spirals down from the throne to reach all the twelve gates. There are three gates on the north, three gates on the south, three gates on the east, and three gates on the west. This one street from the throne reaches all the gates by spiraling. This is for communication. Even today in the church there is only one spiraling street. There is no cross street on which to turn. No one can be lost on this one street. Every entrance can be reached by this one street. This is very meaningful. Quite often, some saints like to turn, but in the church life there is no turn. We just have to go on and on upon the one street.

D. A River of Water of Life

The river of water of life flows from the throne of God and of the Lamb in the midst of the street to the twelve gates of the city to water the entire city (Rev. 22:1a). Where there is the street, there is the flow of life. Where there is the flow of life, there is the street. Our street, our way, is the flow of life.

E. The Tree of Life

The tree of life grows on the two sides of the river of water of life and produces twelve fruits, yielding its fruit each month, to supply the entire city (Rev. 22:2a). The tree of life grows on the two sides of the river, and the river is in the midst of the street. Thus, the street, the river, and the tree are mingled together. These three items are spiraling from the throne through the entire city to reach the twelve gates. The entire city is supplied with the water of life and the fruit of life. This is the life supply of the New Jerusalem.

F. The Uncreated Light
the River of Water of Life, and
the Tree of Life Being
All for the Divine Dispensing

The uncreated light, the river of water of life, and the tree of life are all for the divine dispensing to maintain the New Jerusalem, to supply the necessities of the holy city, and to sustain the divine building for eternity. The light shines to dispense, the river flows to dispense, and the tree grows to dispense. The light, the river, and the tree are for dispensing the very substance, element, and essence of the Triune God into our being. This dispensing mingles the Divine Trinity with the tripartite man. This mingling is the New Jerusalem. The New Jerusalem is the mingling of the Triune God with the tripartite man.

This mingling is not easily carried out or completed. It is not so simple or direct. On God's side there was the need for Him to pass through many processes. On our side, we have to pass through five "-tions": redemption, regeneration, transformation, conformation, and glorification. Every "-tion" is a process. The New Jerusalem is the ultimate consummation of God's new creation work. This consummation is a mingling of the processed, consummated Triune God with the redeemed, regenerated, transformed, conformed, and glorified tripartite man. The mingling of divinity with humanity is the church. This is the intrinsic view of the church as the Body of Christ which consummates in the New Jerusalem, and this is the consummation of the entire Bible. The entire Bible consummates in this mingling, which is signified by the New Jerusalem.

ABOUT THE AUTHOR

Witness Lee was born in 1905 in northern China and raised in a Christian family. At age 19 he was fully captured for Christ and immediately consecrated himself to preach the gospel for the rest of his life. Early in his service, he met Watchman Nee, a renowned preacher, teacher, and writer. Witness Lee labored together with Watchman Nee under his direction. In 1934 Watchman Nee entrusted Witness Lee with the responsibility for his publication operation, called the Shanghai Gospel Bookroom.

Prior to the Communist takeover in 1949, Witness Lee was sent by Watchman Nee and his other co-workers to Taiwan to ensure that the things delivered to them by the Lord would not be lost. Watchman Nee instructed Witness Lee to continue the former's publishing operation abroad as the Taiwan Gospel Bookroom, which has been publicly recognized as the publisher of Watchman Nee's works outside China. Witness Lee's work in Taiwan manifested the Lord's abundant blessing. From a mere 350 believers, newly fled from the mainland, the churches in Taiwan grew to 20,000 in five years.

In 1962 Witness Lee felt led of the Lord to come to the United States, settling in California. During his 35 years of service in the U.S., he ministered in weekly meetings and weekend conferences, delivering several thousand spoken messages. Much of his speaking has since been published as over 400 titles. Many of these have been translated into over fourteen languages. He gave his last public conference in February 1997 at the age of 91.

He leaves behind a prolific presentation of the truth in the Bible. His major work, *Life-study of the Bible,* comprises over 25,000 pages of commentary on every book of the Bible from the perspective of the believers' enjoyment and experience of God's divine life in Christ through the Holy Spirit. Witness Lee was the chief editor of a new translation of the New Testament into Chinese called the Recovery Version and directed the translation of the same into English. The Recovery Version also appears in a number of other languages. He provided an extensive body of footnotes, outlines, and spiritual cross references. A radio broadcast of his messages can be heard on Christian radio stations in the United States. In 1965 Witness Lee founded Living Stream Ministry, a non-profit corporation, located in Anaheim, California, which officially presents his and Watchman Nee's ministry.

Witness Lee's ministry emphasizes the experience of Christ as life and the practical oneness of the believers as the Body of Christ. Stressing the importance of attending to both these matters, he led the churches under his care to grow in Christian life and function. He was unbending in his conviction that God's goal is not narrow sectarianism but the Body of Christ. In time, believers began to meet simply as the church in their localities in response to this conviction. In recent years a number of new churches have been raised up in Russia and in many eastern European countries.

OTHER BOOKS PUBLISHED BY
Living Stream Ministry

Titles by Witness Lee:

Abraham—Called by God	0-7363-0359-6
The Experience of Life	0-87083-417-7
The Knowledge of Life	0-87083-419-3
The Tree of Life	0-87083-300-6
The Economy of God	0-87083-415-0
The Divine Economy	0-87083-268-9
God's New Testament Economy	0-87083-199-2
The World Situation and God's Move	0-87083-092-9
Christ vs. Religion	0-87083-010-4
The All-inclusive Christ	0-87083-020-1
Gospel Outlines	0-87083-039-2
Character	0-87083-322-7
The Secret of Experiencing Christ	0-87083-227-1
The Life and Way for the Practice of the Church Life	0-87083-785-0
The Basic Revelation in the Holy Scriptures	0-87083-105-4
The Crucial Revelation of Life in the Scriptures	0-87083-372-3
The Spirit with Our Spirit	0-87083-798-2
Christ as the Reality	0-87083-047-3
The Central Line of the Divine Revelation	0-87083-960-8
The Full Knowledge of the Word of God	0-87083-289-1
Watchman Nee—A Seer of the Divine Revelation ...	0-87083-625-0

Titles by Watchman Nee:

How to Study the Bible	0-7363-0407-X
God's Overcomers	0-7363-0433-9
The New Covenant	0-7363-0088-0
The Spiritual Man 3 volumes	0-7363-0269-7
Authority and Submission	0-7363-0185-2
The Overcoming Life	1-57593-817-0
The Glorious Church	0-87083-745-1
The Prayer Ministry of the Church	0-87083-860-1
The Breaking of the Outer Man and the Release ...	1-57593-955-X
The Mystery of Christ	1-57593-954-1
The God of Abraham, Isaac, and Jacob	0-87083-932-2
The Song of Songs	0-87083-872-5
The Gospel of God 2 volumes	1-57593-953-3
The Normal Christian Church Life	0-87083-027-9
The Character of the Lord's Worker	1-57593-322-5
The Normal Christian Faith	0-87083-748-6
Watchman Nee's Testimony	0-87083-051-1

Available at
Christian bookstores, or contact Living Stream Ministry
2431 W. La Palma Ave. • Anaheim, CA 92801
1-800-549-5164 • www.livingstream.com